RIBBLE

Other titles by the same author:

Mersey Ferries Vol 1
Transport Publishing Co Ltd 1992
Crosville on Merseyside
Transport Publishing Co Ltd 1992

With J. B. Horne
Liverpool Transport Vol 1 1830-1900
Light Railway Transport League 1976
Liverpool Transport Vol 2 1900-30
Light Rail Transit Association & Transport Publishing Co Ltd 1982
Liverpool Transport Vol 3 1931-39
Light Rail Transit Association & Transport Publishing Co Ltd 1987
Liverpool Transport Vol 4 1939-57
Transport Publishing Co Ltd 1989
Liverpool Transport Vol 5 1957-86
Transport Publshing Co Ltd 1991

With M. Jenkins
The Tramways of Birkenhead and Wallasey
Light Rail Transit Association 1987

Front cover illustration Ribble has had many distinctive vehicle designs over
the years, perhaps none more so than the Leyland Titan PD3 models with full-
fronted cabs of the late 'fifties and early 'sixties. From 1961, the bodywork was
built by Metro-Cammell, derived from the MCW Orion pattern of the period but with
Ribble's style of cab, complete with the neat radiator grille, and deeper skirt panels
to give the Ribble 'look'. No. 1795, seen here, dated from 1962.
Photographed by Roy Marshall, courtesy Photobus.

Typeset and produced electronically for the Publishers by
Mopok Graphics, 128, Pikes Lane, Glossop, Derbyshire
Printed and bound in Great Britain

R<small>IBBL</small>E
Volume One

by
T. B. Maund FCIT
Assisted by
David Meredith
and
Eric Ogden

Principal Photographers in this volume
R. L. Wilson and Roy Marshall

Series Editor

Alan Townsin

VENTURE PUBLICATIONS LIMITED | PO BOX 17 GLOSSOP DERBYSHIRE

CONTENTS

A representative collection of Ribble double-deckers

(Top) Most of Ribble's wartime utility buses were quite extensively rebuilt by Bond of Wythenshaw in 1951/2, thereby surviving in mildly modified form until the mid 'fifties. This Guy Arab with Roe bodywork dated from 1944 and is seen still in Ribble livery complete with fleet number 2441 after sale in 1956 to an East Anglian operator, Jolly of Norton.

(Centre) The Leyland Titan PD2 was Ribble's standard choice of double-decker from 1948 to 1956. Representative of the final batch to receive Leyland bodywork is 1377, a PD2/12 model delivered in 1952. This batch of 30 vehicles was also the last to be supplied to the fleet from new with the traditional form of side-gangway lowbridge bodywork.

(Bottom) In 1955-56 there was quite a large intake of PD2 models with highbridge bodywork, among them 1455, a PD2/12 with Burlingham body dating from 1956 but evidently newly overhauled when seen in the 'sixties. The destination, Gregson Lane, has historic connections for Ribble, for it was the acquisition of J. Hodson's business in that oddly-named village that was the basis of the newly-formed company in 1919.

Photographed by Roy Marshall, courtesy Photobus

CONTENTS

(Top) Briefly, in 1964-5, Ribble chose the Albion Lowlander to meet a need for low-height double-deckers whilst avoiding the traditional lowbridge layout, for this chassis was of layout suitable for low-floor bodywork even though it retained much of the Leyland PD front-end design and layout. Alexander modified its standard body for the model to incorporate the full-fronted cab by then favoured by Ribble, as seen here on 1852, one of ten dating from early 1964.

(Centre) The Leyland Atlantean PDR1/2 was an alternative approach to the low-height requirement, using the Lowlander's rear axle to allow centre-gangway layout in both decks. Seen here is 1960, one of fifteen with Northern Counties bodywork dating from 1967.

(Bottom) The Leyland Atlantean, by then of the AN68 series, came back into favour from the mid 'seventies. Seen here is 1469, one of ten AN68/1R models with Eastern Coach Works bodywork dating from 1979.

Photographed by Roy Marshall, courtesy of Photobus.

Venture Publications Ltd
– a new name in transport publishing

Founded in May 1993 by a group of transport professionals including authors, researchers, historians, editors, publishers, photographers, operators and businessmen, Venture Publications Ltd will serve the needs of the discerning transport enthusiasts, as well as providing material to which the student may turn in his or her research into the history of road transport. Its output will be concentrated mainly on the bus and truck and light rail/tramway scene, but heavy rail subjects will also feature. Quality and accuracy will be its twin aims at all times.

Venture is fortunate in being able to call on the talents of many well-known people in the transport publishing business. Alan Townsin, one-time editor of Buses Illustrated and later for many years with Transport Publishing Company, will be Editor-in-Chief. John Senior, with a lifelong career in print and publishing, will handle design and production, whilst Mark Senior will act as Venture's sales agent. A mail order service will be operated through PO Box 17 Glossop SK13 9FA, and customers will be welcome by prior appointment once the office, shop and warehousing facilities have been established. Trade distribution will ensure Venture's books will be available in leading transport bookshops.

Writers will include Alan Townsin, T. B. Maund, Doug Jack, Neil MacDonald, Maurice Doggett, Richard Hills, Stanley King, John Carroll, Scott Hellewell, Eric Ogden and many other specialists whose names are already a byword in transport publishing.

Venture's first titles will include a two-part history of Ribble Motor Services by T. B. Maund; Blue Triangle; a revised version of the history of AEC buses, by Alan Townsin; Eastern Coach Works 1946-1965 by Maurice Doggett and Alan Townsin; Leyland – the final years by Doug Jack, together with other major manufacturer's histories.

Other titles in the pipeline will be announced in *Classic Bus* and *Buses* magazines, and also in Venture's regular mailing shots. To ensure you receive your copy send a sae to Venture at the address below.

VENTURE PUBLICATIONS LIMITED   **PO BOX 17 GLOSSOP SK13 9FA**

INTRODUCTION

The origins of Ribble Motor Services Ltd. were no different to those of hundreds of other bus companies – a group of newly demobilised entrepreneurs, some ex-army chassis and a good route. However, Ribble was one of the few which forged ahead, outstripped its rivals and gradually built up a reputation based on reliability and service to its customers. In the days before radio time signals, housewives would confidently set their clocks by the Ribble bus, reliability being enhanced by a close relationship with Leyland Motors whose works were situated a mere five miles from Ribble's Preston headquarters. The two developed together and there were few models from the Leyland stable that did not find a place in the Ribble fleet.

The involvement of the British Automobile Traction group from an early date and, later, of the L.M.S. Railway Company, brought financial stability and the managerial guidance of several prominent able men of the bus operating industry. In course of time, the 'red octopus' as its detractors were wont to call it, held a commanding position extending from the Mersey to the Solway. In its heyday, it was the largest operator of long distance services in the country, accounting for 10% of the mileage in that field, and ranking second in the world to the Greyhound organisation in North America. The tentacles of its express services penetrated far beyond its established operating area, reaching north to south from Glasgow and Edinburgh to London, Torquay and Bournemouth and east to west from South Shields, Middlesbrough and Scarborough to Barrow-in-Furness, the Fylde peninsula, Colwyn Bay and Llandudno.

In serving this vast territory, it collaborated with a host of other operators, large and small, company-owned or municipal and was unique in seeking a *modus vivendi* with a greater number of neighbours than any other operator. Several independent proprietors who accepted Ribble's hand of friendship found they had acquired an uncle who offered them many ancillary benefits and always respected their rights.

Ribble was a company which inspired loyalty and its 25-year (and later 40-year) long service presentation events were always great occasions. Several of the original employees remained on the payroll until retirement and established traditions which gave the company an enviable aura of permanence. Ribble was a great training company and many well-known busmen served with the company, passing on to greater things elsewhere.

The social changes which led to the decline of the bus industry inevitably left their mark on the company which was compulsorily dissected into three parts in 1986. Appropriately the third which still bears the old name continues to serve the Ribble heartland and ownership by the Stagecoach group has injected new life into a body which, at one time, looked like a tired old beast waiting to die. Long may its rejuvenation continue.

A fully definitive history of Ribble would fill many volumes and, indeed, a whole book could be filled with tales about the hundreds of interesting people who served Ribble over the years. The object in this volume has been, therefore, to cover the basic facts of Ribble's growth and contraction and to augment the text pages with captions whenever possible. Many of the facts given in Eric Ogden's previous book have not been repeated here and no disrespect is intended to the many prominent people to whom little or no reference is made in this volume. A second volume, in course of preparation, will rectify this present shortcoming. It will also give greatly increased coverage to the fleet

I had the invaluable experience of working for Ribble, one of the stars in the BET firmament, for 18 years. They were years of hard work but there were few dull moments. The Ribble experience was an excellent foundation for any career in the bus industry.

T.B. MAUND.

NORTH WESTERN

There are several references in this book to the North Western Road Car Co. Ltd. and, for the benefit of the uninitiated, it needs to be made clear that there have been two quite separate companies bearing this name. The original company was registered in 1923 and eventually built up a network of services in the Manchester area, Cheshire and the Peak District of Derbyshire, with headquarters at Stockport. It operated several services to Blackpool, jointly with Ribble. In 1972, its bus services were divided between the then SELNEC Passenger Transport Executive, Trent Motor Traction Co.Ltd. and Crosville Motor Services Ltd. and, reduced to a coach operator, it came under Ribble management for a time; its name was changed to National Travel (North West) Ltd. in 1974.

When it was decided to divide Ribble into three companies in 1986, the company which inherited the Merseyside and Wigan areas was named North Western Road Car Co.Ltd. This was a dormant company, Hemptectic Ltd. (formerly Divisional Products [NBC] Ltd.) renamed but for administrative reasons the also dormant Mexborough & Swinton Traction Co Ltd was substituted. Originally, the operating area of the new company, based at Bootle, was quite different from that of the old one, but it has since made its presence felt in Altrincham, Northwich and Warrington, all former strongholds of the old company.

Ribble vehicles were always distinctive in their cherry red livery but none more so than the unique fully fronted PD3s with Burlingham, or as here MCW bodywork. The full front was a curious throw back to the SGs of the 'twenties.

CHAPTER 1
THE FIRST TEN YEARS 1919-29

The Ribble story begins with one James Hodson, of the strangely-named village of Gregson Lane, near Higher Walton, who began a service between Gregson Lane and Preston in 1910. It survived the war and on 15th May 1919, three friends from Yorkshire, Major H.E. Hickmott, John Barras and a Mr Champness, newly demobilised from the forces, made an Agreement with Hodson to take over his business. They formed a company, Ribble Motor Services Ltd., which was registered on 6th June 1919 with authorised capital of £20,000. Hodson remained a director of the company until his death in 1939.

There were rather primitive premises at Gregson Lane and five open-top double-deck buses, four Karriers and one Leyland. Daily services were run between Preston and Gregson Lane and a Sunday service to Longridge.

Until 1930, bus licensing was in the hands of local authorities under a procedure which was similar to that applicable to taxis. Preston issued licences freely, stipulating only that local passengers may not be carried over tram routes, so there was a host of small bus operators running into the town, most of whom terminated in Starchhouse Square, an open space which has since disappeared, or in nearby streets. Preston had a compact

tramway system with no line down the London Road which led to Walton-le-Dale and Chorley so the restricted area was small. Blackburn, 10 miles away, also had tramways but Chorley and the many small towns and villages within ten miles of Preston, relied almost entirely on the railways for transport. Preston railway station was half a mile from the town centre, giving the buses a decided commercial advantage as they could stand close to the market.

The potential for profitable bus operation had also been noticed by the British Automobile Traction Co. Ltd. (BAT), an offshoot of the British Electric Traction Co. Ltd. (BET) which had been formed in 1896 to develop electric tramways, and BAT set up a Preston branch sending buses from their Cheshire base at Macclesfield.

Two of Ribble's constituents can be traced back to 1904, the year when Lake District Road Traffic Co. Ltd. purchased these charabancs, the one on the left, EC 109, being a Clarkson steamer whilst the other two are petrol engined Thornycrofts. Note that the one on the right, registered EC 224, carries a basic curved destination plate for Keswick. The Company was taken over by Westmorland Motor Services Ltd after the latter was formed in July 1925, and in December 1927 the Lancashire and Westmorland Company, as it had then become, passed to Ribble.

This picture shows Ribble's original Preston terminus outside the Harris Library. The leading vehicle is one of the Karriers taken over from J. Hodson; its 43-seat double-deck body having been reseated from 36. It had probably originated on an earlier vehicle bearing the same registration number. The two Daimler 'Y' buses, with Birch bodies, entered Ribble service in 1921 and 1920 respectively and were eventually part-exchanged to Leyland Motors for new buses in 1927. All three had ex-military chassis.

The chassis of this charabanc, built in 1913, originally carried a 33-seat open-top body and was the Leyland double-decker in Hodson's fleet. Sold by Ribble in 1919 after they took over Hodson's business, it passed to Prestonian, being photographed with them by Leyland's photographer in 1921 whilst carrying a rather basic single-deck body and still sporting its wartime markings, showing it to have been requisitioned. Leyland again photographed it, this time in June 1922, by which time it was looking very smart as number 6 in Mashiter's Tra-Bon fleet, destined to become Ribble's first acquisition the following year. The windscreen announces a 2.30 departure for Blackpool, at 3/-, and Lytham, at 2/-, 15p and 10p respectively, and presumably from Preston.

After the initial fleet of five vehicles taken over from Hodson in June 1919, Ribble relied largely on ex-army vehicles sold off cheaply by the government. The Daimler Y and very similar AEC YC were chosen and nearly 40 taken into stock. The body of CK 3297, which was finished in the original grey livery, was built locally by Preston Motor Body Building Co. and the vehicle weighed just under 4 tons 2 cwt.

The Lake District Road Traffic Co. Ltd. with origins in 1904, was, as mentioned on page 9, one of the oldest-established constituents of the Ribble system. Clarkson steam buses were originally operated, though Thornycrofts were later favoured. This charabanc would appear to have been one of those dating from about 1912 (EC 109, 224?, 669) which was kept running during the 1914-18 war with coal-gas carried in the roof-bag.

A Preston-Chorley route was started on 20th December 1919 and, on 22nd April 1920, BAT acquired a substantial interest in Ribble, providing much-needed capital for expansion. The authorised capital was doubled to £40,000. Hickmott continued as managing director but fell out with his original partners after a marital scandal. Champness, who was the engineer, left and Barras resigned as a director of Ribble in June 1920. He returned to his native Yorkshire and started the Don Bus Service, another firm named after a river.

The Preston-Chorley route was extended to Adlington (later to Bolton via Westhoughton) and to Coppull and then to Standish. An intensive service to Leyland started in July 1920, being extended to Chorley via Euxton the following year. The string of villages along the Liverpool road were potentially good traffic generators. Ribble devised a plan to link up all the main towns and extend over the Pennines to Halifax and Huddersfield, hoping the municipalities would be content to serve the people within their own boundaries but, while much of this network came to pass, parochial attitudes frustrated the grand design.

Ribble had severe competition on most routes but concentrated on building up a reputation for reliable, regular time-table operation which was not influenced by the tactics of its many competitors. Until this goal had been achieved, no acquisitions of competitors were made, the first, in 1923, being J. Mashiter of Preston who traded as Tra-Bon Motor Services. In the same year, licences were obtained in Wigan (where a depot was established) and St. Helens. The Chorley-Standish service was extended to Wigan and services to Billinge, St. Helens and Ormskirk started, the latter extending a route between the Wigan boundary and Skelmersdale started three months earlier after the withdrawal of Wigan Corporation buses. Services from Ormskirk to both Southport and St. Helens were inaugurated in May 1923. The Wigan-St. Helens service was extended to Widnes in September 1924 but, after a year's trial, this lengthy extension was confined to Sundays only.

Ribble's first new Leyland vehicle was this SG7, C62, new in the summer of 1923. The dual-door, full-fronted body layout was adopted by Leyland Motors as standard for the SG7. Seats were provided for 39 passengers. It was fitted, in due course, with pneumatic tyres and remained in service until 1931, after which, like many other SG7s, it was converted to a lorry. One of the first production batch of ten SG7s for Ribble was CK 3532, below. Almost identical to the vehicle above, it had arched doorways and seated 38, one less than CK 3513. It was photographed outside the Blackburn Philanthropic Assurance Company's offices in March 1924.

Meanwhile, from Preston, the company had penetrated the Fylde to reach Kirkham and Blackpool in March 1922. In an easterly direction, Ribble buses reached out from both Preston and Chorley to Blackburn and to Longridge and Ribchester.

A depot at Blackburn took over all the equipment from Gregson Lane and a base at Burnley served detached routes to Clitheroe and Accrington. A long route from Blackburn to Haslingden, Edenfield and Rochdale paved the way to a later interchange at Edenfield where buses from Bolton and Rossendale connected.

This early 'twenties view of Castle Motor Services' Garstang bus stand dates from the time when a Preston-Lancaster bus journey involved a change from one company's bus to another. On the left is a 32-seat Leyland G6 of Castle Motors (TC 8704) which passed, with the business, to The Pilot Motors in June 1926 and then to Ribble as C251, three months later. On the right is a Vulcan, TC 6548, of T.E. Smith's Pilgrim Motors of Elswick. This was not one of the six Vulcans taken over by Ribble.

Major Acquisitions

Ribble had become a public company with authorised capital of £100,000 in August 1923 and by the end of 1924 the fleet had grown to 85 vehicles. There followed a period during which major acquisitions were made with a view to consolidating the expansion already achieved and increasing profitability by eliminating the stronger competitors.

February 1925 saw the purchase of the Chorley Autocar Co. Ltd. who had already taken over Parsons' Motor Services, running from Chorley to Whittle-le-Woods, Coppull, Horwich, Wheelton and to Preston on Saturdays. This was followed by Buller's Transport who traded as John Bull Motors on the Preston-Lytham route and then by part of the business of KCR Services (Kenyon, Coleman and Robinson) of Blackburn. Only the stage carriage services and 14 vehicles were acquired, the coach business remaining independent until it, too, was taken over in 1934. This purchase eliminated competition between Preston and Blackburn and took Ribble into Gt. Harwood and connected up the detached Burnley-Accrington route.

In April 1926 there followed Ribble's largest acquisition yet, that of Lancashire Industrial

Motors of Blackburn, trading as Pendle Motor Services. This company had been formed by Bullock and Briggs in October 1922 and had acquired Hodder Motor Services and other small operators. There were services from Blackburn to Clitheroe, Chatburn and Burnley and local routes from Clitheroe to Waddington, Grindleton and West Bradford. Forty vehicles of five different makes were taken over.

Six months later, The Pilot Motors Ltd. of Preston was acquired with 26 vehicles. This firm had been established by Arthur Foley and Co. in 1920; at first it ran between Preston and Longridge but soon started other daily routes to Broughton and Whittingham and to Garstang. The latter became the most important and Saturday branches were soon added to Claughton, Calder Vale and St. Michaels, the last-named also running on Sundays. Also in 1920, J. Stacey and Co. of Garstang, trading as Castle Motors, started a Garstang-Lancaster service by the main road and by 1923 was also running from Lancaster to Dolphinholme and Abbeystead on Saturdays and to

Many independent operators chose Vulcan chassis, then manufactured at Southport, but Ribble bought only six, C47-51/55, in 1922. The 20-seat rear entrance bodies, on a 2-ton chassis, were built by Northern Counties at Wigan, a supplier which Ribble did not patronise again until 1967, except for some wartime allocations.

Mr Dallas made sure no one could mistake his buses. This example, with unusual Leyland bodywork, entered his fleet in July 1924. It is believed to have been an A13 chassis and to have seated 26, but the PSV circle fleet history quotes the registration of No. 4 as TC 8402 and no entry appears for TC 8403, which is believed to be an error.

Leyland C7 No. C351, new in October 1925, poses in Selborne Street, Preston, apparently after being refurbished by Ribble including modification of the destination indicator to Ribble's standard 3in. depth and fitting of the external lamp. Acquired with the Pilgrim business in July 1927, part of its 30-seat capacity was alongside the driver, reached by an outward-opening door. Ribble ran it until 1932.

Cockerham on Thursdays. There was also a Garstang-Scorton route. A Garstang-Knott End-on-Sea route with an associated Knott End-Stalmine service ran for a time but were given up. Pilot acquired Castle in June 1926, putting on a half-hourly Preston-Lancaster service. The Garstang-Knott End service was restarted and there were plans to run direct to Blackpool in 55 minutes, in competition with Pilgrim Motors, who took 90 minutes through all the villages, but licences were refused in Blackpool.

In September 1926 Lancashire and Westmorland Motor Services Ltd. purchased the Lancaster-Preston service of Hodgson and Barnes of Preston and linked it with an existing route to make a Preston-Kendal service. Hodgson and Barnes continued to run a coach business in Preston under the name 'Premier' for many years. On 1st October, Ribble bought Pilot whose Tithebarn Street premises were adapted as Preston's first bus station. Further property was later purchased on the corner of Lord Street to enable the station to be extended.

However, Ribble soon experienced new competition on some routes it had acquired as Dallas Services, quite a substantial Leyland-based operator, started running between Preston and Longridge. This ceased following agreement with Empress Motors, a business founded by ex-Pilot employees who had been dismissed following the Ribble takeover. In the summer, Dallas started running to

Garstang and to Whittingham; the latter prospered but the route to Garstang was still highly competitive and Dallas withdrew early in 1928.

Meanwhile, Ribble set about strengthening its position in the Fylde and Over-Wyre districts where T.E. Smith's Pilgrim Motors of Elswick were well established on the Garstang-Blackpool service. In January 1927, they had taken over the Knott End-Blackpool and Garstang-Hambleton services of E.W. Lewis and Company's Knott End Motors. Pilgrim with six Vulcans, two Leylands and a Dodge was acquired in July 1927 thus consolidating Ribble's position in Blackpool's rural hinterland.

Into Westmorland

Lancashire and Westmorland Motor Services Ltd., like Ribble, was part of the BAT empire. Founded on 13th July 1925 by Mr H. Meageen of Cumberland Motor Services Ltd. as Westmorland Motor Services Ltd. with a capital of £15,000, it served an area with a heavy summer seasonal demand. On formation it took over Kendal Local Bus Co. and Fiern (Ambleside) Ltd; the Lake District Road Traffic Co.Ltd., a firm with origins in 1904 when Clarkson steam buses and petrol Thornycrofts had been operated, followed a little later. The company became public a month later and, on 12th February 1926, changed its name. The 'main line' from Kendal to Keswick started on 15th July 1925, using five AEC 411-type buses based at Kendal, Ambleside and Keswick. Further acquisitions were made in the Lancaster area, principally Lambsfield Motors Ltd., Lancaster and District Tramways Co. and Fahy's Ltd., Mr F.C. Fahy becoming managing director. Although there were small municipal tramway systems at Lancaster and Morecambe and the two towns are only $3\frac{1}{2}$ miles apart, they had never linked up, leaving the through service to private enterprise. This was a horse-drawn tramway until 1921 when it was replaced by a frequent local bus service which was extended to Heysham.

BAT decided that Lancashire and Westmorland should be absorbed by Ribble and this was done in December 1927 bringing the latter new depots at Lancaster, Morecambe, Kendal and Ambleside and extending the operating area north to Keswick, north-east to Kirkby Lonsdale and north-west to Grange-over-Sands. Ribble now had access to all the Lancashire coastal resorts.

The very mixed fleet of 79 vehicles had a strong Leyland element but there were Guys, Thornycrofts, AECs, Daimlers, Tilling Stevens and even a Halley, a Napier and a Pagefield. Most of these had been acquired with other businesses and about 30 were disposed of within the first few months. Ironically, some of the AECs found their way back into the Ribble fleet as a result of a later acquisition, as will be seen.

The Tourist Motor Co. of Heysham operated this Tilling-Stevens TTA1 (apparently registered LF 9208) purchased from the London operation of Thomas Tilling Ltd. It went into the fleet of Fahy's Ltd. and ultimately Lancashire and Westmorland Motor Services Ltd. but did not survive long enough to enter the Ribble fleet on their acquisition on 1st December 1927. Tilling's fostering of petrol-electric vehicles was a trend that never penetrated to Ribble.

Eleven Leyland Lions came with the Lancashire and Westmorland acquisition in December 1927. They were all short-length PLSC1 models with rear entrance 31-seat Leyland bodies. They were numbered C423-9 and 438-41 in the Ribble fleet and most remained in service until 1937-38, several becoming showmen's vehicles.

Into Yorkshire

The company rightly felt that Yorkshire west of the Pennines formed a logical extension of its East Lancashire operating area. On 16th August 1927 it purchased the business of Skipton Motor Co. Ltd. with a Skipton-Earby service which had started in June 1924. This was followed up in November 1928 by putting on a competitive service over part of the routes of T. Wiseman's Old Bill Motor Services who sold out a month later. The Earby route was soon extended to Colne. This area never became very important for the company though a logical traffic boundary was fixed with the West Yorkshire Road Car Co. Ltd. and a base established for routes which eventually reached Manchester, Southport, Blackpool, Morecambe and the Lake District.

In 1928 a Skipton-Ingleton-Lancaster-Morecambe service was started in opposition to Pennine Motor Services of Gargrave who had inaugurated a Skipton-Settle service with a Star Flyer and three 14-seat Overlands early in 1926. County Motors (Lancaster) Ltd. had also been running between Skipton and Lancaster from a garage at Settle since March 1926. A joint working agreement with Pennine was made in 1930, the first of many between Ribble and independent operators. For many years the

anniversary of this event was celebrated by a dinner attended by officials of both operators.

Nearer home, Webster's local services in Wigan were taken over jointly with Lancashire United in October 1927, Ribble taking eight Leyland buses and the routes to Billinge and Ormskirk. J. E. Loynds & Company's Belford Service between Bolton and Darwen, with two local routes in Darwen, was also absorbed in December 1927 with six Vulcans and possibly two Karriers. Their through fare was 1/- single or return but 1/6d was charged on Saturdays. Ribble soon established a through Bolton-Blackburn service via Darwen and Lower Darwen. The Eccleston Motor Co. (W. Solloway and others) was purchased in August 1928 with routes from his home village to Chorley, Preston and Wigan; this facilitated the commencement of a through Preston-Wigan service. The depot was used for storage for many years.

Leyland Lion C160 takes pride of place in front of 1924 SG9 C90 and other early buses outside the Harris Library in 1926. Note the difference in height of the different models. It will be seen that, at this date, Ribble had not yet adopted the reduced aperture destination indicator with external lamp.

Two views of Fishergate, Preston outside the railway station serve to illustrate the rapid advance in bus design in the late 'twenties as both Ribble buses date from 1928. In the upper picture Leyland PLSC3 Lion C515 heads out of town to Leyland with the conductor, wearing summer dust-coat, standing on the step, in accordance with company's regulations. Below, an early Tiger TS2, C488, with 29-seat Leyland saloon body, makes its way to the bus station. Also in the picture are one of the eight PLSC Lions of the Yarrow Motor Co. of Eccleston and a Preston Corporation tram. Note the Eldorado ice cream 'Stop Me' tricycle outside the Victoria and Station Hotel.

Victoria Square was the main town terminus in Bolton until Moor Lane bus station was built. This late-'twenties scene is dominated by PLSC Lions, three Ribbles and two (one a dual-entrance bus) of Bolton Corporation. Also in the scene are a standard open-staircase TD1 of Bolton Corporation and a Lancashire United bus, just to the left of the cenotaph.

Merseyside Area Services

With a population approaching a million, the contiguous Merseyside towns of Liverpool, Bootle, Litherland, Waterloo and Crosby were an obvious goal for Ribble and, having established a network southwards from Preston down to a line drawn through St. Helens, Ormskirk and Southport, the company applied to Liverpool Watch Committee towards the end of 1923 for licences to run three services; to Crosby and Southport, to Ormskirk and to Skelmersdale. After a lengthy delay, these were refused but an appeal to the Minister of Transport was upheld. In 1925, licences were granted for services from Liverpool to Formby and to Ormskirk with a ban on the carriage of passengers point to point within the city and a minimum fare of 6d for all passengers whose journeys originated or ended within the city boundary.

A two-hourly Preston-Ormskirk-Liverpool (Canning Place) service commenced on 8th April 1925 but due to pressure on resources, the plan to run to Formby was not followed up. However, from 3rd July 1925, some trips were started between Liverpool and Scarisbrick via Lydiate and Halsall and some buses ran through to Ormskirk by this route; later it was diverted to Southport. J.S. Bretherton's services from Ormskirk to Aintree and Halsall were acquired in February 1926. The next move came from William Slack, a Glasgow operator, who later traded as Nor-West Bus Services. He applied unsuccessfully for licences for a Liverpool-St. Helens-Wigan service late in 1926 but had better luck with licences for Liverpool-Ormskirk and Liverpool-Southport routes, both of which started in February 1927 using Belgian Minerva vehicles. Ribble fought back and renewed its application for licences

in Crosby which had been refused in earlier. Both the Waterloo and Crosby Councils had contracted with Waterloo and Crosby Motor Services to run a replacement service for their tramway system which had been leased to the Liverpool Overhead Railway and closed on 31st December 1925. The local company originated in 1923, running a service between Seaforth and Crosby over what became the L3 route and this was eventually extended to Woodvale where it connected with Southport Corporation buses.

Ribble started an hourly Liverpool-Crosby-Southport service on 1st June 1927 and, during the next year, both Nor-West and Ribble increased their services, adding short workings to Formby and Crosby. Collingwood Street garage, acquired with the business of Collingwood Motors, was used as a base for these operations. The Waterloo and Crosby company was weakened by this

Nor-West Bus Services was the first operator between Liverpool and Southport and favoured Belgian Minerva vehicles of which there were eight in the fleet. Nor-West came under the control of the Merseyside Touring Co. with whose fleet this Minerva came to Ribble in 1931. It is seen at the old Custom House terminus in Canning Place, Liverpool on the Ormskirk service. The normal-control Minervas received Ribble numbers 1335-40 but were never operated.

competition and Ribble took control of it on 3rd January 1928 maintaining it as a subsidiary during the currency of the five-year Agreement with the local councils but using its Seaforth Sands garage to house buses needed to expand its Liverpool-Crosby network to provide four different routes, designated 'A' to 'D'. Two further operators entered the fray during 1928, Kilburn and Rymer's Ideal Motor Services (who ran through to Southport) on 23rd July 1928 and Wallace Black's Imperial Motorways in November. The latter was a long distance operator (see Chapter 3) and wanted something to occupy his vehicles in the winter; he used a Maudslay and four Crossley luxury coaches on a Liverpool-Crosby service and charged 1d more than the others, a premium on comfort.

Nor-West had originally fixed fares at 1/8d single (1d per mile) and 2/6d return but competition forced fares down, return tickets being issued at single fare plus 1d. This state of affairs still existed in February 1931 when the new national licensing laws froze timetables and fares and it cost only 6d single, 7d return to ride from Liverpool to Crosby and 1/8d single, 1/9d return from Liverpool to Southport until 1951.

In December 1928 the city terminus for both Ribble and competitors' services was moved from Canning Place to the top of Mount Pleasant, the site of the present-day Roman Catholic Cathedral, where there was room for buses to stand. There was a stopping place at the foot of Mount Pleasant where most passengers boarded.

In July 1929 the Ribble services were reorganised to permit the use of double-deck Leyland Titan buses on all routes except 'C' (the later L1) which trees and weak foundations in College Road made unsuitable. The three independents joined forces to provide a six-minute service between Liverpool and Crosby with inter-available return tickets compared with approximately a four-minute Ribble service. Matters came to a head in December 1929 when, following complaints of speeding in Scotland Road, Ideal were refused renewal of their licences in Liverpool. Ribble bought Ideal on 5th December and Imperial sold out on 18th leaving only Ribble and Nor-West in the field.

The latter soon came under the control of the Merseyside Touring Co. which had been formed by Garlick, Burrell and Edwards, Ltd. in March 1929 to operate local services between Litherland, Bootle and Liverpool. The city's Watch Committee refused them licences on the grounds of competition with the tramways but they received strong support from the other councils who accused Liverpool Corporation of neglecting their interests. They therefore worked on the 'return ticket principle' whereby no fare-paying passengers were picked up within the city; they

Eight of the ten AEC 'NS' and three open-top B-type buses of the Waterloo and Crosby Motor Services Ltd. when the former were new, early in 1926. These buses replaced a tramway between Seaforth and Great Crosby, worked by Liverpool Overhead Railway Co. until 31st December 1925. The company came under Ribble control in January 1928 but retained its separate existence until 1930. The ten NS buses became Ribble Nos. 1015-24 and were gradually withdrawn between 1930 and 1933. The B-type had been hired from London General, some being retained.

were thus, technically, not plying for hire. The Merseyside company also became very active in the long distance field as described in chapter 3.

Co-ordination with St. Helens Corporation

Originally, the attitude of St. Helens Corporation towards bus operation contrasted strongly with that of most other municipalities, though it gave Ribble problems later. Their natural desire to protect their own undertaking was not manifested in the all-too-common obstructive tactics but in a recognition of the worth of through bus services and a desire to share the benefits with the company operators. Ribble had been allowed into the town on sensible terms in 1923 and from the following year the Corporation had shared the routes to Billinge and Rainford for which it had obtained statutory powers in 1921. Following the success of a pooled service between St. Helens and Earlestown, operated jointly with Lancashire United (LUT), agreement was reached with Ribble and LUT to extend the Corporation's Burtonwood-Rainford services at both ends to make a Warrington-St. Helens-Southport through route which started on 27th May 1928. This became a highly profitable service, particularly in summer, and paved the way for other agreements with this ubiquitous municipal operator.

Railway Participation

In August 1928, the four main line railway companies who had lost enormous amounts of both passenger and goods traffic to road, obtained Parliamentary powers to engage in road transport and there was considerable apprehension at a potentially serious threat to the established operators. However, in all but a few cases, the railways decided against direct operation of bus services and embarked upon a policy of purchasing shares in the larger companies. In some cases they bought businesses (very often paying too much) and handed them over to companies in which they had shares. Meanwhile, BAT had collaborated with the other major bus holding company, Thomas Tilling, to set up a joint holding company, Tilling and British Automobile Traction Co. Ltd. and it was this company which carried on negotiations with the railway companies. Ribble services lay entirely within the territory of the London, Midland and Scottish Railway Company (LMS) and agreement was reached on 28th December 1929 whereby the railway company would acquire an interest in the Ribble company equal to that of Tilling and BAT. The umbrella agreement made it impossible for the railway ever to obtain control as half the shareholding in any company purchased by them had to be sold to the bus holding company. Standing Joint Committees were set up to co-ordinate road and rail services. Railway tickets were sold at Ribble's Ambleside booking office.

Area Agreements

While broad agreement on spheres of interest had been settled between Tilling and BAT companies in 1921, the railways agreement, the emergence of new companies and acquisition of others made it necessary for territorial boundaries to be reviewed and these matters were settled during 1929-30. These Area Agreements allowed for the minimum penetration of one company's territory by another to reach legitimate traffic objectives. When Tilling-BAT bought a large shareholding in Cumberland Motor Services Ltd., a boundary line was agreed between the Ribble and Cumberland companies which confined the latter to the coastal part of the county. A line through Manchester and Rochdale separated Ribble from North Western while the Pennines formed an effective boundary with the Yorkshire-based companies. Ribble worked out its own agreement with Lancashire United which was independently owned, this being approximately a line drawn through St. Helens, Wigan and Bolton.

Forward to the Scottish Border

Having reached Kendal and Keswick, the company now felt that it could set its sights on pushing northwards to Carlisle. The border city's tramways were worn out and bus services were in the hands of three large companies and numerous small operators. The boundary agreement with Cumberland Motor Services led to Ribble's acquisition in the summer of 1929 (back-dated to 1st April), of Armstrong and Siddle Motor Services Ltd. of Penrith, a Cumberland subsidiary, since June 1928. Fred Armstrong had run an 8-seater Sterling car between Penrith and Pooley Bridge at the early date of 1899 and, by 1912, a regular bus service was in place which was extended to Patterdale by August 1919. The company was formed in 1921 and had established or acquired routes from Penrith to Carlisle (which was the main attraction), Kirkby Stephen, Appleby, Keswick and Windermere via the shores of Lake Ullswater and the Kirkstone Pass. There was also a Kirkby Stephen-Shap route and services between Carlisle, Cumwhinton and Wetheral, previously transferred from Caledonian Omnibus Co. They had acquired several businesses including Lyvennet Motor Services, (Crosby Ravensworth), De Mello (trading as Moore and Baty's Motor Service) of Carlisle, George Taylor and Co. (Motors) Ltd. of Penrith and parts of the businesses of Mandale of Greystoke and Sowerby's of Lazonby. There was a very mixed fleet of 28 vehicles including five new Albions, two new Leylands and two elderly Daimlers transferred from Cumberland following a devastating depot fire in March 1928 in which nine vehicles were lost. There were vehicles of ten different makes including a 13-seat Bean, a 14-seat Dodge and an 8-seat Daimler car. From June 1929 the Penrith-Keswick route was operated jointly by Ribble and Cumberland.

Ribble gained a foothold on the Carlisle city services on 1st December 1929 when the Carlisle-Raffles service of S.P. & T. Adair was acquired with two small Dennis vehicles and a new Gilford 32-seater. The Adairs continued as coach operators and that part of their business was taken over in July 1936. Uncertainty created by the imminence of the new licensing system and the ambition of Carlisle Corporation to become a bus operator prevented any further progress until 1931 (see chapter 2).

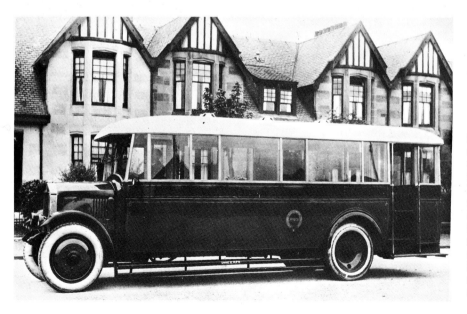

Penrith-based Armstrong and Siddle was another northern area independent with very early origins. The vehicle illustrated is one of a pair of 26-seat Albions delivered in the summer of 1928 which became C687-8 in the Ribble fleet. Note the evidence of Scottish influence, often encountered in Cumberland, in the form of the cutaway rear entrance. Ribble disposed of these buses in 1930 but they had long lives elsewhere, one surviving with Harding of Birkenhead until 1944.

CHAPTER 2
BUS SERVICES 1930-45

Although many of the smaller operators had been taken over by 1930, there was still plenty of competition and some of the more enlightened local authorities tried to maintain some sort of order among the rival operators on the busier routes. As an example, the Chorley Joint Omnibus Committee co-ordinated the licensing activities of several councils including Leyland and Walton-le-Dale and employed an inspector to report on the worst excesses of the contestants. Ribble had challenged their authority as early as 1926 when the company deleted certain of their conditions from licence application forms before returning them. In mid-1929 when Mr Prescott took over Cooke's service and named it Bamber Bridge Motor Service (BBMS), the Committee tried to establish even headways between Bamber Bridge and Preston. BBMS was running five trips an hour, H. Spencer (Brookhouse Motors) ran four and both Ribble and Dallas Services ran short trips on their Chorley-Preston service. Like many large companies, Ribble, whilst maintaining a high standard of regularity, was reluctant to agree to terms which reduced its competitive edge over the smaller operators it sought to eliminate.

The main line railway companies saw the licensing provisions of the Road Traffic Act, 1930 as a means of retarding the growth of road competition. The Act provided for the transfer of bus licensing from local authorities to area Traffic Commissioners who, after publication of applications for road service licences (or amendments), would hold Public Sittings at which interested parties, including other operators, local authorities and railway

An unusual aerial view of Preston bus station taken on 5th May 1930 before acquisition of the buildings on the corner of Lord Street (right rear) enabled the concourse to be extended. Leyland Lion PLSC models predominate, the difference between the short PLSC1 and the longer PLSC3 being clearly demonstrated. In the background can be seen a Lancashire United vehicle on the Manchester-Blackpool joint service, Tigers and two SGs .

Two views of Tithebarn Street bus station, Preston, built in 1928, illustrate progress made during the 'thirties. The upper picture, dating from 1930, shows the traffic offices on the first floor and a selection of single-deck buses. Left to right, there are two 1929 Lion LT1s, that on the left being No. 590; a rear-entrance 1926 PLSC1 (219), ordered by Pendle Motors but delivered after takeover; 1929 PLSC3 Lion No.535; 1930 Tiger TS2 No.729, with bus seats and roof-rack; PLSC3 No.553 and a Lancashire United bus on service X60. Note the supplementary route cards hanging in the rear windows of several buses. These were produced on a Masseely machine by the company's Publicity Department.

The lower view is taken from the Lord Street end on a bright February day in 1939 and shows a standard TD1 Titan double-deck bus, already looking old-fashioned and, in the background, one of the few LT7 buses of 1935-36. On the left are two Cheetah buses, the leader, 1938 ECW-bodied example (probably No.1997) having less downward taper towards the front of the cab roof than 1631, one of the first ECOC-bodied vehicles of 1936.

companies could object to applications. Despite their substantial financial interest in most of the principal bus companies, the railways intended to take full advantage of this right and the spectacle of a railway company objecting to the plans of a bus company in which it held half the shareholding was to become commonplace. The railways believed that they had a better chance of success if some order could be established in the bus industry and they encouraged the companies to buy up as many of their competitors as possible. Some companies had cash available following the sale of shares to the railways, thus accounting for a rash of purchases during 1930-31. Fear of the effect of the new legislation on profitability was another factor in persuading many small men to sell out and this process was manifest during the early 'thirties.

The railways also sought Agreements with local authorities, especially where a hard line or inconsistent licensing policy had interfered with the aspirations of the companies. The best example of this in Ribble territory was Liverpool, and the railways started talking to Liverpool City Council in December 1929, just before they had a shareholding in Ribble. They were already outright owners of the Crosville company and wanted an orderly determination of rights of the various operators. It was not until March 1931 that agreement in principle was reached and a firm Agreement was signed on 2nd July 1931 whereby the areas of influence of the Corporation, Ribble and Crosville were defined. A line along the A57 road was fixed as the boundary between Ribble and Crosville.

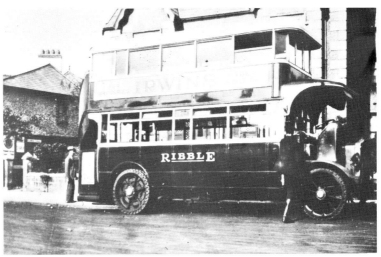

This former Waterloo and Crosby AEC NS bus is shown working the Seaforth Sands-Great Crosby local service about 1931. Whilst buses of the same type working in London were fitted with pneumatic tyres and drivers' windscreens, the Ribble buses remained unimproved. Note the driver's leggings.

Rishton and Antley Motor Co. Ltd.

Ribble already had a strong presence in that part of East Lancashire between Accrington, Whalley and Clitheroe by virtue of its earlier purchases of Pendle and KCR Services but there was still strong competition in the district. Taxi and Motor Transport Co. (Antley Garage) Ltd. had been registered in October 1919 and, after absorbing the Rishton Motor Co. Ltd. in April 1922, it changed its name to the Rishton and Antley Motor Co. Ltd. the main depot of which was at Church, near Accrington. Their main route was from Clitheroe via Whalley to Clayton-le-Moors, then to Accrington or Church and Oswaldtwistle. There were also services to Great Harwood and Blackburn. In October 1929, the services and 10 vehicles of Calder Motor Co. Ltd. of Great Harwood, which had originated in 1921 as W.A. Moore and Co. Ltd., were taken over and the fleet name 'Rishton and Calder' was adopted.

Also active in the area was Claremont Omnibus Co. Ltd., run by F.J. Wood, originally a London independent operator, who started a frequent Burnley-Clitheroe service on 1st April 1927 and then pushed on to establish a network based on Clitheroe, serving Preston, Chaigeley, Grindleton and Pendleton. An hourly Clitheroe-Manchester express and two Burnley-Manchester services – via Todmorden and Rochdale and via Accrington and Bury – were added. The company's name was changed to Claremont Omnibus Services Ltd. on 4th May 1928 and the fleet grew to 37 vehicles – 15 Vulcans, 7 Leylands (1 PLSC Lion and 6 Tigers), 3 Studebakers and 12 McCurds though several of these were in Wood's name.

Following a period of intense competition, Rishton and Antley was purchased by Ribble on 1st March 1930 but maintained as a subsidiary company which immediately bought Claremont. The seven Leylands were taken into the Ribble fleet, the others being disposed of by Wood. Six new Ribble Leyland Tiger TS3s (Nos. 927-32) were given the Claremont fleet name which they carried until October 1930. Rishton and Antley continued as a subsidiary for six months, 43 vehicles, mainly of Leyland and Maudslay manufacture, being absorbed into the Ribble fleet in September 1930.

County, Majestic and Empress

In July 1928 Ribble obtained a controlling interest in the business of County Motors (Lancaster) Ltd., founded on 6th March 1922 under the name of Ex-Servicemen's Transport Ltd. but changed after three months. There were services to Ingleton, Warton, Kirkby Lonsdale and Morecambe. The share capital was increased from £10,000 to £25,000 and, from 1st February 1929, Ribble purchased the remaining shareholding. There was a very mixed fleet of 34 vehicles, mainly of small seating capacity, but including three Thornycroft open-top double-deckers. About 10 vehicles had come with the business of J.T. Atkinson of Skerton. Ribble decided to keep County as a subsidiary; much of the old fleet was withdrawn and replaced by 20 Ribble vehicles, some already second-hand but including three new Leyland TD1s which were registered with Lancashire TE numbers instead of Preston CK numbers, in order to maintain the facade of independence.

It has already been mentioned that Empress Motors had been formed by ex-Pilot employees to compete with Ribble between Preston and Longridge and a limited company, Preston and Longridge Motor Co. Ltd. was eventually formed. Other ex-Pilot men had formed Majestic Motors, under the leadership of Coun. Matthew Wade, a banana merchant, and services were operated to Garstang, Blackpool, Blackburn via Walton-le-Dale and Walmer Bridge, licences for a Bamber Bridge route having been refused. These operators were bitterly anti-Ribble and competition was fierce and unrelenting. Under no circumstances would they negotiate with the company which was anxious to get them out of the way.

In the Spring of 1929, Ribble brought its Trojan Horse, County Motors, into Preston and the latter started an intensive Longridge-Preston-Penwortham service to compete with Majestic and Empress who formed a partnership to combat the threat. County could not get Preston licences but offered a 6d return fare between Longridge and Preston ($7\frac{1}{2}$ miles), compared with 1/2d

21

by Ribble or 1/- by Majestic-Empress. When the latter withdrew their Walmer Bridge service late in 1929, County cut back their service to Starchhouse Square instead of running across town to Penwortham.

Majestic and Empress would still not treat with Ribble so the LMS Railway, probably acting through a nominee, purchased the business on 10th April 1930, withdrawing all but the Longridge service immediately. The latter was handed over to Ribble on 14th April, the County service being withdrawn and the buses returned to Lancaster. Of the 17 Leyland buses acquired, five entered the County fleet. That company continued its separate existence until December 1930 when its fleet was merged with Ribble.

But the Majestic-Empress beast was not yet dead. In October 1930 ex-employees formed a new company, Request Services Ltd. and, with two hired vehicles, started a 45-minute service between Preston and Garstang. By January 1931 there were four buses working a half-hourly service and a shuttle service between Preston and Broughton was run for about six weeks. A road service licence was granted against which Ribble successfully appealed and the service was withdrawn in December 1932, the vehicles having been hired latterly from Viking.

Scout Motor Services

Ribble's monopoly on the Preston-Blackpool road was short-lived as in August 1930, James Watkinson, a farm produce merchant, took over the premises in Starchhouse Square vacated by Majestic and started a half-hourly Preston-Blackpool service under the name of Scout Motor Services. Mr Watkinson had been using dual-body vehicles for goods during the week and as charabancs at weekends since 1919 and, in 1928, had opened a branch in Blackpool from which a Blackpool-London service was started. Four Leyland Lion LT2 buses were used to start the Preston-Blackpool service but a TD1 double-decker was added in November and two more early in 1931.

Starchhouse Square, Preston, which was the headquarters of Scout (and of Majestic before that) has been swept away by redevelopment. This Sunday morning line-up includes eight Leyland-bodied Titans, the newest a 1935 TD4 with metal-framed body; four Lion LT5A and four Tigers (two TS4s and two TS6s) with Burlingham, Weymann or Leyland bodywork. The island platform stands, provided by the Corporation for use by independent bus operators, were situated behind the coaches on the right, the last user being Bamber Bridge Motor Service until 1968.

When application was made for a road service licence under the new procedure, it was opposed tooth and nail by Ribble and a licence was granted only for an express service with one intermediate stop at Kirkham. Scout won a subsequent appeal, arguing that, with new housing developments on the outskirts of both Preston and Blackpool, they had created new traffic. A 30-minute service was licensed against Ribble's 15-minute frequency. A limited company was formed on 24th December 1932 and all single-deck buses had been replaced by double-deckers by 1934. Here was formidable competition which would not go away and Ribble settled down to an uneasy *modus vivendi* with Scout, negotiating, in 1934, an arrangement whereby the existing fares of 1/6d single, 2/3d return were replaced by 1/1d single with no returns so that passengers could return by any bus at busy times when both operators struggled to cope with the crowds. Somewhat hostile co-existence continued until the outbreak of war when co-ordination was forced on the parties by the Traffic Commissioners.

Rationalisation on Merseyside

In June 1930, Ribble purchased the Merseyside Touring Co. Ltd. for £120,000 but retained it as a subsidiary pending confirmation of the licences. Nor-West also retained its identity but its services, by this time worked by some of the Merseyside company's Tilling Stevens buses, were rationalised with those of Ribble with inter-available return tickets. Ribble was now in sole control of the Bootle and Crosby network and, as soon as the Agreement with the local councils expired on 31st December 1930 and a new one had been negotiated, Waterloo and Crosby Motor Services Ltd. was wound up.

The new *status quo* made it much easier to apply the provisions of the 1931 Liverpool Agreement but this had awkward consequences for Ribble in that the Merseyside company's Bootle services mostly fell into the territory of Liverpool Corporation and were reluctantly given up during 1932, only to be partially suppressed by the Corporation who had always considered them to be unnecessary. Competitive applications for road service

Facing page :
A typical leaflet of the mid-thirties, announcing the start of another local service between Liverpool and Crosby. The Crosby routes were lettered A to G until replaced by numbers L1-9 in August 1935.

RIBBLE
MOTOR SERVICES LTD.

NEW DAILY
LOCAL SERVICE
Commencing Saturday, June 29th, 1935.

LIVERPOOL—GT. CROSBY (G SERVICE)

(Skelhorne Street)　　　　　　(Jct. Endbutt Lane and Brownmoor Lane)

Via " D " Route to Crosby Road North, then Kingsway and Stuart Road.

NOTE :—The following Time Table substitutes the Time Table shown on page 265 of the Company's Time Table Books and on the Yellow Handbills dated June 29th to September 29th, 1935.

TIME TABLE.—JUNE 29th to SEPTEMBER 29th, 1935 (inclusive).

Route 67g. LIVERPOOL, BOOTLE, SEAFORTH, WATERLOO and GT. CROSBY, Endbutt Lane (via Kingsway).　　Buses working this service show Indicator letter **G**

	N	N	N	N	N	N		N	F	N	F	N		a.m.	p.m.		
														N			
Liverpool, Skelhorne Street ..dep.	..	735	7 55	8 15	8 35	8 55		15	20	35	50	55		1155	1215	—and	1115
Liverpool, Rotunda Theatre . ,,	..	742	8 2	8 22	8 42	9 2		22	27	42	57	2		12 2	1222	every	1122
Bootle, Bedford Road ...... ,,	..	747	8 7	8 27	8 47	9 7	then	27	32	47	2	7	—minutes	12 7	1227	20	1127
Jct.Linacre Ln.&Knowsley Rd.,,	732	752	8 12	8 32	8 52	9 12	at—	32	37	52	7	12	past each	1212	1232	minutes	1132
Bootle, Norton Street ...... ,,	733	753	8 13	8 33	8 53	9 13		33	38	53	8	13	hour until—	1213	1233	daily	1133
Seaforth Sands Station ...... ,,	735	755	8 15	8 35	8 55	9 15		35	40	55	10	15		1215	1235	until—	1135
Waterloo, South Road...... ,,	741	8 1	8 21	8 41	9 1	9 21		41	46	1	16	21		1221	1241		1141
Gt. Crosby, Jct. Endbutt Lane and Brownmoor Lane .. arr.	744	8 4	8 24	8 44	9 4	9 24		44	49	4	19	24		1224	1244		1144

	N	N	N	N	N	N	N	N	N	F	N	F	N
Gt. Crosby, Jct. Endbutt Lane and Brownmoor Lane ..dep.	7 4	7 24	7 44	8 4	8 24	8 44	9 4	9 24	9 44	9 49	10 4	1019	1024
Waterloo, South Road...... ,,	7 7	7 27	7 47	8 7	8 27	8 47	9 7	9 27	9 47	9 52	10 7	1022	1027
Seaforth Sands Station ...... ,,	7 13	7 33	7 53	8 13	8 33	8 53	9 13	9 33	9 53	9 58	10 0	1013	1033
Bootle, Norton Street ...... ,,	7 15	7 35	7 55	8 15	8 35	8 55	9 15	9 35	9 55	10 0	1015	1030	1035
Jct.Linacre Ln.& Knowsley Rd.,,	7 16	7 36	7 56	8 16	8 36	8 56	9 16	9 36	9 56	10 1	1016	1031	1036
Bootle, Bedford Road ...... ,,	7 21	7 41	8 1	8 21	8 41	9 1	9 21	9 41	10 1	10 6	1021	1036	1041
Liverpool, Rotunda Theatre . ,,	7 26	7 46	8 6	8 26	8 46	9 6	9 26	9 46	10 6	10 11	1026	1041	1046
Liverpool, Skelh'ne St.(bottom)arr.	7 33	7 53	8 13	8 33	8 53	9 13	9 33	9 53	1013	1018	1033	1048	1053

	N	F	N	F	N		a.m.			p.m.			
Gt. Crosby, Jct. Endbutt Lane and Brownmoor Lane ..dep.	1044	1049	11 4	1119	1124	1144	—and every 20 daily until—	1144	1159	....	....	....	....
Waterloo, South Road..... ,,	1047	1052	11 7	1122	1127	1147		1147	12 2	....	....	....	....
Seaforth Sands Station ..... ,,	1053	1058	1113	1128	1133	1153		1153	12 8	1210	....	....	....
Bootle, Norton Street ..... ,,	1055	11 0	1115	1130	1135	1155		1155	1210	1211	....	....	....
Jct.Linacre Ln.& Knowsley Rd.,,	1056	11 1	1116	1131	1136	1156		1156	1211	....	....	....	....
Bootle, Bedford Road ...... ,,	11 1	11 6	1121	1136	1141	12 1		12 1	....	....	....	....	....
Liverpool, Rotunda Theatre . ,,	11 6	1111	1126	1141	1146	12 6		12 6	....	....	....	....	....
Liverpool, Skelh'ne St.(bottom)arr.	1113	1118	1133	1148	1153	1213		1213	....	....	....	....	....

N Not on Sundays.　　　　F Sundays only.

STOPPING PLACES.

As " D " Route to St. Johns Road, then at Junct. Kingsway and Liverpool Road ; Junct. Kingsway and Stuart Road and Junct. Endbutt Lane and Brownmoor Lane.

Fares.

Route 67g. LIVERPOOL, SEAFORTH and GT. CROSBY.
SINGLE FARES.

† Special 1d. Fare.
(E) Jct. Crosby Road South and Cambridge Road and Jct. Kingsway and Crosby Road North.

Special Single Fare.
Liverpool, Skelhorne Street and Jct. Knowsley Road and Addison Street. 4d. ♦

Stage Nos.
1	**LIVERPOOL,** Skelhorne Street									
2	4d. ♦	Scotland Road, Junction with Hornby Street								
3	4	4d. ♦	Rotunda Theatre							
4	4	4	4d. ♦	Woodbine Street or Knowsley Hotel						
5	4	4	4	4d. ♦	**BOOTLE,** Bedford Road or Merton Road					
6	4	4	4	4	4	4d. ♦	Junction Linacre Lane & Knowsley Road			
7	5	5	5	5	3	2	1d.	Seaforth Sands Station, or Trevor Street (A)		
8	6	6	6	6	3	2	1d.	1d.	Jct. Church Road and Crosby Road South (C)	
10	6	6	6	6	4	2	1	1d.	Waterloo, South Road (D)	
14	6	6	6	4	3	2*	2†	1d.	Jct. Kingsway and Crosby Road North	
24	6	6	6	4	2*	2*	1	1d.	**GT. CROSBY,** Jct. Endbutt Lane and Brownmoor Lane (F)	

♦ Day Return Fare 7d. (children 3½d.)

* Indicates that the Ordinary Return Fare is double the single fare shown.

Ordinary Day Return Tickets are, unless otherwise indicated, issuable daily at the rate of single fare plus one penny
Workmen's Day Return Fares are generally superseded by Ordinary Return Fares, except that Workmen's Day Return Tickets are issued at the rate of single fare plus one penny up to 8-0 a.m. departure time, between stages where the Ordinary Return Fare is shown as double the single fare.

LOCAL OFFICES :—LIVERPOOL : 30 Islington (Phone : North 860) and 12a Lime St. (Phone : Royal 5840).
SEAFORTH : Crosby Road South (Phone : Bootle 368).
BOOTLE : Hawthorne Road (Phone : Bootle 339).

licences led to their grant to a newcomer, MacShanes, who sought financial help from the independent Red and White group of Chepstow. A Gilbertian situation developed and following a widely publicised appeal, the services returned to Ribble, acting as agent for Liverpool Corporation, in August 1933. The 1931 Agreement developed a bond of trust between the company and the Corporation and in 1938 a new Agreement established joint working of an extended network on a 50:50 basis.

Meanwhile, with road service licences secure, the Merseyside Touring Co. Ltd. and its subsidiary, Nor-West Bus Services, were wound up on 30th September 1931, 88 vehicles being transferred to Ribble. These included Adair's Gilford and eight AECs acquired with the Pendle and Lancashire and Westmorland takeovers which had been transferred to Merseyside on purchase and which now acquired their second Ribble fleet numbers.

Liverpool-St. Helens

Ribble had received licences in Liverpool for a Wigan service in 1928 but disagreement with St. Helens Corporation, who wanted to establish their own Liverpool service, had prevented its introduction. In an effort to start the service before the new licensing legislation came into force, an application was made for St. Helens ply-for-hire licences for a two-hourly express service, via Billinge. The Corporation refused their application and deadlock ensued to the extent that commencement of the service on 25th October 1930 was announced on the basis that only return ticket holders would be picked up within the borough.

LUT was outraged that Liverpool Watch Committee had licensed Ribble for this route as their own application to extend their Salford-St. Helens service to Liverpool had been postponed several times. At a meeting held at the Park Hotel, Preston on 21st September 1931, attended by the managers of the Ribble, Crosville and LUT companies and Wigan, St. Helens, Leigh and Salford Corporations, areas of influence were agreed on an extended Salford-Liverpool service, a new Wigan-Platt Bridge-Haydock-St. Helens-Liverpool service and the existing express service via Billinge. By virtue of the agreement with Liverpool Corporation, the Prescot-Liverpool section was allocated to Ribble. The Salford route, always worked by LUT, was extended to Liverpool in January 1931, the Wigan via Haydock route started two months later and the three routes were co-ordinated from 1st May 1933, providing a half-hourly Liverpool-St. Helens service. From 10th August 1933, the Billinge route became a stage carriage service thus facilitating universal inter-availability of return tickets. The Wigan-Haydock-Liverpool service was unusual in that all four operators supplied buses though not necessarily simultaneously; Wigan Corporation buses first ran on it in November 1935.

Expansion in the North

The company realised that, in order to exploit fully its presence in Westmorland, Cumberland and the well-populated Furness district, much of the remaining competition needed to be eliminated. The BET had owned

the Barrow-in-Furness tramway system and the BAT had worked a bus service to Ulverston in conjunction with it. This was continued after the sale of the tramways to Barrow Corporation in 1920 but withdrawn because of fierce competition from owner-driver operators of which there were no fewer than 60 by 1925. Five Daimler Y vehicles, including some charabancs, remained in Furness until 29th January 1922 when two were transferred to the Ribble fleet and three to BAT's Macclesfield branch which in 1923 became the North Western Road Car Co. The Kendal Motor Bus Co. Ltd. was purchased on 1st April 1930 with 24 vehicles – 19 Leylands, 4 Thornycrofts and 1 AEC. It had started running between Kendal and Bowness in April 1922, adding a route to Kirkby Lonsdale soon after. The network gradually extended to serve Underbarrow, Grange and Cark, Windermere and Ambleside. An hourly service to Lancaster with two vehicles outstationed in that city, was one of the company's last expansions, together with an extension beyond Ambleside to Grasmere and a half-hourly town service in Kendal. Buses were identified by a white K. Competition now ceased on the Lancaster-Lake District route.

The 24-bus fleet of Rutter's Kendal Motor Bus Co. Ltd. was bought by Ribble in April 1930. Kendal No.27, nearest the camera was a Northern-Counties bodied Thornycroft UB and became No.920; it was withdrawn in 1934. Most of the others were Leyland PLSC or C7 models, some of which continued in service until 1938. Note the 'K' on each bus to distinguish the company's vehicles from those of its competitors. Mr Rutter was Ribble's depot superintendent at Kendal for many years.

The background of hills and drystone wall was typical of Ribble's Lake District operations. This Tiger TS2 was one of 45 (23 with bus seats and 22 with coach seats) new in 1930 (831-75) and one of the last to have the squared-off rear end. This one had bus seats but was still equipped with a roof-rack with rear ladder. Note the destination board and external light to illuminate it at night, the latter a Ribble characteristic until 1940.

The Furness Omnibus Company's fleet, taken over in 1930, contained several modern vehicles, including three Tiger TS2s of which No.22 was to become Ribble 965. It was sold to Western SMT Co. in 1937 but finished its life with Osborne of Tollesbury, with a new body, being scrapped in 1951. Note the distinguishing letter 'F' above the destination.

A month later Ribble acquired the Furness Omnibus Co. Ltd, a company registered on 9th January 1926 by 16 owner-drivers working mainly on the Barrow-Ulverston route. This was a co-operative with all the shareholders working in the business. New, larger buses were purchased and regular time-tabled operation coupled with workmen's and discount tickets led to rapid expansion and the elimination of much of the competition. A thrice-weekly Barrow-Manchester service, started on 19th July 1927, was not a success and was withdrawn for the winter, being operated on Tuesdays and Thursdays only in 1928 after which it was abandoned. The Lonsdale Pullman Bus Co. Ltd., formed in July 1927 as an amalgamation of T. Henderson, H. Such and E. Holme, all of Barrow and W. Jolly and A. Glover, both of Ulverston, was acquired by the Furness Omnibus Co. in 1928 and in the following year the Barrow Bus Co. Ltd. (named for its founder, F. Barrow) and J. Creighton and Sons were purchased. The 36 vehicles taken over by Ribble included 21 Leylands, most of which were retained, and a mixture of ADC, GMC, Chevrolet, Overland and Daimler vehicles, some with only 14 seats.

The Furness company, whose buses were identified by a red F, contributed two routes between Barrow and Ulverston; three between Ulverston and Ambleside; an Ulverston-Millom route and five services based on Dalton, where the rudimentary depot was situated. Ribble built a new depot at

The smartly-maintained chocolate and white buses of Grange Motor and Cycle Co. ran jointly with Ribble on many services in the Furness district and South Lakeland. This 30-seat 1930 TS2, seen in wartime, was later rebodied and survived until 1949, two years before sale of the business to Ribble.

Ulverston which was opened in 1932. The Furness company secretary, Mr J.E. Coward, joined Ribble and managed its affairs in Furness for over 25 years. An agreement with Barrow Corporation gave Ribble access to the shipyards in exchange for a Corporation service to Ulverston. From 28th September 1930 the stage carriage services of Parker and Sons of Grange-over-Sands were taken over, no vehicles being involved in the sale, and with its existing stake in the area, the company became a strong competitor of the only remaining operator of any size, the quaintly-named Grange Motor and Cycle Co. Ltd. A far-reaching co-ordination Agreement was eventually made with Grange, effective from 26th September 1938.

The first and third open-staircase Leyland TD1s are Ribble vehicles seen leaving Barrow shipyard for Ulverston in company with several Barrow-in-Furness Corporation buses.

One of the small Furness vehicles – a Leyland Leveret built in April 1926 – which Ribble replaced with a full size bus after the takeover.

25

Carlisle City Services

In Carlisle, the 3ft 6in gauge tramway system of the Carlisle and District Transport Co. Ltd., a Balfour Beatty group company, ran on six routes, linked in pairs across the city centre. The company had an associated bus company, Richard Percival Ltd., and there were a further 14 independent bus operators. In addition, four major bus companies – Ribble, Cumberland, United and Caledonian – had services into the city. The tram system was worn out and Carlisle Corporation wanted to take it over and substitute its own buses. The Traffic Commissioners refused the Corporation's application in June 1931, suggesting that the operators should prepare a co-ordination scheme. Ribble, acting on behalf of all the Tilling-BAT operators, started negotiations with as many operators as possible and, from September, purchased Carlisle and District Motor Services Ltd. (27 vehicles), G. Bristow (3), White Star Motors Ltd. (9), F. Waugh (3), H. Hayton (1), R. Vickers (1) and Simpson and Thompson whose vehicles went to United. In addition, the tramway company and part of its associated bus operation were acquired, the bus services going to United and Caledonian. Wright of Cumwhinton was purchased separately by Ribble late in November. The City Council accepted £3,500 towards road reinstatement after tramway abandonment. It was agreed that the independent services would cease on 31st August, Ribble being granted temporary licences to run the old services under the name 'Carlisle Joint Transaction', pending settlement of the final scheme which included guarantees about the level of fares.

New services started on 1st November 1931 and the trams last ran on 21st. The city services were run by Ribble except those to Botcherby which were in the territory of United Automobile Services Ltd. Thus Ribble, the last of the big companies to reach Carlisle, got by far the biggest slice of the Carlisle cake and the city services became an important source of revenue. The City Council had a transport committee with an advisory role. Ribble also got the Carlisle-Bowness-on-Solway service which, because of a weak bridge, was limited to 20-seat vehicles. This was really in the territory of Cumberland Motor Services Ltd.

Carlisle was an Albion stronghold. These two PH24 models of 1926 (probably HH 3368-9) are lettered 'Carlisle, Dalston and District Motor Services Ltd.' in a two-line layout though 'Dalston' did not appear in the company's official title at the time of acquisition in 1931. The bodies were probably by Northern Counties and the buses became 1309/08 in the Ribble fleet but they were not operated, both going to Scotland for conversion to lorries.

who did not wish to run small buses. The Albion marque was strong in Carlisle and they figured large in the mixed bag of vehicles acquired so those of White Star Motors were retained for this work until replaced by Dennis Aces in 1934.

With the purchase of the business of H. Lace of Kirkoswald with five vehicles, in December 1931, Ribble's expansion in the Carlisle-Penrith area was complete.

Consolidation in Lancashire

While these momentous events were establishing Ribble's presence in the far north, the company had been consolidating its position in its Lancashire heartland. H. Croisdale's Brunshaw Motors with eight Leylands and a service between Holme Chapel and Burnley was purchased in October 1930 and Freeman's Silver Star service between Chorley, Horwich and Bolton, was taken over a month later jointly with Bolton Corporation who had operated jointly with Ribble since 1st April 1928. Attention now turned to the North Fylde where Councillor F.A. Lawrence had started a Fleetwood-Poulton service in

Councillor Lawrence apparently saw some advantage in using the initials LMS, and his vehicles carried this distinctive livery after the limited company was formed. This PLSC1 Lion was delivered in June 1926.

A Leyland Tiger TS2 all-weather coach of 'the other' LMS Company – the London Midland & Scottish Railway – in Carlisle on a hot June day in 1930. It was UR3783, the body being built by United and the vehicle dating from a year earlier – it being passed to Hebble Motor Services Ltd. To the right a Leyland C1 charabanc of Richard Percival Ltd., HH 2213, awaits departure with its board showing Wetheral. Behind the Tiger a local bus shows 23 on its destination whilst what looks like an ADC bus stands at the left. Wires and rails indicate the trams have some 18 months left before closure.

The Anglo-Scottish services (mentioned on page 35) passed through Carlisle *en route* from Glasgow to Manchester. Joint operation by Ribble and Scottish Transport added more variety to the scene. Here a pair of northbound Scottish Transport Tiger TS1 models with Cowieson bodies to BET Federation design, newly in service, stand at Penrith for the lunchtime break in July 1931. The southbound Ribble vehicles are to the right, behind the gentleman in plus fours. Leyland's new body already looks dated against the Scotsman.

This view of one of the 1930 Leyland Lion LT2s clearly shows the new style Leyland body with curved rear end and slightly arched windows. It is one of the batch numbered 780-4 and was photographed at Leyland on 3rd April 1930, before delivery.

Mopping-up in Central Lancashire

Under the new licensing system the Traffic Commissioners succeeded in co-ordinating services where the local authorities had largely failed. A.E.Brennand's Chipping-Longridge service was acquired in May 1932 but, in the Preston-Chorley-Wigan area, competition continued virtually unabated until 1935. Two small operators, De Luxe Motors (G. & E. Roe) running a Preston-Gregson Lane service and Brookhouse Motors (H. & R. Spencer) sold out in rapid succession in June and July respectively. They were followed by Dallas Services Ltd. which had been one of the largest thorns in Ribble's side with well-managed services between Preston and Chorley via Bamber Bridge; Whittingham, New Longton, Walmer Bridge, Croston and between Chorley and Withnell. Whilst Mr Dallas must have had the sale of his business in mind, it was precipitated by a strike by his drivers and conductors when he refused to recognise their trade union. Ribble took over his services on 10th July 1935; the buses were sold privately and an associated haulage business continued for many years.

November 1925. He was refused licences to extend to Blackpool in 1926 but started a Cleveleys-Thornton-Poulton service in the Spring of 1927. A Fleetwood-Manchester route, worked by a 20-seat Dennis G was not a success, being withdrawn in 1930. A limited company, Lawrence Motor Services Ltd. was formed and the Fleetwood town services of Fleetwood and Knott End Motors were acquired in 1928. The business was sold to Ribble on 10th January 1931 with 13 vehicles mainly of Leyland and Vulcan manufacture. Hourly trips on the Fleetwood-Poulton service were extended to Preston via Elswick and Kirkham in 1933. Ribble also developed the Cleveleys-Thornton local services and the only competing operator in Cleveleys, S. Snape, was taken over on 23rd October 1937.

The following month, Cadman's Services, Ltd. of Orrell, near Wigan was acquired jointly by Ribble, St. Helens and Wigan Corporations for £25,000. The main asset was a Wigan-Southport route and there were other services to Billinge, Kitt Green, Rainford (two routes) and Ashurst Beacon. The Orrell Post garage was used as a store for a many years and the 17 Maudslays were sold.

The fully-enclosed Leyland Titan TD1 lowbridge double-deck bus was the company's standard double-deck bus of the early 'thirties. There were seats for only 48 passengers, the upper deck seats comprising alternate rows of three and four seats to provide passing-places along the offside gangway. Note the route number card for service 154, Blackpool-Burnley, one of the original trunk stage-carriage services. Number 821, new in 1930, was sold to Alexander's of Falkirk in 1938 but finished its days with Kearsey of Cheltenham in 1950.

28

Pilot Motors operated this SG7 with Ribble style bodywork, numbered 19 in their fleet. It was photographed in July 1923 heading for Preston on what was presumably quite a hot day – notice the open windows in the smokers' saloon and all the open top lights. It became C248 and ran for Ribble until 1930.

One of the most competitive routes was between Preston and Leyland on which the number of operators had been halved to four by 1935. Ribble had covered the route since 1920 and there were also J. Fishwick and Sons, J. & R. Singleton and W. Parkinson. Fishwicks was not for sale and it was finally agreed that they would buy the other two jointly with Ribble and set up a pooling arrangement covering all the services to, from or through Leyland. This agreement, effective from 18th August 1935, differed from most of the many others to which Ribble was a party in that Fishwicks was the major partner, having a two-thirds interest. Singleton's continued to run coaches until 1963, being well-known for their three-axle Leyland Tiger.

Apart from Scout, BBMS and Viking, competition in the Preston area had now been eliminated and most of the remaining operators in Ribble's Lancashire area were absorbed gradually over the next four years. A. Parkinson's Knott End Motors (remnant of the larger Fleetwood and Knott End company), with a Knott End-Preesall local service, passed to Ribble on 29th February 1936. In September 1937 the Ormskirk market services and excursions from Rainhill of J.T. Harrison of Prescot were acquired followed, in May 1938, by Hugh Sharrock's market services across the moss from Formby to Ormskirk. Four months later, Harvey's Pilot Motors running from Aintree to Ormskirk via Melling was taken over, giving Ribble a monopoly of services in the area. Wigan Corporation was again involved in the acquisition of H. Tennant's route between Wigan, Wrightington and High Moor from 12th November 1938. Acquisition of the Yarrow Motor Co. Ltd. of Eccleston with services to Preston, Chorley, Leyland and Wigan, followed on 1st April 1939, with some Fishwick involvement, and the Preston-Wigan via Eccleston service was increased from every three hours to hourly as a result, Fishwick buses working through to Wigan. The Wigan-Coppull-Chorley service of M. Corless became the subject of a joint

agreement with Ribble and only the market services to Preston and Wigan of J. B. Jump of Bretherton remained in this area. One of his buses was destroyed by fire and after running for a time with hired vehicles, he sold to Ribble who took over on 1st January 1940.

Other acquisitions during this period were Parker Bros. of Malham in February 1937, his service being merged into the existing Ribble-Pennine operations and J. Edmondson's Clitheroe-Waddington service in March 1939.

In all these transactions between 1935 and 1940, no vehicles were taken into the Ribble fleet. Wherever possible, the vehicles were left for the vendor to dispose of but when their purchase was a condition of the sale, as in the case of Cadman's, they were sold off as soon as possible.

Municipal Agreements

During the 'thirties many Lancashire municipal tramway routes were converted to motor bus operation and routes were extended. Ribble was just as willing to co-ordinate its services with a council as with a company but sometimes councillors adopted a hostile stance, believing that they had the sole right to run the buses within their boundaries. Some councils, such as Bolton and St. Helens, were happy to accommodate the company but on a reciprocal basis, allowing the municipal buses to penetrate far beyond their boundaries. Bolton buses ran to Chorley and Blackburn and when Lewis Cronshaw's Blackburn-Manchester express service was acquired in 1937, it was shared by

The Yarrow Motor Co. Ltd. of Eccleston was another company to be named after a local river. Number 2 was one of five Leyland Lion PLSC3s in the fleet; there were also two of the smaller PLSC1 model and three Tigers. The business was sold to Ribble and Fishwicks jointly in April 1939 but no vehicles went into the Ribble fleet. This one became a showman's vehicle but may have briefly entered the Fishwick fleet. Note the 'Y' symbol, typical of the period.

J. & R. Singleton of Leyland ran a co-ordinated service with Yarrow and Parkinson's as demonstrated by the lettering on the window louvres. Registered TF 47, this 1930 vehicle was a Leyland Badger TA4, common enough as a goods vehicle but rarely used as a bus, though it had some affinity in design to the Lion LT1. Its 20-seat body was built locally by Fowler who, many years later was taken over by Fishwicks. It became a lorry when sold after the Singleton service was taken over in 1935, though coach operation continued into the post-war era.

W. Parkinson of Leyland was perhaps impressed by Singleton's Badger and purchased this somewhat similar vehicle a few months later. The body had 24 seats and although differing in various respects, the appearance and circumstances make it likely that Fowler may have built this one, also – there is a hint of the PLSC about the rear which ties in with local influences.. It was apparently scrapped following the sale of the business in 1935.

Viking Motors had its headquarters in Woodplumpton Road, on the northern outskirts of Preston and this all-Leyland Lion LT2, new in December 1930, was a typical choice for an independent operator. Note the folding door on the outside of the entrance, an optional alternative to a door at the top of the steps favoured by most operators. The destination reads 'Great Eccleston via Elswick' in an arched form and the route was not taken over by Ribble until November 1952.

Ribble, Lancashire United and Bolton Corporation.

Ribble services penetrated the Rossendale area extensively, competing with the buses of Bury and Rawtenstall Corporations and Ramsbottom Council. Bury had a period of empire-building when it joined in Manchester's 'Co-ordinated Motor Bus Service', linking a Stockport-Bury route with another from Bury to Burnley in which Rawtenstall Corporation and Ramsbottom UDC also participated. In 1932, the routes between Bury and the former tram termini at Water and Crawshawbooth were pooled with Ribble and Bury ceased to run to Burnley. The arrangement whereby Ribble limited stop buses on the Clitheroe or Great Harwood to Manchester services carried local passengers through Haslingden was a sensible one which avoided the need for Haslingden Corporation to run a loss-making service through to Edenfield. Accrington Corporation had obtained powers in 1929 to run to Clitheroe and Ribble's predecessor, Rishton and Calder, had come to terms. A new agreement made with Ribble in 1931 established joint working over a wide area.

Some Ribble local services in Blackburn and Darwen were sold to those authorities when they started running their own buses. The formation in 1933 of the Burnley, Colne and Nelson Joint Transport Committee by amalgamating the three towns' tram and bus undertakings was followed by complete abandonment of the tramways and Ribble had to come to terms with a municipally-owned bus system with ramifications stretching from Padiham to Keighley. A joint area was defined and an agreement signed on 18th February 1935. This enabled both operators to develop services to their mutual benefit and when the businesses of E. Jones of Newchurch-in-Pendle and the Barley Omnibus Co. were taken over in 1945, the acquisitions were made jointly.

The Fylde coast operators were generally less co-operative and an early Ribble service between Preston and St. Annes was curtailed at Lytham. In the 'thirties, both the LMS Railway Co. and Ribble unsuccessfully attempted on a number of occasions to buy the Lytham St. Annes municipal transport undertaking. Blackpool remained hostile, resenting the Ribble-Scout monopoly of traffic on Preston New Road and Ribble's more direct routes between Blackpool and Poulton-le-Fylde. An offer to purchase the small Lancaster Corporation system was also abortive.

Traffic Development

The acquisitions of the late 'twenties and early 'thirties facilitated the rationalisation of services, and frequencies were increased, double-deck buses being introduced on many interurban services following the appearance of the low-height Leyland Titan bus in 1928. The four 'trunk' services linking Bolton and Burnley with Blackpool and Morecambe (and Heysham for a time) used double-deckers from their inception and in days when speed was less important, many people were content to make long, leisurely journeys and the trunks certainly encouraged through traffic. This was helped by the 'All Route Ticket' introduced at 15/6d in 1927 allowing eight days' unlimited travel; it was increased to £1-12-0d in 1929, by which time the company's territory had expanded, and remained at that price until 31st March 1966. In later years it was never advertised and few knew of it. However, by 1966 fares had risen to such an extent that commuters were using it as a cheap season ticket and it was abolished.

Suburban housing development in the various towns where there was no municipal transport prompted Ribble to develop extensive local networks in Chorley, Fleetwood, Crosby, Kendal and Carlisle. Loss-making services received no revenue support from local councils but relied on cross-subsidisation from other profitable routes.

The low height of the TD1 Titan, and its much improved performance and comfort compared to earlier double-deckers, made it suitable for use on interurban services and No. 814, one of 56 put on the road in 1930, is seen on the Garstang-Preston road when new. It had the later style radiator, as introduced that year. Withdrawn in 1938 it then served another 11 years with W.Alexander and Sons Ltd., Falkirk.

Leyland Lion LT2 No. 781, new in 1930, heads north up a deserted A6 to Brock, a village between Preston and Garstang which was a popular starting point for hikers and fell-walkers. This bus, like many others of its vintage, was withdrawn in 1939 and saw further service with three operators in the north-east. Former Ribble vehicles often saw extended service but away from their former haunts, Scotland or County Durham being likely new homes.

The War, 1939-45

During the months preceding the outbreak of war on 3rd September 1939, detailed plans were made for dealing with the effects of war if it came. In days when there was no domestic oil production and every drop of liquid fuel and rubber for tyre manufacture had to be imported across seas likely to be infested with enemy submarines, it was essential to limit consumption to the absolute minimum. In the summer of 1939, bus operators were told to submit plans to the Traffic Commissioners for services which would require only 60% of the current fuel consumption. The wartime role of the Chairman of the Commissioners was Regional Transport Commissioner with virtually absolute powers and full control of the fuel ration to bus operators. Express services were to be cut even more savagely so Ribble, the largest operator of such services in the land, was to be especially hard hit and, in fact, when war came, the company was faced with a fuel allocation of 50%, 1,543 drivers and conductors being laid off in September 1939. Following an appeal to the Commissioner, this was increased to $62\frac{1}{2}$% in October and some late journeys up to 10.30pm and peak hour duplication were restored. Very soon there was a need for many new factory services as the economy was switched to wartime production.

Many marginal services were totally suspended, others were run on fewer days of the week while frequencies were reduced on virtually every route. As the war progressed, late services were withdrawn and Sunday services suspended on many routes to discourage travel. Blackout conditions reduced demand and placed a heavy burden on platform staff. From a short-term economic point of view, the suspension of loss-making services and the greater utilisation of what was retained, coupled with reduced maintenance costs, were an accountant's dream but all had to be paid for in the long run. Fares remained at their 1931 level throughout the war. There was some relaxation of fuel supplies for summer services in 1940 but this was not repeated in subsequent years. In 1939, the company carried 106.7 million passengers over 42.6 million miles. The comparable 1945 figures were 143.6 million passengers and 25.3 million miles, an increase in productivity from 2.5 to 5.7 passengers per mile.

During the peak production period, Ribble conveyed 40,500 passengers per week on 900 bus journeys to and from Royal Ordnance Factory, Euxton and 12,000 on 250 bus journeys for Bristol Aeroplane Co at Clayton-le-Moors. Shift working in factories spread the peak load but in some cases the company was unable to cope with the demands of large new war factories and other operators had to be asked by the Commissioner to share or take over the responsibility. A good example was the ROF at Kirkby, near Liverpool which was served by Liverpool

For the most part, Ribble's fleet remained quite smart in wartime. This 1938 Titan TD5 carried its years well in the April 1944 picture taken in Carlisle. In the late 'thirties Ribble had adopted its own styles of bodywork, in accordance with the ideas of Captain Betteridge, who was Chief Engineer at the time. The slightly arched cream band below the front indicator identifies this as a Brush body. The squat, square-cut driver's windscreen was a feature of the Betteridge designs.

Tiger TS8 bus 2167 was one of an order for 129 diesel-engined examples which entered service in 1939 and one of 89 bodied by Burlingham. Its seating capacity was increased from 32 to 34 in 1949 and it was withdrawn in 1951. It is also shown working a Carlisle city service in 1944.

and St. Helens Corporations and eventually the former built a lengthy tramway extension with government money. Other factories and military establishments were partially served by independent operators who were allocated work by the Commissioner in as fair a way as possible in order to keep them in business. Blackpool Corporation served some RAF camps in the Fylde until some time after the war ended.

In districts where there were corporation bus systems, the company often had serious staff problems as municipal working conditions tended to be better. Conscription of workers, mainly women, to bus work was not a success, producing a poor standard of work from a resentful staff. Strikes were narrowly averted at some depots and, at Bootle, the company's share of the joint services with Liverpool Corporation was handed over to the latter for several months in 1942-43 because independent services could not be adequately served with the staff available;

32

Ribble buses which could not be manned were hired to the Corporation. The air raids of 1940-41, which devastated the inner areas, tended to disperse the population, placing unprecedented demands on company services.

Increased demands were met to some extent by converting more routes to double deck-operation, an expedient helped by the delivery of new buses. Despite these problems, the company responded very well to the challenges of wartime operation, putting on extra works services and vehicles for troop movements, very often at extremely short notice. The consequences of wartime conditions affected the company, however, for many years into the peace as will be seen in later chapters.

Generally speaking, only double-deck buses with utility bodywork were finished in wartime grey livery. However, this 1940 Leyland Tiger TS8, seen in Blackburn, seems to have suffered from some deterioration of its cream areas and was painted brown or dark grey while retaining the original red paint on the lower panels.

One of Ribble's wartime priorities was to provide transport for those working at Leyland Motors' various factories. In this early post-war view outside South Works the Cheetah, one of a 1938 batch with body by Eastern Coach Works, heads a line of grey double-deckers, the first two of which, at least, are utilities. The cold, wet, workers at the head of the queue will probably notice that the bus they are about to board is a wartime rebodied Titan TD1, one of five thus treated, by Northern Coachbuilders – they were fitted with diesel engines at about the same period. The Cheetah was still petrol-engined at the time, Ribble having been unusual among major companies in continuing to place full-sized petrol single-deckers in service up to 1939, choosing the Cheetah thus powered generally for more rural services.

During the early- and mid-'twenties, there was a great expansion of the services provided by charabancs and motor coaches and, in the absence of modern legislation, there was nothing to distinguish between the regular time-tabled service and the type of tripper excursion which operated only if sufficient numbers of passengers were persuaded to book. Most services fell into the latter category and, in practice, on quiet days, there was co-operation between competing operators who pooled their passengers to make up economic loads. In the terms used after the passing of the Road Traffic Act, 1930, these activities were 'excursions and tours' and the first regular inter-city express service was started by Greyhound Motors Ltd between Bristol and London on 11th February 1925.

A direct service between Glasgow and Liverpool was started on 7th April 1927 by Anglo-Scots Motorways Ltd. of Glasgow who, by its association with Scottish Clan Motorways Ltd., could provide an onward connection from Glasgow to Aberdeen. During 1927, several other long distance services commenced, worked by fast, imported lightweight vehicles such as Lancias, Fiats, Reos and Studebakers. The tempo increased in 1928 and, while most of the initial activity had been by private operators, many of whom quickly slid into insolvency, the larger companies such as Ribble now began to take an interest.

Ribble entered this sector of the market in July 1927 with the purchase of Collingwood Motors (Liverpool) Ltd. who ran four 1920 Daimler charabancs, mainly between Liverpool and Blackpool. They advertised under the not-too-original slogan 'one or twenty we go' and had a better reputation for reliability than some others. The

purchase included a city centre booking office at 127 Dale Street, (a site later occupied by Higson's Brewery offices) and garages in Collingwood Street which, despite their inadequacy, remained in use until 1960. Ribble substituted saloon buses for the charabancs.

Lancashire to the Lakes

The acquisition of Lancashire and Westmorland Motor Services Ltd. during the winter of 1927-28 extended Ribble's area of influence into the Lake District. A comprehensive integrated network of long distance services was devised and brought into operation on 23rd May 1928 as follows:-

1ex	Manchester-Bolton-Chorley-Preston-Blackpool	2-hourly
2ex	Manchester-Bolton-Chorley-Preston-Lancaster-Kendal-Ambleside	2-hourly
4ex	Liverpool-Preston-Lancaster	

Three days later, North Western started a competing Manchester-Blackpool service with buses running through from Macclesfield, Urmston and Altrincham and, as both operators were in the same financial group, a joint half-hourly service, bringing in also the independent Lancashire United company was agreed to start on 6th July. Initially, North Western could not obtain licences in Bolton but this problem was eventually resolved. An alternative route through Swinton, Walkden and Westhoughton was served as a result of Lancashire United participation.

The 1ex and 2ex routes were initially timed to give an hourly Manchester-Preston service, the Liverpool-Lancaster trips co-ordinating to provide connections

This Leyland Lion LT1, No. 706, with standard Leyland body pictured in Manchester's Lower Mosley Street bus station, came into service in 1929 and is seen loading for Clitheroe on one of the frequent East Lancashire limited stop services. Note the company's name on the bulkhead window where it would be illuminated by the saloon lights at night, and the 'Duplicate' label, displayed in order to let passengers waiting en route know that another bus was following. After 10 years' service with Ribble, it was sold to Davies of Summerhill, Wrexham for whom it operated for another fifteen years.

between Liverpool and Blackpool or Ambleside. The latter were extended to Morecambe in July and the following month the co-ordinated network was expanded to give direct services between Liverpool and Blackpool (7 trips) or Ambleside (5 trips); Southport-Blackpool (every 2-hours) and Blackpool-Morecambe (roughly every hour). During the winter, there were reduced services and the Ambleside route was curtailed at Kendal.

A little-known service was 11ex between Seaforth Sands, Liverpool and Manchester which started on 20th August 1928 and was withdrawn within three months following agreement on spheres of influence with Crosville and North Western. The Seaforth Sands-Liverpool section was really for depot running purposes and was covered only on the first and last journeys, with several Liverpool-Manchester journeys during the day.

From 20th April 1929, the Liverpool-Preston section gained an hourly service for most of the day comprising a 2-hourly service to Ambleside and four through trips to Blackpool via Kirkham but, from 22nd June, many adjustments were made in the realisation that, useful as connectional facilities were for a minority, the majority of passengers disliked changing, even under supervision, and wanted through journeys. The half-hourly Manchester-Blackpool service had been an enormous success and soon justified a 15-minute frequency at weekends. A new Liverpool-Blackpool service via Lytham St. Annes was introduced, worked by two buses from Preston and one from Liverpool; Liverpool-Ambleside was extended to Keswick with fewer trips, some of the discontinued times being taken over by a new Manchester-Keswick service. There were also through journeys from Liverpool and Manchester to Morecambe.

It is doubtful if such a structured, inter-connected network, put into operation more or less simultaneously, could be found elsewhere and it typified Ribble's disciplined, methodical approach to service planning. In the meantime, competitors had not been idle. Lowland Motorways of Glasgow, Eniway Motor Tours, and W. & G. Coachways of Manchester started daily Manchester-Glasgow services in 1928; The Liverpool-Glasgow service

was resumed by another company named 'Anglo-Scottish' with competition from Wallace Black of Seaforth trading as Imperial Motorways. The following year both Imperial Motorways and C.F. Rymer of Liverpool started Liverpool-Edinburgh services.

The Scottish Services

From 13th May 1929, Ribble and Scottish General Transport of Kilmarnock commenced daily Glasgow services from Manchester and Liverpool leaving those cities at about 8.45am and running in tandem between Preston and Carlisle whence the Manchester coach followed the direct route via Lockerbie while the Liverpool coach ran via Dumfries and Kilmarnock, the same route as the Liverpool competitors. Both coaches continued beyond Glasgow to Paisley where the SGT depot was situated. The running time from Manchester to Glasgow was 10hr 10min; from Liverpool by the longer route it was 11hr. The through fares were £1 single and £1.11.0d return. Lunch was taken in both directions at Penrith and there were other short refreshment halts. In order to provide a morning trip southbound, an additional Carlisle-Liverpool trip commenced on 26th July 1929, returning from Liverpool at 3.40pm.

The Glasgow services continued throughout the winter of 1929-30 and from June 1930 the Ribble network was greatly expanded. The Liverpool-Glasgow service now took the direct road north of Carlisle but ran an hour later to establish approximately an hourly service between Preston and Carlisle. The Dumfries and Kilmarnock road was taken over by a new Blackpool-Glasgow seasonal

The bus stand at Sandgate, Penrith, was used as a refreshment stop and a crew changeover point on the Lancashire-Scottish services. This 1931 scene shows a newly-delivered TS3 26-seat coach (No. 1124) leaving for Glasgow, displaying not only an Express board but a supplementary card showing intermediate points. On the far left, a Scottish Transport Tiger and another Ribble Tiger are also en route to Glasgow while, right, a 1928 Tiger with rear-entrance body, awaits departure on the local service to Carlisle. Note the driver with summer white top and dustcoat and the different styles of Leyland body on the Ribble vehicles.

service which ran twice daily in the high season and followed the route through the Lake District. A new network of Lancashire-Edinburgh services, run jointly with the Scottish Motor Traction Co.Ltd., was introduced. These followed the same pattern as the Glasgow services with a Blackpool route via the Lakes and direct Manchester and Liverpool routes running an hour apart. The latter had lunchtime departures from both ends, giving arrivals around 11.0pm demonstrating an extreme application of establishing a regular interval network through Ribble territory to the detriment of the through traffic. The service was retimed to run about 90 minutes earlier in 1931.

The winter of 1929-30 had given the company a measure of the winter traffic potential and the time-tables for the 1930-31 and subsequent winters were more realistic. There were Manchester-Glasgow and Liverpool-Edinburgh services with connections at Preston and thereafter the Liverpool-Glasgow, Manchester-Edinburgh and both Blackpool services ran only seasonally. The afternoon Blackpool-Glasgow service was also dropped. The Carlisle-Liverpool facility was continued throughout the year. Imperial Motorways' local operations in Liverpool were acquired by Ribble in December 1929 but the goodwill of their Scottish services was sold to MacShanes' Motors of Liverpool who curtailed the Edinburgh service at Keswick but continued the Glasgow route, a night service being added in either 1930 or 1931. Rymer's Edinburgh service was replaced by a Glasgow service in 1930 but he was soon in financial difficulties and passed it to Imperial Motor Services (E.J.Jones) which had no connection with Imperial Motorways.

Ribble's Liverpool terminus was transferred to Skelhorne Street in 1931 and to the former Merseyside office at 30 Islington a year later. The Anglo-Scottish service ceased in September 1932 and Ribble and Western SMT Co. (successor to Scottish Transport) bought the goodwill jointly, suppressing the Liverpool-Glasgow via Dumfries route. In 1933, MacShanes' services were run by Red and White Services Ltd. of Chepstow and under an agreement with Ribble in January 1934, these licences were surrendered. Lowland and W. & G. Coachways sold their Manchester-Glasgow routes to Ribble alone in 1934 and Lowland's service became the basis of the night service which continued independently for the next 20 years. The company, in effect, had its own Glasgow depot and staff based there. Ribble and its Scottish joint operators were now in sole possession of the Lancashire-Lakes and Scottish network which remained unchanged except for minor alterations until the outbreak of war in 1939 brought an end to these long-distance services.

Dalton Square, Lancaster was the principal loading-point in the city before Damside Street bus station opened. A Ribble Tiger of 1928 to 1930 takes a break on the way to Keswick. Note the 'Express' board. The vehicle behind is a Scottish General Transport coach bound for Glasgow.

An elegant Leyland Tiger TS3 of Scottish Motor Traction Co. Ltd. with 26-seat Cowieson body, stands in Hatton Garden, Liverpool about 1930, probably waiting to pull round the corner to load outside the Ribble office at 127 Dale Street. Note the curtains and sheeted luggage rack.

The Merseyside Touring Co.Ltd.

The Merseyside Touring Co. grew out of the well-established motor dealer and haulage contractor, Garlick, Burrell and Edwards Ltd., of Bootle and, as a member of the Vestey group, with its shipping and meat interests, it had the advantage of considerable financial resources. In its short life it grew into a very large and important operator which demonstrated much greater professionalism than most of its contemporaries. Private hire and excursion work started in 1928 and the name 'Merseyside Touring Co.' was registered though a limited company was not formed until August 1929. Vehicles were originally registered in the name of the parent company or various GBE officials. A city office was opened at 30 Islington, on the corner of Fraser Street.

From March 1929 a controversial network of services was built up between Litherland, Bootle and the city centre, working on the 'return ticket principle' whereby only return ticket holders were picked up within the city of Liverpool where licences were consistently refused. The company also acquired control of Nor-West Bus Services Ltd. with local services from Liverpool to Crosby, Southport and Ormskirk.

A stylish leaflet announcing the programme of Lancashire-Scottish services for 1930, the first year Ribble ran to Edinburgh. On the original, the Ribble and Scottish Transport vehicles are printed in red and the SMT vehicles in blue. Note the red rose of Lancashire and the Scottish thistle in the border design.

In the Spring of 1929 the company launched an extensive programme of excursions and extended tours, the latter forming the nucleus of Ribble's Liverpool-based excursion and tour business in later years. For the Cup Final on 27th April 1929 a special weekend trip was organised, costing £2.12.6d, including hotel accommodation, four meals a day, light refreshments on the outward journey and a two-hour tour of London on the Saturday morning. The company issued contribution cards for weekly payments to be made.

An express service was started from Liverpool to Scarborough via Warrington, Manchester, Oldham, Huddersfield, Leeds and York on 11th May 1929 with journeys to Bridlington and Filey on peak Saturdays. The company acted as agent for other operators, one of which was John Pike's 'Claremont' service to London. The latter had been running buses in London since 1924 and another partner started another 'Claremont' business in Burnley in 1927 (see page 21). Pike was retained by Merseyside to advise on the expansion of their Bootle bus business and eventually sold his London service to the company who took over from 19th August 1928. The service which, like many others on the route, had been running via Stratford-on-Avon and Oxford was altered by the new owners to run via Lichfield, Northampton, Newport Pagnell and Dunstable.

The Scarborough and London services were cancelled in the winter but from April-May 1930 the express network was expanded to include services to and from Gt. Yarmouth (later also to Lowestoft); Bristol and Weston-super-Mare; and Torquay and Paignton, the West of England services being worked in conjunction with Greyhound Motors Ltd. of Bristol who ran the Torquay route via Chester, Shrewsbury, Ludlow and Bristol while Merseyside ran to Weston via Warrington, Bridgnorth, Kidderminster and Cheltenham. Limited winter operation during 1930-31 was unprofitable and was not repeated. The Weston service was diverted to Ilfracombe from 23rd May 1931. A further development in 1930 was the conversion of the Blackpool excursion into a regular service picking up in Bootle and Crosby.

In 1930, the Merseyside Touring Co. took delivery of several coaches with this style of Massey 26-seat bodywork, some on Bristol B and others, like this one, on Tilling-Stevens B10A chassis. It carries headboards for the Liverpool-Great Yarmouth service which Ribble disposed of to the North Western and Eastern Counties companies. This vehicle became Ribble No. 1270 and was sold to a dealer at the end of the 1935 season. It returned to Liverpool and ran for W. Sudlow until 1949.

A line up of Merseyside Touring Co. coaches in Fraser Street, Liverpool is headed by a 1930 Bristol B with Massey body. The Merseyside company was purchased by Ribble in June 1930 but operated separately until September 1931. Their extended tours were used as the foundation of Ribble's programme, the company not having attended anything of this nature hitherto.

Ribble purchased the Merseyside company on 8th June 1930 but, in order to ensure a smooth transfer of licences at a time when the licensing provisions of the Road Traffic Act were coming into effect, retained it as a separate company until 30th September 1931. The takeover was heralded by the opening of booking for Ribble services at Merseyside offices and footnotes about the London services in Ribble publicity. The London service was diverted into London Coastal Coaches' Lupus Street station and there were two departures a day, the early one from Liverpool arriving in time to give connections for many south coast resorts. However, the London service was handed over to Crosville on 9th November 1930 under the Area Agreements between Tilling & BAT companies. The Lowestoft service also offended against these Agreements and, after operating it in 1932, Ribble sold it for £1,500 to the North Western Road Car and Eastern Counties Omnibus Companies; they ran it jointly until 1936 after which it was discontinued. Liverpool-Scarborough, too, could have been claimed by North Western but this was avoided by rerouting it via St. Helens, Bolton and Rochdale.

At its peak, the Merseyside fleet (including 16 in the Nor-West name) comprised about 90 vehicles of 12 different makes including 10 transferred by Ribble from acquisitions in the North. Only 32 were coaches and it was the practice to use service buses for weekend duplication, with a van to carry the luggage.

The Central Lancashire-London Operators

The services between Blackpool, Preston, East Lancashire and London originated in the long distance mania years of 1928-29. Chorley, Wigan and Warrington were served *en route* and a service originating at Colne and serving Nelson, Burnley, Accrington, Blackburn, Darwen and Bolton was also of importance. There were also variations which combined elements of both routes such as Yelloway's Blackpool-Rossendale-Manchester-Leicester-London and John Bull's Blackpool-Preston-Blackburn-Bolton-London route. Unlike the Liverpool-London services they mainly passed through the centre of Birmingham which was unusual as Birmingham Watch Committee normally only licensed operators with premises in the city. Needless to say, they were highly competitive and little, if any profit was made during the winter. The contenders in this race were W.C. Standerwick Ltd., C. Smith, Wood Bros. (Blackpool) Ltd., (trading as John Bull Coaches), and Scout Motor Services. Eniway Motor Tours of Manchester are said to have been the pioneers, running on to Blackpool as an extension of their London-Manchester service.

Joseph Bracewell Ltd. ran the Colne-London service but also had a Blackpool-Birmingham via Wolverhampton route with a morning departure from Birmingham. They took over Charlie Smith's in August 1928 but continued to use the name for some time. Ribble was interested in getting control of the Lancashire-London services and, once licences had been granted by the Traffic Commissioners, started negotiating. After Standerwicks' business, which had been founded by 1904, had been advertised for sale, there were negotiations for its purchase jointly by Ribble and North Western, transfer being effected from 11th November 1932. The Birmingham and Midland Motor Omnibus Co. Ltd. (Midland 'Red') who were joint operators of the Manchester-London route with

North Western, were piqued at being left out but it seems probable that it was done to avoid a conflict of interest as they were acting as agents for Bracewell's. A third share of Standerwick was then sold to them but this tripartite control proved to be cumbersome and Ribble bought out Midland Red in 1933 and North Western in 1934.

It was decided to keep W.C. Standerwick Ltd. as a subsidiary company and Wood Bros. and Bracewell's services, which had been acquired on 1st February 1933, were transferred to Standerwick in 1934. Services to Liverpool via Wigan and to Oldham were abandoned or merged with other routes. Scout and Yelloway were not for sale so there were still three operators on the London road.

Coach operation in Blackpool was fiercely competitive in 1929-31, particularly on the London and Yorkshire services. Upper left; this Leyland Tiger for Wood Brothers, trading as John Bull Coaches, dated from 1929-30. Bodywork of this character, with deep seats having headrolls and the two-door layout was typical of this period. The Wood Brothers business was acquired in February 1933 and transferred to Standerwick in 1934. Lower left; Standerwick's fleet had been quite mixed in the 'twenties, including several Albions. Seen here is FV49, a rare normal-control version of the Viking Six model, dating from early 1929. The photograph is a Leyland official view of November 1930 and may indicate that it had been part-exchanged against new Tigers. Right; these views of a 1931 Standerwick Tiger show the roll-back canvas top and the interior with toilet compartment at the rear nearside.

The Yorkshire-Blackpool Pool

Another lucrative market was the group of services between the West Riding industrial towns and Blackpool, sometimes taking in some East Lancashire towns on the way. From the Blackpool end, three operators were running by 1928-29, Wood Bros. (John Bull) mentioned above; W. Armitage and Son Ltd., (Progress Motors) and Walker Taylor and Sons. (Pride of the Road). All three served Leeds, some by rather devious routes, while Progress also ran to Dewsbury, Ossett, Wakefield and Barnsley. From the Yorkshire end, West Yorkshire Road Car Co. Ltd. was running six times daily from Bradford via Skipton and Whalley from 16th July 1928, and from Leeds the following year. R. Barr (Leeds) Ltd., an ancestor of Wallace Arnold, was also early in the field together with B. & B. Tours, J. Bullock and Sons (1928) Ltd. from Wakefield, Hansons Buses from Huddersfield, Hebble from Bradford and Halifax, W. Pyne and Sons from Harrogate and several others. In 1930, Ribble started a twice daily Blackpool-Leeds service via Clayton, Burnley, Colne, Keighley and Bradford, all the independents continuing to use the route through Todmorden and Halifax. As in the case of the London services, the profits from summer operation were to some extent dissipated in the winter.

Ribble and West Yorkshire agreed to run joint services between Leeds and Blackpool, Morecambe and Keswick, the latter absorbing a Ribble Skipton-Ambleside service, started in 1930 and several West Yorkshire services. Joint working started in May 1932 and the agreement also covered the Scarborough services from both Blackpool and Liverpool.

The federated companies were talking among themselves with a view to co-ordinating their Yorkshire-Blackpool activities but there was a lack of agreement, mainly about the share which each operator should have. Meanwhile, early in 1933, the three Blackpool firms were purchased by Ribble (acting for the potential pool partners) but retained their identities. The Traffic Commissioners were making threatening noises but the first pooling scheme submitted to them, which was estimated to save 100,000 miles per annum, was turned down, largely because of strenuous railway opposition. The Commissioners then prepared a revised scheme which, after much argument, was agreed by the operators, the main bone of contention being the compulsory winter co-ordination between the Tilling-BAT and independent operators.

The result was that the five Tilling and BAT companies formed the Yorkshire-Blackpool pool with shares of Ribble (30%), West Yorkshire (27%), Yorkshire Traction (23%), Yorkshire Woollen District (11%) and Hebble (9%). During the winter, Bullock's Wakefield-Blackpool service and Hanson's and Yorkshire Woollen District/Hebble's Huddersfield-Blackpool services were worked on a three-week rota, only one vehicle running through to and from Blackpool. Pyne's Harrogate-Blackpool and the Leeds-Blackpool via Skipton routes of the Pool, R. Barr and B. and B. Tours were also co-ordinated on a similar basis, but with each operator running through on agreed days. Local feeder services were run as necessary.

These arrangements came into force in two stages in

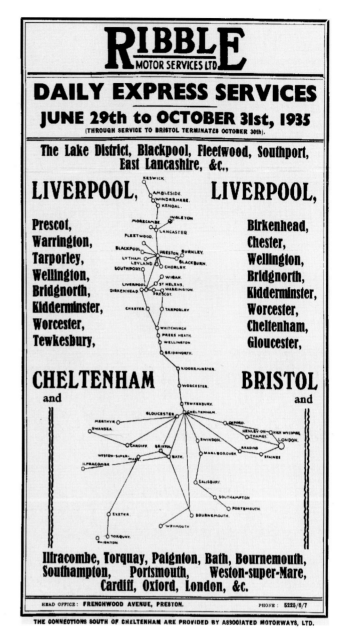

The Liverpool-West of England services were curtailed at Cheltenham and Bristol from 1935 by order of the Traffic Commissioners, onward connections being provided by the newly-established Associated Motorways network. The map on the cover of this leaflet shows connecting routes from Keswick in the north to Bournemouth and Torquay in the south though the longer journeys were impossible in one day at that time.

January and October 1935, all the previously licensed services continuing unaltered for that summer though John Bull, Progress and Pride of the Road mileage was counted as part of the Ribble share. These three companies were wound up and some of the indirect routes eliminated. All the services were given numbers with a J prefix. The Agreements stood the test of time, continuing until services were suspended during the war and resuming in substantially the same form after 1946; West Riding Automobile Co. eventually took the place of Bullock.

The 36 Leyland TS6 coaches of 1933 were Ribble's first venture at the operation of coaches quite distinct from and superior to the ordinary saloon buses. The body order was equally divided between Leyland and English Electric and, while the overall impression was similar, there were many detail variations, particularly in the window treatment. Number 1383 had a 26-seat English Electric body and was withdrawn in 1940, seeing further service with Victory of Ibstock, Leicestershire.

The Duple-bodied version of the Tiger TS7 coaches delivered in 1936 was identical to that built by English Electric to Ribble specification the previous year except for the reversal of the livery and a revised rear mudguard outline. Duple's standard coaches of the time often incorporated some similar features – notably the use of alternate plated and painted pillars – but the Ribble design, the first manifestation of Captain Betteridge's ideas, was quite distinctive. The shallow rear window was unusual for the period – it became fashionable 45 years later. The coach shown is 1539 which remained in service until scrapped in 1951.

Wright Bros. (Burnley) Ltd. ran this Leyland PLSC Lion with an unusual sunshine roof. The body is believed to have been built by Strachan and Brown. Wright's main contribution to Ribble was the site of the Coliseum Coach Station, Blackpool.

Consolidation on the Fylde Coast

The acquisition of Wright Brothers (Burnley) Ltd. in January 1934 included the Coliseum site in Blackpool on which a much-needed coach station was built. Wright's four seasonal services between Colne/Bacup and Blackpool/Morecambe were transferred to Standerwick. In addition to the express services already mentioned, all the Blackpool operators acquired had excursion and tours licences. More were added with the joint acquisition by Ribble, North Western and Lancashire United of M. and H. Motors Ltd. of Jubilee Garage, Blackpool from 9th March 1935. There were also services to Manchester and Oldham by two routes and these were consolidated into a route to Oldham via Chorley, Bolton, Bury and Manchester which became route X9.

William Salisbury and Sons Ltd., with a Blackpool-Manchester service and an excursion licence, was taken over in 1935. Salisbury's retained their identity, acquiring J. Jenking (Queen of the North) in April 1936, being merged with Standerwick in July 1937 when the latter also purchased Waddington and Sons Ltd. (Union Jack). There was thus a very confused situation with both Ribble and Standerwick operating excursions in Blackpool and, in February 1939, all the Ribble excursion licences were transferred to the subsidiary.

The North East

The Area Agreement companies were late starters in the race to link the Tyne and the Tees with Blackpool, a host of small operators having started services in the late twenties. Star Motor Services, Primrose, Wilkinson's, Scott's Greys and Darlington Triumph Services immediately come to mind. In order to stake a claim before the appointed day under the Road Traffic Act, Ribble and the Northern General Transport Co. Ltd. started joint services between Newcastle upon Tyne and both Blackpool and Keswick on 31st May 1930, replacing seasonal services run in 1929 by NGT alone. In due course Northern General developed a series of feeder services extending to South Shields, Sunderland, Houghton-le-Spring, Consett and Stanley and in practice there was much through running. These services were well planned and continued without any appreciable change until interrupted by the war.

United Automobile Services Ltd. was a late-comer to the Tilling camp and this may have retarded efforts by Ribble to establish direct links with Teesside. When agreement was reached, an ambitious scheme comprising four joint seasonal services was introduced in June 1932. There were two Middlesbrough-Blackpool routes, one via Ripon, Harrogate, Skipton and Whalley (started by Smith's Safeway Coaches in 1928) and the other via Darlington, Richmond, Hawes, Ingleton and Lancaster. A Middlesbrough - Barrow-in-Furness service with connections at Kendal for the Lakes was abandoned at the end of the 1932 season and a Darlington-Carlisle route via Barnard Castle, Brough, Appleby and Penrith lasted for only one more year, being replaced in June 1934 by a Darlington-Keswick route which was withdrawn permanently in September 1935. The Blackpool via Hawes route was diverted via Sedbergh and Kendal to replace part of the Barrow facility. This curtailment of the grand plan meant that Ribble had to take on some operations from the Middlesbrough end and it became the practice to out-station a crew at Middlesbrough to work the Hawes service and, in some years when the mileage was seriously out of balance, the Skipton route also.

The Short Express Services

During the summer months there was a close-knit network of limited stop services of 30-60 miles in length linking the Lancashire towns and, year by year, more of it fell into Ribble hands. The objective was to provide what would now be called 'user-friendly' facilities to travel to the seaside resorts of Blackpool, Lytham St. Annes, Morecambe and Southport and to the cities of Manchester and Liverpool. In the winter, the network was less complete but, nevertheless, there was a very adequate all-the-year-round framework. Many of these services were a result of Ribble enterprise, examples being the three services between Widnes, St. Helens, Wigan and Blackpool which, in addition to these towns, provided direct coaches from several large villages such as Sutton Manor, Billinge, Coppull and Eccleston. As the network developed, the company published composite time-tables for sections such as Burnley-Blackburn-Preston and Preston-Lytham St. Annes-Blackpool which were common to a number of services, with a view to filling empty seats and receiving a higher fare than that charged on the local buses in exchange for a swifter and more comfortable ride.

The year 1934 saw the purchase of the express services of Kenyon, Coleman and Robinson (KCR) between Great Harwood, Accrington, Darwen, Blackburn and Blackpool with two AEC Regal coaches. It will be recalled that the stage services had been taken over in 1925. Ribble staff were still referring to these services as 'KCRs' over 30 years later. The 1935 acquisition of Pearson's 'Happy Days' (jointly with Crosville), Mrs. S.S. Wilson of Edge Lane, Liverpool and an express service of J.T. Harrison of Prescot brought the company additional Liverpool-Blackpool services with a host of new picking-up points in the suburbs and at the Pier Head. From 1st June 1937 the Blackburn-Bolton-Manchester express service of Lewis Cronshaw Ltd. was purchased jointly with Lancashire United and Bolton Corporation. Cronshaw was a London operator who carried on trading at Hendon after the sale of his Blackburn business. Ribble then withdrew its Blackburn-Haslingden-Bury-Manchester service.

The 1938 purchase of two Bolton coach operators, Arthur Christy (Bolton) Ltd. (jointly with LUT), and F. Snaylam brought two new Bolton-Lytham St. Annes-Blackpool services, one via Belmont and the other via Horwich and completed the Ribble monopoly on this section. Strangely, these services were not integrated into the existing facilities, remaining much as they were before takeover until the late 'fifties.

The Lancashire holiday scene was dominated by the Wakes Weeks whereby all the industries in a particular town closed down for one or two weeks and often, also, for a weekend in September. This meant that enormous resources had to be concentrated at different points each

Saturday. Ribble was now in a strong position to minimise dead mileage as the vehicles which took one town's holidaymakers to the coastal resorts could be used to bring another town's people back. The Yorkshire-Blackpool pool had the same effect as vehicles of any of the five companies could be used on all the routes. The regular express services were augmented at holiday weekends by period excursions and holiday expresses; the latter often operated on one day licences applied for each year.

Nowadays, it seems strange that people from Preston would book seats on a double-deck bus to go for a week's holiday to Blackpool, 18 miles away, but hundreds of people did just that. They were issued with special card tickets valid only on a particular bus and similar arrangements were made for the return journey.

The Manchester services acquired with the Rishton and Antley and Claremont businesses were developed into intensive routes to Clitheroe (with connections to Gisburn and Skipton) and Great Harwood, the latter carrying some local traffic by agreement with the Rossendale municipalities. Some of the Manchester-Rochdale-Todmorden-Burnley journeys were extended to Blackpool or Morecambe.

Lower Mosley Street bus station, Manchester could often present a contrast in vehicles as demonstrated by 1927 Leyland PLSC1 Lion 285, with a later Lion behind, both bound for Great Harwood, and 1936 Brush-bodied Cheetah LZ2 coach 1584 on the Blackpool stand about 1937, shortly before the withdrawal of 285. The PLSC would be based at the former Rishton and Antley garage at Church and it was a tribute to Ribble's maintenance standards that such an elderly vehicle should be allowed to venture so far from home.

Bolton town hall is the backcloth to this 1930 line-up of the fleet of Arthur Christy (Bolton) Ltd. whose business was acquired by Ribble in 1938. However, all the vehicles shown had been sold by 1934 as Christy's policy was to keep his fleet modern. Shown are an Austin 20 car of about 1927, a 1926 Lancia, two 1929 Tiger TS2s with canvas-roofed bodies by a local firm, Bromilow and Edwards, and two 1930 Tiger TS1s with modern Duple bodies. Christy's business contributed the X90 summer express service between Bolton and Blackpool via Lytham St. Annes, together with excursions and tours. In the illustration below drivers can be seen arranging cases in the roof-mounted luggage holder – the large rear boot had yet to come.

Ribble rarely took vehicles from acquired businesses into stock in the later 'thirties, but Christy's fleet of eleven Duple-bodied Tigers, none more than three years old, was too good to miss. Most survived until 1950 or later, generally having been transferred to Standerwick in 1948, as in the case of this 1936 TS7, still petrol-engined when seen in Victoria Coach Station, London in July 1949.

Wartime Express Services

The outbreak of war in September 1939 curtailed the summer season abruptly and many seasonal services were terminated early. Others were severely curtailed but the Commissioner realised that many of the medium-distance limited stop services catered for essential travellers and were in no way pleasure-orientated. These included the East Lancashire-Manchester services X3, X4, X13, X23, X43 and X66 and the Wigan-St. Helens-Liverpool services.

For the 1940 summer season, the following services were allowed to run on Fridays, Saturdays, Sundays and Mondays only:-

X42	Blackpool-Morecambe (8 trips)
X60/70	Blackpool-Manchester (1/2 hourly Mons & Fris; 20 minutes Sats & Suns)
X62	Blackpool - Newcastle-on-Tyne (1 trip and 1 additional Sat., July & Aug)
X63	Keswick - Newcastle-on-Tyne (1 trip)
J1-2	Fleetwood-Blackpool-Leeds (4 trips)
J3-4	Blackpool-Leeds via Halifax (1 trip with extras Sat)
J6-9	Blackpool-Bradford/Leeds via Skipton (1 trip)
J7/12	Blackpool-Barnsley-Doncaster (2 trips)
J8	Blackpool-Ossett-Wakefield (2 trips)
J16	Blackpool-Harrogate (1 trip)
	Colne/Bacup-Blackpool/Morecambe (Standerwick services) (1 trip each)

Services J5, J10 and J15 ran on Saturdays and J11 on Saturdays and Sundays. The weekend Yorkshire-Blackpool time-tables were little different from the summer of 1939 though duplication was severely restricted.

No Lancashire-Scottish services were permitted, operation on the 'main line' being confined to return journeys between Manchester and Carlisle, Keswick and Manchester and two trips between Liverpool and Carlisle.

For the winter of 1940-41, daily operation was resumed on X60/70 (hourly); X42 was given four daily trips and X4 was curtailed to run between Manchester, Todmorden and Burnley only with 6 trips. X13/23, X21, X30, X43 and X66 continued unaltered but X40 was withdrawn. Summer 1941 saw a half-hourly Blackpool-Manchester service and a less extensive Blackpool-Yorkshire timetable on Fridays to Mondays. The four Standerwick services were also run as in 1940. On Tuesdays to Thursdays a service (X61) ran four times daily between Blackpool and Preston via Lytham St. Annes and a Preston-Burnley service (J1-2) which was run as a through service, indicators being changed at Preston and separate tickets issued. These continued during the winter of 1941-42 when there was also an hourly X60/70 service at weekends only. The latter was withdrawn on 30th March 1942 by order of the Ministry of War Transport.

There was no summer augmentation in 1942 and, from 27th July, to discourage non-essential travel, all Sunday services on limited stop services were withdrawn except between Lancaster and Carlisle. There were further reductions in April 1943 when the last buses on X13/23 and X43 were timed about one hour earlier, between 8.0 and 9.0pm from Manchester. The 'main line' services were reduced to three trips between Lancaster and Carlisle (X21), on weekdays only. Late buses and Sunday services were reintroduced on X13/23 and X43 from 8th December 1945 on which date some services suspended since September 1939, X3 Great Harwood-Manchester, X53 Manchester-Burnley and X55 Burnley-Blackpool were reinstated. Lancaster-Carlisle and the Blackpool-Preston-Burnley link-up continued to run on weekdays only.

The return of peace brought plenty of passengers for leisure travel and this was the scene at Aintree on Grand National day, 1949 with a Ribble Brush-bodied Daimler CWA6 leading an ex-Sheffield Crosville Titan TD4. The stream of traffic also includes a Lancashire United Titan, an unidentified coach and contemporary Austins and a Vauxhall. Others include a rare Avon-Standard, mid-thirties Buick, ex-army Ford V8 with estate car body, Triumph roadster and a Riley. Aintree depot was to be built just across the bridge within two years.

CHAPTER 4
POST-WAR EXPANSION – STAGE CARRIAGE

The end of the war in August 1945 replaced one set of problems by another. Fuel was still rationed and, because of the emphasis placed on exports by the government, virtually everything was in short supply. A Labour government, committed to doctrinaire socialist policies, threatened to nationalise all means of transport and, in the meantime, imposed bureaucratic controls on virtually every commercial activity. There was a pent-up demand for travel which created a virtually insatiable call on the company's resources which showed little sign of abating for the next five years. During the war, many coaches had been commandeered by the armed forces and were in need of heavy refurbishment on their return. The company had concentrated its limited resources on the mechanical parts of the vehicle, bodywork receiving less attention, and much of the fleet was in need of urgent attention.

There were manpower problems, too, as many of the company's pre-war staff decided not to return to bus work, grasping new opportunities in fields of endeavour with less unsocial hours. Gone, too, were the compliant men of pre-war days as the complexion of the government encouraged militancy.

The first relaxation in fuel supplies came in December 1945 when many suspended late buses and Sunday facilities were restored. The company then concentrated on reinstating suspended services and increasing frequencies, the trunk routes between Burnley/Bolton and Blackpool/Morecambe and Lancaster to Keswick being given priority. The summer of 1946 was marked by long queues as harrassed officials endeavoured to shift the crowds with an aged and inadequate fleet. The following year, glorious summer weather taxed the fleet even further. Tree-lopping

In 1938, a massive order for 132 Leyland Cheetah LZ2A buses, with vacuum-hydraulic brakes was bodied by Eastern Coach Works. Number 1850 was one of 31 with sliding roofs for use in the Lake District and is seen after the war in Carlisle. It still had a petrol engine but had lost its black mudguards and gold lining-out. A distinctive 1936 Dennis Ace (1657) is visible in the background.

Blackburn Boulevard about 1950 with Blackburn Corporation Crossley DD42s on the left and Ribble buses at the unprotected centre stands. On the left are 2484, a Leyland PD1A with Brush body, new in September 1947, *en route* to Chorley and preceded by a Tiger PS2 on the Rochdale Service. The TD7s facing the camera date from 1939-40 and are operating local services to Oswaldtwistle and Great Harwood. The cream flash on the single-deck bus, below the domed building, identifies it as a Tiger TS8 of the ACK-registered batch delivered in 1940.

45

crews were out all over the system as problems were eased by converting more and more routes to double-deck operation. By 1950, the company had a policy calling for a maximum of 600 double-deckers but it was hard to keep the demand within this number. In spite of opposition from the conservative Lakes UDC, double-deckers were introduced to the Lancaster-Keswick service; the council, having been successful in obtaining green telephone kiosks, then demanded green Ribble buses! The company agreed not to carry advertisements above lower deck window level, but the livery remained unchanged.

The gradual extension of the five-day working week throughout industry altered the pattern of weekend traffic. The operators lost one sixth of their peak hour revenue but the Saturday demand was spread throughout the day and operators such as Ribble, with a heavy recreational traffic, had more vehicles available for it. The use of ordinary double-deck buses on medium distance limited stop duplication increased as a result of this social change.

To ease its serious vehicle shortage, Ribble hired 16 Wigan Corporation Titan TD1s in July and August 1947 and operated them at Bootle (13) and Wigan (3) to release single-deck buses for express duplication. Number 45 is seen on the L9 Crosby-Seaforth Sands shuttle, bearing two fleet names – Ribble and Wigan Corporation. The destination aperture has been partially masked to take the then standard Ribble three inch blind.

Leyland Cheetah 2101 dated from 1939 and was one of 40 fitted with diesel engines in 1946-48, thus transforming a quiet, smooth-running vehicle into a noisy brute. The post-1950 livery with the cream upper-works and black mudguards repainted red was less attractive than the original paint scheme. It is seen at Keswick bus station, apparently carrying the body from an earlier batch, duplicating a PD2 on the Keswick-Lancaster service as far as Ambleside.

All the wartime utility buses underwent some degree of rebuilding after the war. The Duple body of Guy Arab 2406 (below left) had been fitted with a rounded rear dome and sliding windows and generally smartened up by Bond of Wythenshawe while Daimler CWG5 2393 (below right) lost its Brush body altogether and acquired a second-hand Metro-Cammell body from Wallasey Corporation.

Ribble's workshops at Frenchwood Avenue were kept busy catching up with wartime arrears of maintenance, in addition to more routine work. Eastern Coach Works and Brush bodied double-deckers, the former a rebodied pre-war Titan, and the latter a 1949 PD2/3, flank a Burlingham PS1 coach in the paint shops in this photograph taken during 1951.

Ribble bought second-hand Tiger TS7 chassis from the Devon General and Yorkshire Woollen District companies in 1948 and, after a thorough overhaul, fitted them with new 35-seat Burlingham bus bodies. Number 215 (previously 2706) was originally Devon General XL121; it is seen on the Ambleside-Dungeon Ghyll service on 1st September 1951 and was to give another nine years' service.

New Burlingham saloon bodies (below) were fitted to pre-war Tiger chassis, replacing the existing coach bodywork, in addition to being fitted to new Tiger PS2s and the ex-Devon General TS7s. A re-numbering scheme brought the various batches together in the 2xx series. The rebodied buses received 7.4-litre diesel engines of the type used in the post-war PS1 model. This view shows their original livery, differing only slightly from the pre-war style.

Bootle depot received PD1s, as seen above, fitted with 56-seat highbridge Burlingham bodies which were the first post-war additions to the fleet in 1946-47, and ran them on the Bootle services joint with Liverpool Corporation. Number 2467 had lost its upper cream band when this picture was taken in 1957, near the end of its life. Ribble never came to terms with Liverpool's suffixed route numbers as letters appeared only on the 'hundreds' blind. Generations of buses were doomed to show 'A57' instead of '57A'.

Stanley Road, Bootle, below, near the junction with Linacre Lane, was an important connecting point between Liverpool Corporation and Ribble services. The large number of half-drop windows identifies these Leyland Titan PD2/3s with 8ft wide Leyland bodies as part of the batch of vehicles which were originally destined for Cape Town. Note the non-standard destination layout on No. 2649 for which special service number blinds were needed; these boxes were modified at overhaul time. The bus on the left is 2618, the first of the batch, and is working the peak hour L90 shuttle between Linacre Lane and Crosby bus station.

All-Leyland PD1A 2475 was working a Chorley local service when photographed in 1959. It was one of a batch of 10 buses which were the last in the fleet with 7ft 6in Leyland bodies. Its life with Ribble lasted from 1947 to 1961 after which it moved north and saw a further five years' service in Scotland.

In 1950, Ribble placed in service 50 PD2/3 double-deck buses with hand-operated platform doors (1301-50) and No. 1320 is seen when 11 years old, leaving Preston bus station for Bolton via Westhoughton. It ran until 1965 and then went to Scotland for a further four years' work.

More Joint Services

From 1st January 1948 Ribble and Preston Corporation commenced operation of four joint cross-town services – Frenchwood-Lea (P1), Lightfoot Lane-Penwortham (Plough Inn) (P2), Lightfoot Lane-Penwortham (Crookings Lane) (P4) and Ribbleton-Hutton (Anchor Inn) (P5). After a few months P4 was withdrawn in favour of an increased P2 service. The latter was normally worked by Ribble, who also had one bus on P1, the only route to pass the company's head office, while the Corporation ran the P5. However, peak hour trips were run by either operator. Scout also had an interest in P1 but did not operate. In later years, following new housing developments west of Preston, the P1 service was split into two branches (P1 and P3) and a new service to Ingol (P6) was added.

Oliver Hart and Sons had a run a service between Southport and Croston via Hesketh Bank since 1928 and a joint agreement came into force on 12th November 1949 whereby it was extended via Eccleston and Park Hall Lane to Standish (106). The obvious course was to extend it further to Wigan but Ribble did not want a joint service competing with its own independent route via Ormskirk. The extended service was a dreadful failure and Harts complained that they were losing money. Ribble then released them from the agreement, curtailing the service to reduce the mileage and eventually bought it from Harts in May 1953. The last Standish journeys were withdrawn at the end of the 1954 summer season.

More Acquisitions

The Magnet Service of C. Head, with a local service between Windermere and Bowness, was acquired from 1st February 1946 followed by J. Fawcett and Sons' Dallam Service of Milnthorpe on 1st December 1950. The jointly operated stage carriage services of the Grange Motor and Cycle Co. Ltd. were taken over from 1st July 1951, that company continuing as a coach operator until 1st January 1958 when Ribble took over the excursion and private hire business. The penultimate stage carriage operator running into Preston without any formal association with Ribble, Viking Motors Ltd. was taken over from 16th November 1952, though some Ribble vehicles ran on hire before that date.

The services, worked to a large extent by double-deckers, traversed sparsely populated country between Preston and Woodplumpton, Great Eccleston and Salwick. There was a multiplicity of local shareholders, all of whom had free passes. It was far from being an attractive commercial proposition and Ribble was asked to take it over by the Traffic Commissioners. The firm had originated in the businesses of G. & W. Whiteside (Royal Blue) in 1919 and R.A. Tootell in 1921 or 1922, the company being registered by Tootell in 1924. There was short-lived competition from Ribble who ran a 2-hourly Preston-

Brush-bodied Titan PD2 No. 2672 is seen at work at Darwen, following the rerouting of the Bolton-Blackburn service to avoid a low bridge at Darwen Station. These buses were supplied in 1949-50 and were an 8ft wide version of the bodies supplied on PD1 chassis in 1947. Rubber glazing modernised their appearance. After withdrawal in 1960, it saw further service with the South Notts Bus Co.

Great Eccleston-Fleetwood service in 1926 but withdrew it for lack of support. Royal Blue and Viking amalgamated in 1929 and the service began to resemble the pattern of later years.

One by one, more of the remaining stage carriage operators were taken over – Bolton-by-Bowland Motor Services, based on Clitheroe, in September 1955 and M. Corless and Sons of Charnock Richard from 1st January 1957. The latter's Wigan-Chorley service had run jointly for 20 years and he had been persuaded to run through to Blackburn when services had been linked. Hadwins' local services in Ulverston were acquired in July 1956. The take-over of Scout Motor Services in 1961 is described in Chapter 6. McGregor's Ambleside-Hawkshead service, the last to remain in private hands in the Lake District, was acquired from 30th June 1962 and R. Prescott and Sons' Bamber Bridge Motor Service on 1st April 1967. The latter was the only one to contribute

any vehicles to the Ribble fleet and, except for Fishwicks, was the last independent stage carriage operator working into Preston.

The east shore of Lake Windermere was a magnet for tourists. The upper picture, taken at Bowness Pier in the early 'fifties is indicative of the transition from traditional front-engined single-deck buses to the underfloor type with greatly increased seating capacity. On the right is a 1936 Tiger TS7, originally a coach, which was fitted with a new Burlingham 35-seat bus body and a 7.4 litre diesel engine in 1949. Originally No. 1446, it was renumbered 2712 and then 221 in the 1950 scheme; Ribble ran it until 1960 after which it was used by the British Aircraft Corporation, Warton until 1967. The newer bus on the right is one of the 40 Leyland-MCW HR44 integral Olympics delivered in 1951. The lower picture shows Ambleside Cross and the bus station, a tastefully designed structure which blended well into its surroundings. From left to right are one of the 14 post-war Tiger PS1 coaches with 31-seat Burlingham bodywork; all-Leyland PD2/3 1338, with platform door, on the Lancaster-Keswick service; Olympic 273 loading for Coniston and one of the 1951 Leyland-bodied 41-seat Royal Tiger coaches.

Underfloor engined buses arrive – more seats give greater economy

The availability of chassis fitted with the engine mounted below the floor, coupled with an increase in permitted length, offered great scope for economy of operation – up to 44 seats could be installed instead of the previous 32-35 on a conventional bus. Sentinel were first off the mark, in 1948, and collaborated with Beadle to produce an integral vehicle based on Beadle's development of lightweight designs. Ribble took six 40-seat Sentinel examples in 1949 followed by a further fourteen 44-seaters as seen here, in 1951, but then, having stirred Leyland's sales force no doubt, purchased several hundred of the local marque.

Leyland's first venture in the design of an integral vehicle was built in conjunction with MCW. The Olympic, using a horizontal version of the 0.600 engine of the PD2 double-decker, was ahead of its time for companies like Ribble who still lifted bodies from their chassis at overhaul. Thirty Olympics entered the fleet during 1950/1 and the clean, uncluttered interior is noteworthy. Ribble's standard leather-trimmed moquette gives a reminder of just how smart vehicles of that era really were. Although the entrance/exit was at the front, one-man-operation was some way in the future – economy would come initially from the extra seats, for a conductor was still carried.

Leyland next offered the Royal Tiger chassis using much the same mechanical design as the Olympic and Ribble took 110 with Leyland's own 44-seat bus bodywork in 1951 and 1952. The Royal Tiger was a heavyweight, and was somewhat under-endowed in the brake department. Number 349, still looking typically smart though now around eight year's old, is seen on X43 service to Skipton.

In 1952 Leyland produced its lighter weight chassis – the Tiger Cub. The decision to cease body building at South Works meant that there would be no Leyland-bodied Tiger Cubs and other manufacturers were quick to step in to fill the gap. Weymann bodied this demonstrator with a body having much in common with the MCW-Olympic. During July and August of 1952 Ribble ran the vehicle for evaluation but in the event decided not to order the Weymann bodywork.

Instead Ribble's Tiger Cub buses carried stylish bodywork built by Saunders Roe at Beaumaris in Anglesey. The first vehicle was displayed at the Commercial Motor Show in 1952 and a further 49 of these handsome 44-seat examples entered the fleet during 1954. They operated for some 15 years, the last ten years being with one-man-operation. Saunders Roe, whose main business had been in the aircraft industry, went out of business altogether a year or so later. The photograph was taken at Grange-over-Sands. The early post-war Jaguar saloon belonged to Leyland's publicity chief of the time.

The Great Link-up Operation

By 1953, the post-war boom had cooled off and the company was seeking ways of encouraging additional traffic. General manager H. Bottomley believed that an untapped demand existed from a section of society which was free to travel at off-peak times but was discouraged by the fear of the need to change buses at unfamiliar places. This fear, confirmed by the number of times enquiry office staff were asked 'Do we have to change?', was sufficient to deter these mainly middle-aged or elderly people from travelling at all. He directed that, wherever possible, services crossing centres such as Preston, Chorley and Blackburn should be linked together, pointing out that unproductive layover time could often be reduced by creating long routes. During the winter of 1952-53, the Schedules Department applied itself to this task, producing a number of operational link-ups in time for the 1953 summer season. Through licences were not applied for immediately, destinations and numbers being changed at intermediate points, the ultimate destination often being shown on a paper label thus 'For Blackpool'. This gave time to make any adjustments in the light of experience and to allow the licensing procedure to take its sometimes leisurely course. Despite some opposition from such operators as Yelloway, all the stage carriage link-ups were eventually licensed as through services.

Whilst some economies in scheduling were doubtless achieved, there was disagreement as to the real value of these facilities, some believing that they were more appropriate to the 'thirties when time was less important and there were fewer daily express services than 20 years later. Problems were created, too, particularly at large depots with one common rota which meant that platform staff might encounter a trip to, say, Rochdale only once in several months. On the link-ups covering the Chorley-Wigan section, there was the hazard of the low bridge at Coppull which dictated the use of far more special lowbridge vehicles than would have been the case if the section had been isolated. Local passengers between Cleveleys and Thornton had to put up with bench seats on the upper deck because of this bridge 30 miles away! Delays on one section were passed on to the others and, on a bright but chilly winter's day, it was difficult to persuade passengers waiting at Wesham for a bus for Blackpool that its non-appearance was due to snow on the road between Edenfield and Norden.

The link-up operation was spread over five years – 1953-57. One of the last was 122, Bolton to Southport, which brought Bolton Corporation double-deck buses into the rural villages of West Lancashire and to Southport. However, within another five years traffic congestion was playing havoc with the through routes across Preston. Furthermore, changes in demand led to the need to reduce frequencies on some sections but not others. Bottomley was dead and could no longer support the policy and most of the through routes were broken up, starting with those crossing Preston in June 1965 and ending with Liverpool-Blackburn in September 1971. Some remnants, such as Preston-Chorley-Wigan remained. A full list of these through services will be found in Table 1, below.

TABLE 1: CREATION OF THROUGH ROUTES 1953-57

Date	Service No.	Route	Through Service	Service No.
19.12.52		Birmingham-Manchester-Glasgow	21.12.53	X20
23. 5.53	162 + 113	Fleetwood-Preston-Wigan	9. 1.54	162
	281 + X43	Skipton-Colne-Burnley-Manchester	10. 4.54	X43
27. 6.53	158 +1 +244	Blackpool-Preston-Blackburn-Rochdale	16. 4.55	158
	215 + 212	Bolton-Blackburn-Clitheroe-Chatburn	9. 1.54	215
	98 + 367	Preston-Croston-Chorley	———	—-
1. 8.53	155 +123 +308	Blackpool-Preston-Chorley-Wigan	6. 2.54	155
	308 + 239	Wigan-Chorley-Blackburn	1. 8.53	249
	123 + 313	Preston-Chorley-Westhoughton-Bolton	6. 2.54	313
15. 8.53	X50 + X2 *	Morecambe-Manchester-Nottingham (Smr SaSu)	———	—-
14.11.53	X60 + X2 *	Blackpool-Manchester-Nottingham (Daily)	———	—-
5. 6.54	X60 + X1 *	Blackpool-Manchester-Derby (Smr daily)	———	
30. 4.55	X27 +19 +296	Liverpool-Southport-Preston-Clitheroe-Skipton	7.56	X27
19. 5.56	152 + 167	Lytham-Preston-Burnley	9. 8.58	152
	X60 + X2*	Blackpool-Manchester-Nottingham-Gt.Yarmouth (SmrSa)	———	—
30. 6.56	B4 +298 +106	Oswaldtwistle-Blackburn-Leyland-Southport	1.10.56	298
	311 +331 +239	Liverpool-Ormskirk-Chorley-Blackburn	6.12.58	311/331
30. 3.57	122 + 347	Bolton-Chorley-Southport	30. 3.57	122
29. 6.57	180 +123 +308	Cleveleys-Preston-Chorley-Wigan	6.12.58	180

NOTES: * North Western-Trent joint service. Smr – Summer, Sa – Saturdays, Su – Sundays

The cross-Manchester facilities to Nottingham, Derby and Great Yarmouth remained as unlicensed link-ups.
Birmingham-Glasgow was extended to run from Coventry from 30. 3.53.

Ref. No. 5240

RIBBLE

Commencing Saturday, 30th April, 1955
NEW SERVICE 19
PRESTON — CLITHEROE
via SAMLESBURY, MELLOR BROOK, OSBALDESTON, LANGHO and WHALLEY

REVISED SERVICE 296
CLITHEROE — SKIPTON
PROVIDING THROUGH FACILITIES
with Service X27 Liverpool — Preston,
BETWEEN
LIVERPOOL and SKIPTON

With the introduction of the above, the through operation between Preston and Skipton on Services 9 and 296 WILL BE DISCONTINUED.

Time Table :—30th APRIL until 24th JUNE, 1955

	RIBBLE MOTOR SERVICES LTD.		Phone
LOCAL OFFICES ...	LIVERPOOL ... 30 Islington	... ...	North 2127
	SOUTHPORT Bus and Coach Station	... ...	55114
	AINTREE ... Ormskirk Road	... ...	1733
	BOOTLE ... Hawthorne Road	... ...	1161
	CROSBY ... Omnibus Station	...	Gt. Crosby 2699
	PRESTON ... 30 Lancaster Road	... ...	4272
	CLITHEROE ... 16 Wellgate	... ...	176
	SKIPTON ... 65 High Street	... ...	3407
HEAD OFFICE ...	FRENCHWOOD, PRESTON...	... ...	4272

Tickets are issued and passengers are carried subject to the General Regulations and Conditions of the Company contained in its Official Time Tables available on request.

mb. 5M. 20/4/55.

The long limited stop service X27 between Liverpool and Skipton was built up in stages and this leaflet announces the introduction of the 'missing link' between Preston, Whalley and Clitheroe in 1955. Indicators were changed twice en route until a through licence was granted. It replaced a link-up via Longridge.

Replacing the Trains

The Beeching plan to rationalise the railways led to the company being asked to provide replacement services to meet the alleged needs of the residual passengers, a chore which resulted in much unremunerative operation. These requests affected most parts of the company's territory and ranged from the provision of a few workmen's journeys, for example W13 Burnley-Great Harwood in December 1957 to a major reorganisation following the closure of the Preston-Southport line in September 1964. The main service (100) was diverted via Hesketh Bank and limited stop commuter services (X47, X57) were provided. Elsewhere, station closures on lines which remained open led to additional or diverted trips being demanded on existing services, which were invariably poorly patronised. Thus some Rainford-St. Helens journeys were rerouted via Crank when the Ormskirk-St. Helens line closed in 1951 and Chorley local service C6 to Heapey was slightly extended in 1960.

Fares

Between 1939 and the days of the post-war boom, fares were kept at their pre-1931 level by high levels of traffic and stringent economy measures. However, when the boom tailed off, there were annual demands for higher wages and fuel tax rose virtually with every budget; the company was obliged to bring the 20 year period of

stability in fares to an end. With costs running at about $2\frac{1}{2}$ times the pre-war level, it was remarkable that fares had remained the same for so long. Workmen's daily return tickets had largely been replaced by weekly tickets and some fares had gone up in other operators' areas. In 1951-52 increases were made in return tickets and contracts; singles remained largely the same and there were still 1d fares at a time when $1\frac{1}{2}$d and 2d minima were the norm. One of these, on the outskirts of Preston remained for some years after all the others had gone but Ribble retained a low minimum fare for longer than most by introducing additional stages. This created a conductor's nightmare – 62 stages between Blackpool and Preston instead of 31! – but retained low fares for short journeys.

Ever increasing costs and falls in traffic created by the social changes which followed the coming of television and personal transport, made the fares increase almost an annual event, relentlessly opposed by a host of local authorities who would have recoiled in horror if anyone had suggested that their annual rates increase should be made the subject of a Public Enquiry. The bus operators had to lay bare their accounts before the Traffic Commissioners to prove that their application was justified. Higher fares led to consumer resistance and the lower level of traffic fed the spiral which led to the next increase.

Like all bus companies who worked closely with municipal operators, Ribble was at a disadvantage in having no rate fund to absorb some or all of the extra costs. Municipalities usually preferred a tapering fare structure whereby, in effect, the short distance passengers who were in the majority, subsidised the longer riders and thus made residence in outlying housing estates more affordable. Ribble, with its complex network and with parochially-minded councillors looking over its shoulder for evidence of favouritism towards a neighbouring authority, found that anything other than a logical mileage structure was liable to create all kinds of anomalies, particularly when there was more than one route between the same places. Under co-ordination, Ribble had to keep its fares to the same level as the joint operator so if the fare to the boundary point was below standard, there was then a big jump in fare to the next stage. This brought the company into bad odour with its passengers who could not understand the economics of the situation. Many years were to pass before this situation could be remedied.

Increased Productivity

As bus operators approached the situation whereby salaries and wages absorbed 70% of revenue, it was essential to increase the productivity of the road staff. Relaxations in the permissible dimensions of buses and design changes had resulted in increased seating capacities, from the pre-war single-deck 32-34 seats to 44 and from 53 in a double-deck bus to 61. The 30ft long forward-engine double-

The last rear-entrance double-deck buses in the fleet, on Leyland Titan PD2/12 or PD2/13 chassis, the latter with air-pressure brakes, were delivered in 1955-56. The order for 61-seat highbridge bodywork was divided between Burlingham and Metro-Cammell, both types having open- and closed-platform versions. The Merseyside depots had a large allocation though they could be found all over the system, including Carlisle. The upper left picture shows an open-platform Metro-Cammell bus, 1411, in Lime Street, Liverpool on a joint service while, above right, is a rather dented enclosed platform Burlingham, No. 1461. The latter remained in the fleet until 1973 but 1411 was withdrawn two years earlier.

Ribble broke new ground in 1957, with a design of full-fronted forward-entrance double-deck buses, evolved in conjunction with Burlingham. These were the first 30ft. double-deckers in the fleet, being based on Leyland Titan PD3/4 chassis, with seating for 72 passengers. Number 1554, seen in Lower Mosley Street bus station, Manchester was one of those from the first 69 that were delivered in 1958 – a further 36 had arrived by the end of the year.

The rear engined Atlantean was welcomed by traffic managers, seeking to get more passengers into their vehicles. Engineers were more cautious and Ribble reverted to front-engined PD3s for several years after the arrival of the first Atlanteans in 1959-60. The bodywork on these was by Metro-Cammell. Number 1617 became the first Ribble one-man double-deck bus and is seen on a Lancaster University service when first converted in March 1969. It remained on the road until 1978.

In 1961, Ribble reverted to the Titan for its main double-deck requirements, though choosing the PD3/5 with Pneumo-cyclic gearbox after the introduction of this on the Atlantean. Burlingham was no longer building double-deck bodies so Metro-Cammell produced a special version of its contemporary style with full-width cab, deeper skirt panels and Ribble-style grille. Some 131 were built, 1769 dating from 1962.

The entrance layout of the PD3, loading – one of the Burlingham-bodied batches is seen below.

decker on Leyland PD3 chassis was whole-heartedly embraced by Ribble in 1957, giving a seating capacity of 72 ; the subsequent appearance of the Atlantean increased this to 78. The latter started entering service on the 'trunks' in November 1959.

Changes in legislation whereby buses with a seating capacity greater than 20 could be used without a conductor led to the introduction of one-man buses on trips with poor loadings and easy schedules. The first one-man buses came into service at Clitheroe on 9th August 1958 and spread to Fleetwood, Preston and the northern depots. Royal Tigers, Tiger Cubs and a few Olympics were used, ordinary Setright machines, driven by an electric motor, and Syro change-giving machines being fitted. One-man operation was theoretically accepted by the trade unions but, in practice was usually opposed at depot level. One-man duties tended to consist of odd trips on different routes strung together in the best possible way and little real progress was made for almost a decade. When 53-seat Leyland Leopard saloons were proposed for one-man operation, the unions refused to accept them for one-man duties, declaring a maximum seating capacity of 45. Several Leopard saloons had eight seats temporarily removed to meet this situation until the shorter PSU4 saloons were received.

These 110 Leyland-bodied 44-seat service buses mostly dated from 1952, and had allowed the last unrebodied pre-war single-deck buses to be withdrawn. Their extra capacity enabled some marginal duplication to be withdrawn and they were to be found all over the Ribble system. Many of the existing Royal Tigers were converted to one-man operation, as indicated by the yellow triangle in the nearside front windscreen. The electrically-operated Setright machine can be seen beside the driver on No. 324 as it leaves Appleby for Penrith on the Saturday-only route 675 on 11th August 1962

From 1963, the 36ft long Leyland PSU3 Leopards, with 53-seat Marshall bodies, started to replace lowbridge double-deck buses of the same capacity. There was no agreement on one-man operation of these vehicles and No. 209, seen in Tithebarn Street bus station, Preston when new, was delivered in 1967 with equipment for one-man operation but with only 45 seats and two large luggage pens. It was eventually re-seated to 53 in 1974 and ran in this form until withdrawn in 1982.

Bolton town hall clock looks down on Moor Lane bus station with a cross-section of Ribble's mid-'sixties fleet in evidence. Left to right are 1964 Leyland-Albion LR1 low-floor double-decker with 72-seat Alexander bodywork; 1965 Weymann-bodied 49-seat Leyland dual-purpose vehicle 814 and Plaxton-bodied coach 788 both on Leopard chassis. Both the latter carry route numbers for Bolton local services. A bus-bodied one-man Leopard brings up the rear.

The Changing Scene

The 20 years after the end of the war brought constant change. Changes in leisure pursuits and the growth of car-ownership were not the only factors which impacted upon the bus industry. The five-day 40-hour week combined with urban sprawl and the spread of factories into non-traditional areas compressed the peak hours so that more buses were needed to do less work. Changes in education brought demands for special school services which the company had to provide at its own expense, subsidies from education authorities being directed to the pupils in the form of free or reduced fare contracts. The combination of afternoon school trips and workers' journeys was often economical but as industrial hours were reduced there was a tendency for the two peaks to overlap, placing the company in a position when it could not find sufficient buses economically. A good example occurred in 1965 when Leyland Motors' finishing time was advanced to 4.18pm when the buses previously used were all at work on school journeys.

Throughout the 'fifties and 'sixties many depots experienced a chronic shortage of drivers and conductors resulting in service unreliability and literally driving passengers to private transport. At some depots it was not uncommon for up to 40 drivers and conductors to fail duty or report late in the morning, leaving the luckless duty inspectors to run the best service they could devise.

Ribble policy had always been to accept the responsibility of providing for all reasonable needs within its area, irrespective of profitability and, in return, the Traffic Commissioners protected the company's quasi-monopoly. This policy extended to retaining services which had outlived their usefulness for fear that some other operator would apply for a surrendered licence and use it as the thin end of the wedge to expand within the company's area. With hindsight, it is possible to query the wisdom of this thinking as few operators would have been likely to want to take on unremunerative routes. In cases where a Ribble bus had to be sent out empty from an urban depot to a village to work an inward trip and vice versa at the end of the day, it might well have been more economical to withdraw and allow the original type of village-based carrier to re-emerge.

Bus Stations

In many towns, the growth of both bus and car traffic made it essential to adopt revised terminal arrangements and there was often a need to take the buses off the streets in order to reduce traffic congestion and provide better facilities for waiting passengers. Ribble had built its own bus stations at Preston and Chorley in the 'twenties and Morecambe and Crosby in the 'thirties, and co-operated in a number of municipally-sponsored schemes in the 'thirties. These included Bolton (Moor Lane), Lancaster (Damside Street), Burnley (Cattle Market) and Blackpool (Talbot Road). Payment was made on the basis of the number of vehicle visits.

New stations were opened at Skipton in May 1950 and Whalley in April 1954 but of greater interest are the large schemes financed solely by the company over the next seven years. The first was at Southport where the municipally-owned Coronation Walk stand had been in use since the early 'thirties. Whilst conveniently located for the promenade, it was exposed and lacking in all but the most basic passenger facilities. Following the closure of the former Cheshire Lines extension railway to Southport, the company purchased Lord Street station, situated at the southern end of that prestigous thoroughfare. The former rail track-bed was brought up to platform level and the run-down facilities were refurbished. It came into use on 26th June 1954, being the first combined bus station and depot though its use as the latter was delayed for three months and it was also unusual in including a licensed bar with the company secretary, Harold Westall Miller, as licensee.

The next scheme was at Preston where congestion at busy times had reached intolerable levels, a number of standmen being employed to control buses reversing from the platforms. The express services, herded into one section at the southern end, were frequently delayed because of the inability of vehicles to reach the platform. Lord's Walk Coach Station, adjoining and parallel to the old station, was opened on 2nd April 1955, Preston Corporation having made a short new street to connect Tithebarn Street and North Road. This enabled a gyratory system to be adopted by all buses. The new station accommodated all express services and also the Longridge and ex-Viking groups of stage carriage services. Passengers waited under cover though construction was basic because the Corporation's plan for a new central bus station was already known. The latter, built at a cost of £1.1 million and opened by Lord Stokes on 22nd October 1969, replaced both stations and all the town centre stands for all operators' services, including excursions. It included a car park for over 1,000 vehicles and offices for both the Corporation and Ribble. The removal of the town centre stops for local services was criticised as the new station was some distance from many of the principal shops.

The largest of the company's schemes was at Liverpool where a site in Skelhorne Street had been acquired in 1939 but the outbreak of war and various other factors delayed construction. Since 1931, the company's services had terminated in Skelhorne Street, a steep street alongside Lime Street station, without serious mishap though at least one case is known of a driver who, seeing an empty bus slowly rolling backwards downhill towards him, drove his bus into its path, thus averting a serious accident. Express services loaded in Fraser Street (and, unofficially, on busy days, on various sites cleared by bombs during the war). The new station was built into the hillside, with the stage carriage services on the lower level and the expresses above. Opened in stages between April and June 1960 it was also used as a depot when an adjoining washing and service facility was built, the woefully inadequate Collingwood Street garages being closed at last.

Chorley was one place where the increase in bus width from 7ft 6in to 8ft was noticed and the island-platform station was rebuilt during 1964-65.

A new bus station at Ormskirk opened in December 1981 but its avowed purpose as a road-rail interchange was prevented when there was no money to move the railway station.

ENTER THE LEOPARDS – FOR STAGE CARRIAGE & EXPRESS WORK

The 36ft long Marshall-bodied Leyland Leopard PSU3/1R model had a sombre appearance in their all-cherry red livery. The first 40 entered service in 1963, their 53-seat capacity matching that of many double-deckers still in service. Number 460, new in June 1963, remained in the fleet until 1980, having been renumbered 685 in September 1973 when numbers caught up.

The Marshall body adapted well to a dual-purpose role, 49 coach seats replacing the normal 53 and still giving a roomy and attractive interior. The first ten (764-73) went into service in 1964 being used mainly on the shorter express services though it was not unusual for them to go further afield at very busy weekends. Several were converted for one-man operation in 1966 and withdrawal was spread over 1973-75.

The demand for long distance travel in the post-war period was insatiable and the company was severely handicapped by the depleted coach fleet. The principal express services were reinstated for the 1946 summer season but some had to wait until 1947 and it was not until 1950 that the list was complete, the last being X17 Southport-Morecambe and X183 St. Helens-Blackpool. Service buses were utilised as far as possible for medium length journeys but they sometimes strayed further afield when nothing else was available and a red bus was better than no bus. One gentleman, after enduring a rough ride from Kidderminster to Liverpool on an elderly Leyland Cheetah wrote to say that he thought the company's name should be changed to 'Terribble'. The fleet position improved marginally each season as a few new and reconditioned coaches came into service but the demand increased each year so little progress was made. The 49-seat 'White Lady' double-deck coaches, of which the first entered service in June 1948, greatly reduced costly duplication on many limited stop services such as East Lancashire-Manchester, Liverpool/Manchester-Blackpool, Manchester-Morecambe/Kendal and Great Harwood/Darwen-Blackpool. Behind the scenes, Ribble was urging Leyland Motors to hasten the production of an underfloor engined coach and, when delivery was near, a demonstrator,

painted grey, was sent on a publicity tour. Delivery of Ribble's order for 120 Royal Tigers had not commenced when Scout took delivery of their first and cheekily had it driven past the Frenchwood Avenue headquarters, with resounding blasts on the horn. The 41-seat Royal Tiger provided a 32% increase in seating capacity and, for the 1951 season, all the principal routes were equipped with them.

People began to look further than Blackpool and Morecambe for their holidays and the demand for West of England and the South Coast resorts increased. There was a willingness to recognise the benefits of overnight travel not only as a means of arriving at the chosen destination sooner but also as a saving of a night's accommodation cost.

Before the big 1951 intake of underfloor-engined coaches, Ribble had only 14 new coaches in the post-war years, all Leyland Tiger PS1s with 31-seat Burlingham bodies, which entered service in 1948-49. However, 48 identical vehicles were allocated to the Standerwick fleet. Originally numbered 2548-61, they became 701-14 in the general renumbering and were withdrawn in 1960, seven of them being exported to Yugoslavia. In this scene showing 713 at Skipton a vehicle of Pennine Motors, one of several independents which enjoyed friendly relations with Ribble, is also visible on the right

DOUBLE-DECK SEMI-COACHES – THE WHITE LADIES ENTER THE FLEET

The original double-deck 'White Lady' coaches made a big impact on the public and increased the capacity of vehicles on the medium-distance limited stop services from 31 to 49 – 58%. The original vehicle, BRN 261 (2518, later 1201 on Leyland PD1/3 chassis with Burlingham bodywork, was photographed behind Frenchwood offices when new in 1948. Left to right are A.S. Woodgate (Chief Engineer, later to be Assistant General Manager), J.W. Womar (Managing Director), R.P. Beddow (Chairman), E.L. Taylor, T.W. Royle, W.E. Yates (directors) and H. Bottomley (General Manager). Below, the front of the Burlingham body with original radiator grille (left) is compared with the East Lancashire body on the 1950-51 PD2/3 deliveries with modified grille which was applied to all 50 White Ladies.

THE ROYAL TIGERS TRANSFORM THE SINGLE-DECK COACH FLEET

The prototype Leyland Royal Tiger PSU1/15 coach is seen in original condition before its fleet number (781) had been applied. These heavy, all-metal, centre-entrance Leyland-bodied 41-seat coaches transformed the Ribble fleet, no fewer than 120 entering service in 1951. The front skirt panels were deepened on the Ribble vehicles though other fleets, such as Trent, North Western, Hebble and Southdown, retained the original design. The bodies were the first coaches to be built by Leyland since pre-war days. The Royal Tiger coaches achieved big mileages and withdrawal was spread over 1962-66, 781 being exported to Malta and rebodied there.

The very first Royal Tigers in the Ribble empire were the six front-entrance Duple-Roadmaster bodied coaches originally in the Standerwick fleet as 120-5. They all finished their service in 1963-64 with Ribble as 1054-9 and number 121 is seen outside the Duple factory when new in 1951 They were among Duple's first metal-framed bodies and caused a 38-week strike over demarcation and working practices. On a happier note, they were immortalised by the Dinky model which accurately portrayed the vehicle, though in red and cream.

The first batch of 'White Lady' double-deck coaches had five-bay Burlingham bodies mounted on Leyland PD1 chassis. The front grille was remodelled as shown to provide better cooling, (see page 60). Number 1215 (originally 2532) is shown working the X42 Blackpool-Morecambe service.

The 'White Lady' double-deck coaches were often used on local services, either as part of an mainly express duty or to meet unforeseen demands. At Blackpool depot, their duties were so mixed that local destination blinds were fitted. Titan PD2/3 No. 1248, with 49-seat East Lancs. body, was new in 1951 and is seen in Cambridge Road, Seaforth in March 1953 on the L3 Crosby service, one of Ribble's busiest routes.

The nearside view of Royal Tiger coach 812 in original condition when new in 1951 and before modification of the front skirt panel. Note the air intakes beside the front destination indicator which supplied air to ventilators under passengers' control above the seats.

'Westlinks'

The Ribble Liverpool-Cheltenham-Bristol services fed into the seven-company Associated Motorways network at Cheltenham which acted as a hub for coach services converging from all directions. They were timed to connect during four periods throughout the day and night – around 4.0am, 11.0am, 2.0pm and 4.30pm, the 2.0pm interchange being the most important. Between these times the coach station was largely deserted. The 7.30am Liverpool-Cheltenham service fed into the 2.0pm departures and the return trip was fed by the 4.30 arrivals but there were no connections at Liverpool. In 1948, an 8.0pm Friday night service from Liverpool to Cheltenham and a connecting 2.0am Cheltenham-Ilfracombe service brought the West Country within one-day reach of places further north though there were difficulties in the northbound direction.

For the 1951 season, the introduction of a 6.0am Preston to Liverpool journey brought the 2.0pm departures from Cheltenham within reach of Glasgow people. The following year, certain services were retimed and a two-way Liverpool-Cheltenham night service introduced on Fridays and Saturdays. Connections from Scotland were afforded by the old-established Manchester-Glasgow and a newly granted Liverpool-Edinburgh night service which absorbed the 6.0am departure from Preston during the summer only. Other 1952 adjustments were made in connection with the introduction of the Keswick-London service with connections at Keswick from West Cumberland by Cumberland Motor Services, at Kendal from Carlisle and at Lancaster from Barrow, a feeder revived in 1950. This range of facilities fed, at Preston, the 10.0am Blackpool-Liverpool-Bristol coach. Such marathon journeys as Glasgow to Torquay and Edinburgh to Ilfracombe, both in under 24 hours and with day and night services on certain days, were now possible.

For publicity purposes, this network was dubbed 'Westlinks' and, after adjustments to services within Scotland, Ribble produced a time-table showing connections from Scrabster in Orkney to Penzance. How many hardy folk made this trip is unknown but the Cheltenham traffic continued to expand and in 1955, through Liverpool-Paignton and Liverpool-Bournemouth weekend services were introduced, run by Ribble and Black and White Motorways respectively. This was the first Ribble one-man operated express service, the Blackpool to Newcastle-upon-Tyne, Middlesbrough and Scarborough services being similarly soon converted.

Coach-Air

The Coach-Air link at Blackpool Airport for the Isle of Man originated in 1951 and was greatly expanded in 1953 when larger aircraft working a more frequent service were introduced. The airport was right on the coach route and coaches on the principal express services from Blackpool Coliseum diverted briefly to pass a special loading point inside the airport perimeter. It was agreed that coaches would wait up to five minutes and this usually worked quite well. As the traffic developed, Ribble found it necessary to employ a standman at the airport and there were some chaotic summer Saturdays when, the airline having scheduled an hourly service, a plane breakdown resulted in hundreds of passengers being hours late. Special arrangements were often necessary to get people home to Lancashire and Yorkshire destinations, with duplicate vehicles held back for lengthy periods. The through bookings were extended to Jersey flights but this traffic never rivalled that to the Isle of Man.

Easy Way Holidays

Much marketing effort was put into a scheme for promoting centred holidays under the 'Easy Way' name. An inclusive charge covered travel to the holiday destination by Ribble and associated companies' regular express services, hotel accommodation and optional excursions. Holidays were not only available at the resorts in the Ribble area but at places as far away as Brighton, Eastbourne, Bournemouth and the Isle of Man. Some joint operators were persuaded to book holidays from their territory into the Ribble area. The project was successful in attracting thousands of holidaymakers to the company's services.

The Burlingham Seagull body was one of the most successful of the early coach styles for underfloor-engined chassis. Ribble chose it for touring coaches on the Royal Tigers there being fifteen in 1953, and a final five, including 940 seen here, in 1954 – these were on PSU1.16 air-braked chassis. This coach was the first PSV to run on a British motorway (see page 73).

The first Leyland Tiger Cubs had 41-seat centre-entrance Burlingham Seagull bodies, similar in general appearance to the Royal Tiger touring coaches but with plainer mouldings. They were much lighter in weight and returned a good fuel average on the most arduous of duties.

The later Tiger Cub coaches had front-entrance Burlingham 41-seat bodies. These vehicles had flat windscreens and more bus-like side windows. Number 988 is seen in Lancaster on the Glasgow-Manchester-Birmingham through service.

Midland Connections

The established companies were given a jolt in 1952 when a virtual newcomer, Northern Roadways Ltd., was granted a licence for a service between Birmingham and Glasgow with refreshment facilities on board. For the Christmas and New Year period 1952-53, Ribble and Midland Red collaborated to provide a through Birmingham-Manchester-Glasgow overnight link-up, operated by Ribble with Midland Red duplicates, and from March 1953 a Coventry-Glasgow link-up was put in place, a through licence eventually being granted; Northern Roadways was bought out and in 1963 their service was extended to work between Coventry and Glasgow via Wolverhampton and the M6 motorway.

Other link-ups were introduced in 1953, in conjunction with the North Western and Trent companies, coaches running across Manchester and carrying hire labels as appropriate. The first was a summer weekend Nottingham-Morecambe service, followed in November by a Blackpool-Manchester-Nottingham facility running three times daily throughout the year. A similar facility between Blackpool and Derby followed in 1954 in the summer only. In 1956, a North Western coach worked right through from Blackpool to Great Yarmouth via Manchester and Nottingham each Saturday in the summer. These unlicensed link-ups angered other operators such as Robin Hood Coaches but they were perfectly legal so long as separate fares were charged on each section of route and the appropriate destination was displayed.

Internal link-ups were also devised as shown in the table on page 53. The most ambitious was between Liverpool and Skipton via Southport, Preston and Clitheroe (eventually X27), running every two hours with a journey time not much short of four hours. Bearing in mind its stopping-service role over much of its length, many thought that the general manager's soubriquet 'Yorkshire-Mersey Express' was somewhat hyperbolical.

Within Lancashire

The popularity of the Blackpool-Manchester service continued well into the sixties. With a basic hourly winter frequency stepped up to half-hourly in summer (but both doubled on Saturdays and part of Sundays), it was said to be the most intensive express service in the world. There was some scheduled duplication throughout the year but at holiday periods, special schedules were drawn up by Ribble, allocating duplicate journeys to Ribble depots and to North Western and LUT, neither of whom would ever agree to a schedule which allocated more than their three-and two-twelfths respectively. The day viewed with the greatest apprehension by the Blackpool control staff was Easter Monday as, if the weather was fine, some period traffic would arrive every day, then heavy day traffic on the Monday and it would all want to travel back together on Monday afternoon and evening. Their 'finest hour' was Easter Monday 1964 when, with a schedule showing 192 duplicate journeys from 11.30am, 193 were operated and the queue was clear by 8.45pm. No fewer than 12,000 people left Blackpool on this one service on that day, 25 double-deck buses being loaded between 6.30 and 7.0pm.

Progress was also made in putting Morecambe further on the express service map. The Scottish day and London services had been rerouted through the resort in 1953 and this was extended to the night services and the Manchester/Liverpool-Keswick seasonal routes in 1956. One of the benefits was the relief of congestion at Lancaster caused by passengers changing to and from local buses. A summer weekend St. Helens-Morecambe service (X163) was added.

New Ventures

The run down of railway facilities was presenting new opportunities for long distance coach services. Excursion operators were applying for weekend summer services and, despite Ribble opposition, some were successful. Ribble saw the solution in joint ventures, the first of which was brought to fruition when competing applications for an East Lancashire-North Wales service were resolved by granting a joint licence to Ribble, Standerwick, Crosville, Ribblesdale Coachways and Bracewell's (Colne) Ltd. X35 ran from Skipton to Llandudno but it was not unusual for coaches to run through to and from points off the route such as Blackpool. This set the scene for future joint ventures and, in 1965, separate applications by competitors led to a joint Colne-Skegness service being licensed to Ribble, Bracewell's, Ellen Smith Tours and David Tattersall.

After trials with the Ribble Atlantean 'Gay Hostess' double-deck coaches had been carried out on the Standerwick London services (see Chapter 6), Nos. 1251-2 were transferred to the Manchester-Glasgow services, followed by Nos. 1253-4 to Blackpool-Liverpool-Bristol in June 1960. There were, of course, no motorways on these routes at the time and public reaction was to say the least, mixed. The suspension was such that on roads where the surface was less than perfect, the ride rivalled a roller coaster and there were many examples of passengers being ill when riding on a lightly-loaded top deck. The administration of the catering and toilet-cleaning arrangements was expensive and time-consuming. All these factors, coupled with the lack of enthusiasm from joint operators, combined to influence the decision to transfer all the Ribble vehicles to Standerwick and Scout for the 1963 season. However, the second generation of 'White Lady' double-deck coaches, also on Atlantean chassis, was more successful. Almost a ton lighter and with 59 seats, they started to replace the White Ladies on medium distance express services from May 1962.

The spread of the motorway network changed the character of many coach services, reducing running times but constantly raising the dilemma of how best to serve the places on the old roads or whether it was worthwhile serving them at all. Falling traffic all too often provided the answer. The new road network also brought new destinations within one-day range.

For the 1966 season, there were new weekend motorway services between Manchester, Blackpool, Morecambe and both Glasgow and Edinburgh and the duplicates on many other services were able to use sections of motorway, thus speeding up journeys considerably. New services to Manchester Airport from both East Lancashire towns and Blackpool were started but were poorly supported except

THE GAY HOSTESS ATLANTEANS BRING AIR SUSPENSION AND TRUE COACH SEATS TO DOUBLE-DECK EXPRESS TRAVEL

The use of 50-seat double-deck coaches on such lengthy routes as Manchester-Glasgow was a revolutionary step and Ribble's enthusiasm was not shared by its joint operators. Number 1251 was Ribble's first Atlantean and was used on various trials. Their limitations on ordinary roads soon became apparent and all 15 Ribble 'Gay Hostesses' were transferred to Standerwick or Scout.

Left, the lower deck interior and, lower left, the upper deck showing the individual adjustable aircraft-style seating and folding tables. Lower deck passengers' view forward was obstructed by the stairwell and by luggage in the rack above the nearside wheel-arch. Below, the galley showing storage and public-address microphone. Though based on a standard Metro-Cammell shell, the pioneer vehicle was sent to Weymann, more experienced in coach trim, for completion in the summer of 1959.

THE SECOND GENERATION WHITE LADIES ARRIVE IN 1962

The second generation 'White Lady' medium distance double-deck coaches were active from 1962 to 1976-77 and were never down-graded to service buses. Number 1277 stands at Blackpool Coliseum in 1972 on the accelerated Manchester-Blackpool motorway service, appropriately numbered M61; it has acquired the lower-case fleet title but otherwise remains in original condition. Poppy red livery had been applied to No. 1285 when seen in Portland Street, Manchester in 1973, after the closure of Lower Mosley Street coach station. The 59 seats were fixed and less luxurious than on the 'Gay Hostess' coaches.

at times of peak demand. Holiday camps were popular and the following year a direct Saturday facility between Colne and Butlin's, Pwllheli (X45) was commenced by the same joint operators as the X35 Llandudno route. This followed a joint Ribble-Western SMT service from Manchester to the camp at Ayr which was extended to Largs in 1968. To take full advantage of the motorways, the traditional route pattern often had to be forsaken and this resulted in there being several services direct to the South West, avoiding both Liverpool and/or Cheltenham

such as X34/44 Blackpool-Paignton with reciprocal through running with Black and White Motorways.

With a Pontin's holiday camp nearby, Southport was placed more and more on the express map with through coaches from Glasgow from the late 'fifties. Direct services from Newcastle-upon-Tyne and Cheltenham started in 1969 and from Middlesbrough in 1971.

Several medium distance services, including Skipton/Bolton/St. Helens-Blackpool, were converted to one-man operation in 1967, using dual-purpose 40-seaters.

THE LEOPARD ERA BRINGS VARIETY IN COACH BODYBUILDERS

BET Coach body orders tended to be spread around several suppliers in the 'sixties. One consequence was the appearance of Harrington, hitherto regarded as a 'southern' bodybuilder, among Ribble vehicles. The first Harrington-bodied coaches came in 1961. Mounted on 30ft-long Leopard L2T chassis, the first 20 (1019-38) had 32 individual seats for extended tour duties, the next 15 being 41-seaters though 10 were reseated to 32 in 1962. The seats from 1019-38 were transferred to new Bedford chassis in 1966 and the whole batch finished service in 1969-72 with 39 or 41 seats.

The Burlingham factory in Blackpool had become Duple (Northern), for a time building designs quite different from the parent company's output from Hendon. Duple (Northern) bodies were carried by six Leyland Leopard 40-seat coaches with toilet ordered by Scout Motor Services but transferred to Ribble in November 1962 as 701-6 after having been provisionally numbered S63-8. They lacked route number indicators at the front and, after spending the winter of 1969-70 on the Standerwick London services, four were permanently transferred in 1970 as Nos. 113-6.

Plaxton of Scarborough was the rising star among coach body specialists, its Panorama designs, with their big windows proving especially popular, Plaxton Panorama 49-seat bodies on Leyland Leopard PSU3/3RT chassis entered the Ribble, Standerwick and Scout fleets in 1963-64 and there were several repeat orders. With the growing network of motorways, they provided the power and speed necessary to accelerate many express services.

Accelerated Services

With traffic congestion a serious problem, the accent was now on speeding up services by avoiding congested areas which produced little revenue and 1970 saw many route changes on what were essentially non-motorway services. Thus X6 Blackpool-Middlesbrough ran direct from Skipton to Ripon, missing out Otley and Harrogate; X15 Blackpool-Scarborough made a similar short cut avoiding Harrogate and X72 Blackpool-Filey ran non-stop from Clitheroe to York. Cheltenham services avoided Tewkesbury, a notorious traffic bottleneck. The Blackpool-Newcastle weekend services were reorganised to provide a non-stop Blackpool-Durham ride with the intermediate points served by a separate coach starting at Lancaster. Some poorly patronised services such as X17 Southport-Morecambe and X22 Keswick-Blackpool were suspended altogether. This trend continued the following year when X1 Liverpool-Glasgow was rerouted via Skelmersdale, Preston, M6 and Carlisle, saving 83 minutes and X10 Manchester-Edinburgh followed a similar route from Preston, saving 1hr 40 minutes. New summer Saturday non-stop services connected Blackpool and Morecambe with Glasgow and Edinburgh. The famed X60/70 remained basically hourly for the winter of 1971-72 but X70 omitted Chorley and Preston, calling at Leyland instead and a new M61 motorway service took over the linked Nottingham trips, saving 55 minutes, the through facility to Derby being dropped. Leeds-Blackpool motorway services saved one hour. The ex-KCR services X8/18 between Great Harwood/Darwen, Blackburn and Blackpool were pooled with Ribblesdale Coachways and Holden's Tours (Oswaldtwistle) Ltd., the same operators combining their excursions licences from the same area and from Clitheroe.

Ribble was now on the threshhold of major changes consequent upon the fragmentation of the old North Western Road Car Co. Ltd., the passing of Lancashire United into the ambit of the Passenger Transport Authority in Manchester and the introduction of the National Express network.

Excursions and Tours

During the 'thirties, day excursion facilities were gradually expanded, to a great extent through the acquisition of other businesses. The Merseyside Touring Co., for example, had a substantial day and extended tour business which was the basis of the enormous Merseyside tours programme of later years. Lancashire United had been excursion operators from Liverpool since 1919, employing Avery and Roberts to manage that part of the business for several years and Ribble and LUT pooled their resources under Ribble management. At busy times, coaches were brought in from Ribble depots as far afield as Blackpool, Burnley and Fleetwood, assembling at Aintree and then being allocated to various day trips. The two companies also pooled their resources in a similar manner at Bolton while Skipton had a tripartite excursion programme embracing Ribble, West Yorkshire and Pennine.

In the Lake District there were several popular tours, many including short lake cruises. Some of these were run in conjunction with the railway, coaches sometimes meeting trains at one station, taking passengers on a tour and returning them to a different station. Some of these programmes had been originated by Ribble's predecessors early in the 'twenties.

In the immediate post-war years, restricted fleet availability limited the amount of excursion work which could be undertaken at some depots but the 'fifties brought a new awareness of the potential profitability of this type of work which was increasing the strength of several competitors. During the next few years, several of these firms were taken over including Howard Coaches of Southport (1954), Auty's Tours Ltd., Bury (1956), Grange Motors, G. Moore and Sons, St. Annes, and three Morecambe operators, Florence Motors, Kia-Ora Ltd. and F. Binns Ltd. (all in 1958). Parkers Motors Ltd., Grange-over-Sands followed in 1964 and Lake Hotel Coaches and Weightmans Coaches, both of Keswick, in 1965. Moores' business went to Standerwick and the two Keswick operators were acquired jointly with Cumberland Motor Services Ltd.

Extended Tours

Ribble's extended tours were based on those originated by the Merseyside Touring Co. and operated wholly within the British Isles. The company developed a superior class of tour with all meals included, using high quality hotels, and 14 to 16 itineraries were offered each year, using well-appointed dedicated coaches.

Auty's Tours was run as a subsidiary company until 1959; in addition to day excursions, it provided a programme of popular tours competitive with Smiths, Pleasureways and other well-known Lancashire tour operators. From 1960, these tours continued to be directed at the same clientele and were marketed by Ribble as 'Kingfisher Tours', using less luxurious coaches.

Less well-known were the tours licensed to Standerwick and operated only during 'Tradesmen's Holiday', a traditional break before the beginning of each season which gradually faded out in the post-war years. The company would pick one or two itineraries from those available and advertise them locally but by the mid-'fifties, the 'tradesmen' wanted something more sophisticated and operation all but ceased.

Private Hire

Most Ribble depots undertook private hire work though there was a general embargo on using coaches on anything other than express services on Saturdays during July, August and early September. Periodically, massive hires were undertaken which only a very large undertaking could tackle, the best known being Littlewoods Pools outing from Liverpool to Blackpool, involving between 70 and 100 vehicles. This job was undoubtedly operated at a loss but was regarded as a publicity exercise as such a long convoy inevitably attracted a great deal of attention. Coaches were brought in from as far away as Lancaster, Blackpool and Burnley, running empty to Liverpool and returning empty to their depots at the end of the day.

Usually, the convoy included a few Crosville coaches because of a territorial agreement between the two companies. Double-deck buses became popular for children's outings and some depots advertised special rates, emphasising the economies to be obtained from these vehicles. This was a highly competitive field and, especially during the winter months in the seaside resorts where there were large fleets of coaches, competitors would quote very low rates just to obtain some cash flow.

The annual outing for members of the staff of Littlewoods Pools from Liverpool to Blackpool required much ingenuity in assembling the number of vehicles needed. In this scene on an overcast 23rd August 1951, a convoy of Leyland Royal Tigers, all almost new at the time, is led by two with Duple bodywork from the Standerwick fleet hired in for the occasion. The dead mileage in such cases, with many vehicles effectively doing the round trip twice, swallowed most if not all the profit. Because of the Area Agreement, passengers from South Liverpool and Wirral were always carried in Crosville coaches.

Auty's Tours, purchased in 1956, had offered a lower-priced range of tours and Ribble continued this policy, using a fleet of new 36-seat front-entrance Tiger Cub coaches with less decorative mouldings embellishing their Burlingham Seagull bodies. From 1960, Auty's was wound up and the range of tours was marketed under the Kingfisher name. Number 979 carried Auty's as both fleet name and statutory owner; others with the Auty fleet name were legally owned by Ribble and all carried the Ribble name from 1960.

(Opposite page) Ribble influence on the Standerwick fleet was evident from 1937 but a degree of individuality continued, not least in 1939 when 22 AEC coaches were placed in service. They were on the rare Regal Mark II chassis, slightly lighter than the standard Regal, with a six-cylinder engine of a nominal 6.6-litre capacity, the Standerwick vehicles having the even rarer petrol version. The 31-seat bodywork, built by Burlingham, was similar to contemporary Ribble coach standards. The vehicle shown, No. 105 (registered in Preston like other Standerwick coaches of the period, in this case as RN 8523) was one of those not returned after requisitioning along with the rest of the batch by the War Department, being one of eight which were acquired by the Northern Ireland Road Transport Board, this one being re-registered GZ 712.

CHAPTER 6
STANDERWICK & SCOUT

During the later war years, Standerwick was virtually dormant, all its regular services having been suspended. The Blackpool and East Lancashire-London services were re-introduced on 15th February 1946 and, following the success of the Ribble-Scout joint services, (see below), a Standerwick (75%) and Scout (25%) pool came into operation from that date. Standerwick coaches were now found on the seasonal Blackpool-London night service whilst Scout coaches occasionally ran on the Colne-London and Blackpool-Birmingham via Wolverhampton services.

The demand for excursions from Blackpool was virtually insatiable. The main stands were on Central Promenade (the Golden Mile); Chapel Street, Pleasant Street (North Shore) and Dog and Partridge (South Shore) and there were a number of other stands used only at the height of the season. Passengers were ferried between stands in an Austin 16 car (AFR 2) and later in an Austin station wagon (NTB 859) also. Whilst there was a comprehensive range of full-day trips, there was a particularly heavy demand for Fleetwood Market and for Morecambe and Blackpool Illuminations, over 100 coaches being despatched on each of these on busy days.

The decision to keep W.C. Standerwick Ltd. as a separate company was reaffirmed after the war, being based on the more relaxed working practices in the subsidiary. It was important that working costs should equate with those of the other Blackpool coach operators rather than with the parent company.

The wisdom of maintaining Standerwick as a separate company was demonstrated by the liberties that were taken with the timetable which the Ribble Unions would never have accepted. It was quite normal for a man to work a 'Blackpool-Birmingham return' and even a Coventry return. According to the the timetable, the coach arrived at Birmingham at 2.5pm and left at 1.55pm! The secret was that duplicates did not need to follow the whole of the timetabled route; in pre-motorway days, Blackpool to London (12 hr) could not be legally done by one driver, but it was – every day. Usually the coaches arrived up to an hour early.

From 10th April 1952, a Keswick-London service was introduced, licensed to Ribble, Standerwick and Scout. During the winter time-table, the Standerwick vehicle replaced a Ribble coach between Keswick and Preston, spare Standerwick drivers acting as conductors on this section only. Ribble feeders from Carlisle to Kendal and, in the summer, from Barrow to Lancaster, brought Cumberland, Westmorland and Furness into direct contact with the Midlands and London.

In the 'fifties, much of the Standerwick fleet was grossly under-used, most of the PS1s doing insufficient mileage in a whole season to justify one dock. The least used of the fleet were six open Tiger TS2 runabouts (Nos. 1-6) which had been rebuilt by Ribble in 1939. They could well have been called the 'rainmakers' as it was sure to pour down if they were brought out for excursion work, forcing them to spend much time sheltering under bridges.

Six 1931 Brush-bodied Leyland Tiger TS2 Standerwick coaches were converted by Ribble in 1939 to 31-seat open runabouts and were numbered 1-6. They saw little use in the post-war years, performing local Fylde excursions and Illuminations tours though, on rare occasions, they ventured as far as Burnley and Warrington on express services.

On the morning Birmingham-Blackpool service on summer Saturdays, it was the custom to allocate 29 seats to the Warrington agent and send a Bedford-Duple coach empty from Blackpool for this load. On one memorable day in August, the Bedford broke down and an open Tiger was the only vehicle available to go to Warrington. Fortunately it was a glorious, hot day and the passengers were apparently delighted.

New Services

In 1953 an agreement was made with Southdown Motor Services Ltd. for through running across London between Blackpool and the South Coast, each operator going on hire to the other north or south of the metropolis. Surprisingly, a Blackpool-Portsmouth service was to be run by a Standerwick vehicle daily while a Blackpool-Brighton-Worthing service was run by Southdown on Thursday, Friday and Saturday nights northbound and Friday and Saturday nights and Sunday mornings southbound. the Sunday morning coach being taken to

This Leyland Tiger with Burlingham body was supplied to the then independent W.C. Standerwick Ltd. in January 1931. Note the twin, outward-opening doors and the toilet compartment. Such facilities, increasingly fashionable in modern times, were by no means unknown 60 years ago.

Wood Bros. (Blackpool) Ltd., 'John Bull Motors', operated express services from Blackpool to London, Leeds, Oldham and Liverpool and was acquired jointly by Ribble, North Western and Midland Red in 1933. The company was wound up in 1934 and some of its coaches, including this Leyland Tiger with partial canvas roof, were transferred to the Standerwick fleet.

London by a Standerwick driver. These arrangements started on 25-26th June 1953. The Portsmouth coach ran on the night service from Blackpool, continuing on the 9.0am departure from Victoria Coach Station; a Standerwick driver was stationed in London to work the London-Portsmouth section and there were occasions when the Standerwick coach was the service vehicle.

There were weekends when full loads were carried but very often, particularly midweek, there were no through passengers and after two seasons the arrangement was discontinued. A further attempt was made in 1969 with through Colne and Blackpool to Eastbourne weekend services.

In 1954, Ribble, Standerwick and Scout applied jointly for a Blackpool-London service via Stratford-on-Avon and Oxford which was fiercely opposed by the railways. The hearings before the several Traffic Commissioners on the route lasted several days and a host of witnesses was called in support. One could almost feel sympathy for the railway representative faced with the unenviable task of arguing the adequacy of a journey involving a change of trains at Crewe or Stafford and a transfer from Wolverhampton High Level to Low Level with its myriad steps. The licence was eventually granted with a duplication restriction and a complete bar on setting down or picking up between Oxford and London. This service commenced on 28th May 1955.

From 1st April 1955, the services of Ribble, Standerwick, North Western and Yelloway between Oldham, Rochdale, Rossendale and Blackpool were all placed in a new pool, comprising three services between Oldham and Blackpool – X9 via Manchester and Bury, X79 via the Rossendale Valley and X89 via Edenfield. The main operators were North Western, Standerwick and Yelloway and there was some Ribble duplication and a dormant LUT financial interest. This agreement was a great step forward between companies who had been traditional rivals for many years. The Hyde-Cleveleys service of T.H. Parker's Blue Bird Motors was taken over and added to the pool as were North Western's Glossop/Stalybridge-Blackpool services and some journeys on X79 were extended to Fleetwood.

The Colne/Bacup-Morecambe services continued to be worked by Standerwick until merged into Ribble services X14 and X55 on 1st June 1968. By this time, traffic had fallen to the extent that the separate services were in competition with each other.

Motorways and Double-Deck Coaches

Contrary to popular belief, the M1 was not the first British motorway, the honour going to the Preston by-pass portion of the M6 on which the first PSV to run was Ribble Royal Tiger 940, conveying an official party on 8th October 1958, two months before the opening. When the first part of the M1 was opened on 2nd November 1959, the first PSV to enter from the Luton spur was a Ribble Atlantean double-deck coach, thus establishing a double first.

The trials of the Atlantean double deck 'Gay Hostess' coaches were done between Blackpool and London and between Manchester and Glasgow, using Ribble 1251.

The class was designed with motorway travel in mind but only the Preston by-pass existed when trials started so testing was done on ordinary roads including passing through several towns on the A6. The Glasgow route involved the long haul over Shap, sharing the narrow highway with all other traffic including many underpowered but heavily-laden trucks. Often the drivers of 1251 had to resort to the use of bottom gear for several miles. Its standard MCW body had been trimmed and fitted out by Weymann so its power-to-weight ratio was therefore inferior to the standard Atlantean buses. The trial runs were often accompanied by management trainees whose job it was to assess customer reactions, suggest improvements and generally iron out any problems which arose.

One suggestion was that its O.600 engine should be replaced by the 11-litre O.680 unit thus enabling it to overtake some of the crawling trucks on Shap and climb in second gear instead of first. When motorway operation started, a higher cruising speed would be possible. The Ribble managing director, A.F.R. Carling, decided to sample the double-deck coach himself and boarded at Kendal one hot September day. The trainee reserved seats for him in various parts of the coach and he chose to travel on the offside upper deck. Being Sunday, there was little lorry traffic so 1251 was unlikely to be baulked on Shap as on a weekday but a quiet word to the driver by the trainee ensured that the revs gradually faded, necessitating a change down to first gear before reaching the summit. On arrival at Glasgow the managing director expressed his satisfaction at what he had seen and, soon after, authority was received to install an O.680 engine in 1251. All subsequent models were similarly equipped.

Standerwick took delivery of 22 Atlantean coaches in 1960-61 and when the unsuitability of the vehicle for Blackpool-Bristol and Manchester-Glasgow had, at last, been conceded, 11 of the 15 Ribble vehicles were transferred to the Standerwick fleet, the remaining four going to Scout. This was sufficient to equip the Blackpool, Colne and Keswick-London day and night services and provide much of the regular duplication. They continued in service until 1969-70 when all but four were sold. These four were used by Ribble on 'White Lady' duties in 1970-71 before sale to Hong Kong.

Whilst it was several years before the motorway network was sufficiently extensive to provide really fast services between the Lancashire towns and London, the opening of the initial stretch of the M1 and the associated M45 enabled two hours to be cut from the time-table. There was, of course, a reluctance to abandon the stopping places along the A5, in particular Dunstable, and one coach continued to follow the old route. On the night services, the departure times were retarded by two hours to avoid unacceptably early arrivals. As more sections of motorway were opened, the dilemma of providing the fastest possible service while maintaining services to all points en route was repeated and various combinations of route were devised from time to time. Inevitably some places eventually lost their direct services.

An experimental 36ft long Bristol VRLL double-deck coach with an Eastern Coach Works body seating 42 on the upper deck and 18 downstairs with toilet and large

Two 1936 Duple-bodied Standerwick Tiger TS7s in Penrith on a private hire. The leading vehicle (10) was originally Ribble 1535 being one of 12 transferred to Standerwick in 1937. The second was theoretically Ribble 1544 but always carried Standerwick No. 87. Note the subtle differences in the styling of the Duple bodies, the second vehicle to a Duple rather than Ribble design.

Two Standerwick TS8 coaches with post-war 8ft wide Duple bodies stand on the forecourt of Devonshire Road garage, Blackpool. The body of number 43 was originally on the chassis of RN 7785, a 1936 TS7 which was Ribble No. 1535. It was the third body for the chassis of RN 8788 which originally had a 32-seat Burlingham bus body (Ribble No. 2223) in 1939 and a modernised 7ft 6in Duple coach body in 1951 (Ribble No. 777).

Six Duple-bodied Leyland Royal Tiger coaches (120-5) entered the Standerwick fleet in 1951, followed by 30 with Ribble's standard centre-entrance Leyland bodywork.

luggage compartment entered service in 1968. It was numbered 50S in the Standerwick fleet and differed from the VR service buses in that the engine was mounted lengthwise on the offside. By this time on-board catering had ceased as there were adequate facilities on the motorways. There were various teething problems and it was 1971 before a further 11 similar vehicles (51-61) were placed in service. They were unreliable in service and a serious overturning accident on the M1 added to their unpopularity. In April 1974, they were all transferred to National Travel (North West) who withdrew and sold them prematurely. One of the problems associated with their use was that, in the event of a fully loaded vehicle

failing far from home, two vehicles were needed to accommodate the passengers.

The End of Standerwick

When Scout Motor Services finally ceased trading in 1968, Standerwick took over the Salwick works services, their only stage carriage services, and the former Scout excursions from Blackpool. As more and more people took their cars on holiday, the excursion business was in decline and the Standerwick fleet with it. Some stands were disposed of as they were inaccessible to 36ft long coaches; others were sold for development. Standerwick

Gay Hostess coaches at speed on the motorway. Scout S68 (originally Ribble 1264) overtakes Standerwick 29. Note that it had been considered worthwhile to have special metal 'Scout' plates made to replace the original 'Ribble' plates on the front of the vehicles.

Standerwick No. 63 is seen on the X79 Blackpool-Oldham service at Mumps roundabout, Oldham in 1971. This Plaxton-bodied 49-seat Leyland Leopard was originally Scout No. S741, part of a batch shared between Ribble and its two subsidiaries. Under George Brook's accounting policy, these coaches were owned by Ribble and leased to the subsidiaries. In 1971, it was renumbered 15 and eventually reverted to Ribble as 741.

Two Standerwick Leopards with Plaxton Panorama 49-seat bodies, new in 1965, were caught by the camera while on a meal break at Coventry. Number 795S was successively renumbered 65 in October 1968, 17 in August 1971 and Ribble 795 in March 1974.

was joined with Ribble in several new services such as Banbury-Nuneaton-Morecambe on summer Saturdays, which was joint with Midland Red and Colne-Pwllheli (Butlin's Holiday Camp), shared with Ribblesdale Coachways, Crosville and Bracewells of Colne.

In 1972, when the National Bus Company decided to set up regional National Travel companies to establish a nationwide express network, Standerwick ceased to exist in everything except name. By this time, its coaches were hired from Ribble and they were sold to the North Western Road Car Co. Ltd. (the original, not the present, company of that name). The shareholding was transferred to that company in December 1972 and to National Bus Company in July 1973. North Western, which had already disposed of its bus services, was renamed National Travel (North West) Ltd. in February 1974 and absorbed Standerwick which was formally dissolved on 3rd August 1979. The Standerwick fleet of 90 vehicles was transferred to the new company in April 1974. Thereafter there were frequent reorganisations, the company being merged with others as National Travel (West) in 1977 and National Travel (NBC) in 1979. The Manchester-based fleet was transferred back to Ribble on 20th May 1984.

Scout

Throughout the thirties, Scout Motor Services Ltd. built up a successful business. Its sole stage-carriage service between Preston (Starchhouse Square) and Blackpool (Talbot Road) via Wrea Green held its own with Ribble and its Blackpool-London service (by day all year and night in the summer) was reasonably prosperous, though the scale of its operations was small once many of the previous operators had been combined under the Standerwick umbrella.

The company built up a substantial private hire and excursion business in Preston and a modest operation in Blackpool where it had a garage in Foxhall Road.

Upon the outbreak of war, the Regional Transport Commissioner insisted that Ribble and Scout should pool their resources on the Preston-Blackpool road and the first stage of co-ordination started in September 1939. Ribble buses started calling at Starchhouse Square and Scout buses ran through to the Ribble bus station. Scout also appeared on the route through Weeton which had hitherto been a Ribble preserve. These *ad hoc* arrangements led to a formal agreement being signed on 19th December 1941 establishing a pool with 60% to Ribble and 40% to Scout. The latter's waybill analysis was undertaken by Ribble and Scout conductors issued Ribble tickets and paid in at Ribble offices. A good working relationship developed between the two companies.

Post-War Expansion

The establishment of the Atomic Energy factory at Salwick just after the war led to a big increase in vehicle requirements for the Ribble-Scout pool, some of which was satisfied by the use of Scout coaches running without conductors. Most of the labour came from Blackpool and Lytham St. Annes and, as there was shift working round the clock, much of the work was out of the peak.

In 1952, Scout purchased the excursion and tour business of Whittaker Brothers who had a centrally situated

(Facing page) The successor to the Atlantean 'Gay Hostess' class was this striking Bristol VRL with 60-seat Eastern Coach Works body and, like its predecessors, powered by the Leyland O.680 engine. The prototype (50S) was exhibited at the 1968 Commercial Motor Show but the 29 production vehicles were not delivered until 1971-72. The engine was mounted longitudinally behind the off-side rear wheel and the centre-entrance layout avoided the obstruction of the view which made lower-deck travel on the Atlanteans unpopular. A low floor level gave easy access and there were flat centre gangways on both decks, but with overall low height. Number 72 is shown loading in Accrington on the Colne-London service. This vehicle overturned on the M1 in July, 1974 but was rebuilt and returned to service. All 30 were transferred to National Travel (North West) in April 1974, looking very bland in their all-white livery.

The last batch of coaches to carry the Standerwick name from new were 1973 Leyland Leopard PSU3B/4s with Duple 49-seat bodywork. They were part of an order for 28 placed by Ribble, nine (Nos.32-40), being allocated to Standerwicks, and were delivered in the white National livery. They were transferred to National Travel (North West) in 1974.

Scout bought six of these Leyland Tiger TS2 coaches with half-canopy bodywork by Spicer of Southport in 1930, mainly for use on their Blackpool-London service. The livery was a plum-coloured roof, black band and cream skirt and this was maintained throughout the firm's independent existence.

office and excursion stand in Adelaide Street, Blackpool virtually in the shadow of the Tower and this placed them firmly on the map as a Blackpool coach operator. Many of the short excursions could be sandwiched in between Salwick trips so that some coaches were running more or less continuously for 18 hours a day.

Before the extension of through running across Preston, the 15-minute Preston-Blackpool service was run by four Scout buses working the 155 and 158 local trips and Ribble buses running the 'trunks' through to Bolton and Burnley. When through running was extended to cover all trips, Scout readily agreed to run through to points east and south of Preston. A previous scheme for them to participate in service 126 to Bolton fell through but Scout PD1s 1-5 had destination blinds which included 'Bolton via Horwich' and 'Chorley via Bamber Bridge'. Eventually Scout supplied two buses for 154 Blackpool-Burnley, one for 158 Blackpool-Rochdale and one for 167 Preston-Lytham. Scout buses would occasionally cover some Ribble duties on 154 and 158 to release Ribble double-deckers for express duplication.

Scout regularly borrowed Ribble conductors to cover short peak hour duties worked by coaches.

Scout-in-Ribble

There was excitement within Ribble when it became known that Scout was to be bought out. Take-over date was 5th December 1961 when, somehow or other, over 50 Scout vehicles were crammed into what were already considered overcrowded depots at Preston and Blackpool (Devonshire Road). The decision to keep the company as a subsidiary was a wise one as, during the exercise to convert all the Scout duties to Ribble format, it was soon apparent that many stage-carriage trips (particularly Salwicks) had less than the standard running-time though they had no difficulty in performing the work safely. In the prevailing climate, Ribble men would have demanded the full running time and several additional peak hour vehicles would have been needed to do the same work

Scout vehicles were given fleet numbers with an 'S' prefix and, before long, buses appeared in Ribble red with a 'Scout' fleet-name in Ribble style. Older Scout double-deckers were eventually replaced by vehicles transferred from the Ribble fleet. These also had 'S' numbers and those that eventually came back into the Ribble fleet received a second Ribble fleet number. Coaches were repainted in Ribble style and new coaches had fleet numbers in the Ribble series with an 'S' prefix. There were several transfers between coach fleets.

Scout operations finally ceased on 25th October 1968, the Blackpool excursion business being transferred to Standerwick who also took over the Salwick coach operations. After a dormant period, the company was renamed Scout Computer Services Ltd. which undertook data-processing for Ribble and other companies. In 1977 it became NBC Computer Services Ltd.

Blackpool Omnibus Stations Ltd.

The Blackpool Coliseum site was acquired in 1934 with the business of Wright Bros. (Burnley) Ltd. who had used it as a coach station. There was a huge octagonal building on the site (the 'Colosseum') which had latterly been used as a skating rink. A new company, Blackpool Omnibus Stations Ltd. was formed to own and operate the coach station. Ribble subscribed 50% of the capital, the rest being held by the principal users, North Western and the four Yorkshire-Blackpool pool companies. BOS was not, therefore, strictly a subsidiary but it was always managed by Ribble, the general manager being the managing director of BOS. There was a manager, one inspector, booking clerks and general hands who cleaned up and staffed the left luggage room.

After the end of the Illuminations in October 1935, the site was closed and demolition of the building commenced, difficulties in dismantling the roof being solved by a Blackpool gale. Work on the construction of a new station, designed by the Ribble Architect, was not finished until September 1936. A series of parallel queue barriers were capable of being linked together by manipulating a series of chains but, at first, the platforms were only partially roofed causing problems in wet weather. The roofing was extended about 1950. Land at the Rigby Road end of the site, known as the Coach Park, was unsurfaced until the late 1950s. The Coliseum was unfortunately built on shifting sand and tons of concrete had to be pumped into the foundations to prevent it collapsing.

In its earliest pre-war days the station handled 32,000 vehicles and overflow parking was provided on railway-owned land near Bloomfield Road. A field telephone was used to summon vehicles when required for loading. In the 1950s the station was handling 70,000 vehicles per year and, towards the end of that decade, additional space was hired in an old tram shed in Blundell Street and, on occasions, the main Corporation bus garage in Hopton Road.

In the summer season, one of the most profitable sources of BOS revenue was the ladies' toilet to which access was gained through a turnstile accepting one old penny. On busy days, the cash box would need to be emptied two or three times, a job done by the manager in person who said that he would readily accept the proceeds instead of his salary. The rattle of the pennies cascading into a metal container was a familiar sound all over the station.

Standerwick's control offices were moved from Chapel Street to temporary buildings at the north end of the site and it was used as a Ribble depot from 1987 when it was substantially rebuilt with an upper floor to house traffic offices. The fall in traffic made the station uneconomic and it was closed in 1991 for conversion to a car park.

(Right) Scout's first five Leyland Royal Tigers were these PSU1/15 models with 41-seat Duple Ambassador bodies which were placed in service in 1951. Fleet numbers were not carried on Scout coaches in independent days and this one was numbered S33 by Ribble but was soon withdrawn.

(Below) Scout S4 was one of three Metro-Cammell bodied Leyland Atlanteans delivered in 1961, just before the company came under Ribble control. It acquired a Ribble indicator layout on overhaul and became Ribble 1972 in October 1968. After withdrawal in 1974, it was exported to New South Wales, Australia.

(Upper) Leyland PD2/12 S20 was Scout's first highbridge double-deck bus; it was new as a Leyland demonstrator in 1953 and sold to the company the following year. It is seen leaving Devonshire Road garage, Blackpool on a contract service to the Atomic Energy factory at Salwick. It was withdrawn shortly before the company's operations were merged with Ribble in 1968.

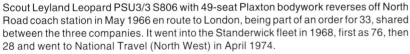

Scout Leyland Leopard PSU3/3 S806 with 49-seat Plaxton bodywork reverses off North Road coach station in May 1966 en route to London, being part of an order for 33, shared between the three companies. It went into the Standerwick fleet in 1968, first as 76, then 28 and went to National Travel (North West) in April 1974.

(Lower) Scout placed five 72-seat Leyland PD3s in service in 1958-59, No. 21 being the first. They differed from the Ribble vehicles in having a half-cab layout which the management preferred for accessibility to the engine. They even had the standard Ribble destination indicator layout. This vehicle became S21 in 1961 and Ribble 1974 in 1968; it was withdrawn in 1974 and worked for an operator in Cornwall until 1980.

By the mid-'sixties, service frequencies were being reduced all over the company's system and in 1966-67, several services in the Carlisle and Penrith area, one of the most sparsely populated regions in the company's territory, were withdrawn altogether. Wherever possible, a minimum basic service was maintained to all the communities, sometimes only on one day of the week.

Elsewhere, evening and Sunday services were reduced and some routes such as Warrington-St. Helens-Southport, which had enjoyed an increased summer service, had the same frequency throughout the year. One-man operation increased slowly and some of the long, linked services (see Chapter 4) were broken up because one section of the route could be economically converted to one-man working. Following changes in the law, the first one-man double-decker, Atlantean 1617, appeared in March 1969.

Bus Industry Reorganisation

Meanwhile, the Transport Bill, 1968 contained wide-ranging proposals for public transport. Conurbation transport authorities were to be created in and around large cities and there was a danger that these relatively profitable parts of the large company undertakings such as Ribble would be excised. As their profits were essential to cross-subsidise the rural services, BET, for whom buses were now a minority investment, viewed the situation with some apprehension. An approach by the state-owned Transport Holding Company resulted, after lengthy negotiations, in the sale of the BET shareholdings in the bus companies for £36 million in November 1967. Continuity of management was guaranteed until the end of 1968 and from 1st January 1969, the BET and former Tilling companies were brought together in the state-owned National Bus Company (NBC). The operating companies retained their separate identities and there was no immediate effect on day-to-day operations. Two of the original four Passenger Transport Authorities impinged upon Ribble's operating area. The Act also introduced financial support for loss-making bus services from county councils and capital grants for new buses of approved design. The latter was calculated to encourage the purchase of buses suitable for one-man double-deck operation.

One of the first results of the NBC's formation was the tidying up of areas between former Tilling (THC) and BET companies and the Carlisle area of United Automobile Services Ltd. with 24 buses was transferred to Ribble on 5th January 1969, only five days into the new era. Ribble now had full control of the Carlisle city services and rural routes to the east of the city.

The Passenger Transport Executives for South East Lancashire and North East Cheshire (SELNEC) and

Merseyside took over the municipal bus services in their areas late in 1969. Both had a statutory duty to co-ordinate road and rail services and the company services continued undisturbed for the time being. In the SELNEC area a deal between the PTE and the NBC resulted in the services of the North Western Road Car Co. Ltd. being shared between the PTE, Crosville and Trent, Ribble being involved only with the express services (see below). The Merseyside PTE was content to arrange for the NBC, represented by Ribble and Crosville, to operate as agents and under an Agreement signed on 30th January 1972, Ribble was entitled to run 13.074% of bus mileage within the PTE area. In theory, this could be run on any route but the attitudes of the trade unions reduced the intended flexibility and attempts to run Ribble buses on unfamiliar routes led to labour disputes. The entitlement was reduced to 12.89% with the enlargement of the area in 1974.

Merseyside PTE pursued a pro-rail policy, favouring schemes to feed bus passengers into the stations on the electric rail system to which extensions were put in hand. Ribble had already introduced local circular services feeding railway stations at Formby and Freshfield in 1967 and Waterloo in 1968 and feeders to Maghull were added in 1970. The PTE proposed to reduce bus services running parallel to these railway routes, replacing some routes with feeders with through bus and rail tickets. Ribble's frequent Crosby and Maghull area services were seriously affected and this was seen as a threat to their jobs by Ribble men on Merseyside who refused to handle any through tickets. Nevertheless, the Crosby network was substantially reduced in January 1977, traffic being fed into Waterloo station. Ribble men at Bootle struck on the first day and the PTE eventually overcame the veto on through tickets by selling zone and unlimited travel tickets at shops and post offices. In the meantime, fares throughout the area were standardised and local passengers were carried on Ribble buses on sections of route hitherto restricted.

SELNEC PTE wanted full control of the bus services within its area and had already concluded agreements with Lancashire United Transport whose routes were closely entwined with those of the PTE. A complicated exchange of routes took effect from 27th April 1974. Lancashire United withdrew from the Manchester-Blackpool/Blackburn express services X60/66/70. Certain Warrington local services were handed to Crosville while Ribble withdrew from the Liverpool-St. Helens-Wigan/Manchester services 39/317/320 in favour of LUT and handed all its services wholly within the PTE area over to that body. These comprised routes between Bolton and Bury and Edgworth, Walshaw, Holcombe etc. In return, Ribble received the Lancashire United share in the Tyne-

The 1952 all-Leyland lowbridge PD2s continued in service until 1967. Number 1380, numerically the last, is seen working a Fleetwood local service against a background of the, by then, closed Fleetwood railway station.

The 1951 Weymann-bodied Olympics were withdrawn gradually in 1964-68 and No. 277, seen at Lancaster when 15 years old, was the last of all, working latterly at Preston as a one-man operated bus.

Leyland PDR1 Atlantean No. 1973 was rebuilt to make it indistinguishable from Ribble's standard Metro-Cammell bodied vehicles. It was new in 1961 to Scout Motor Services (No.5) and outlasted all the other ex-Scout double-deck buses by several years, being sold for preservation in 1981.

(Above) The chill of the Cumbrian winter is conveyed by this picture of Marshall-bodied Leopard PSU3 pictured at Armathwaite in 1975. The absence of passengers underlines the company's difficulties in the sparsely-populated northern districts. Note the 'Pay as you Enter' sign and the advertisement on the lower panels.

(Left) Trade union restrictions on vehicle capacity on one-man operated services were a contributory factor in the choice of the 30ft 10in long Leopard PSU4 with Marshall 44-seat body, rather than the 36ft long PSU3. Number 635, entered service in April 1966, but is shown much later in poppy red livery carrying the NBC, Merseyside PTE and British Rail logos. In this guise it was used on Formby circular services.

The 72-seat Alexander-bodied Albion Lowlanders were preferred by passengers to the low-height Atlanteans as their flat saloon floor enabled centre gangways to be provided on both decks. Ten arrived in 1964 and a further six, of which No. 1866 was the last, came the following year. The grille and full-front were to Ribble's specification, being similar to those on the PD3s. W. Alexander & Sons (Northern) Ltd. purchased this vehicle and 1865 as a source of spares in 1976.

Tees-Mersey, Liverpool-Nottingham, Liverpool-Skegness, Rochdale-Leigh-Paignton express services, some recently licensed summer routes not then commenced and excursions from Liverpool. Crosville also replaced LUT as a joint operator on 309/319/329 Warrington-St. Helens-Southport but its participation was confined to one early morning journey between Warrington and Rainford worked on behalf of Ribble. A few Ribble journeys continued to run on the Liverpool-St. Helens routes for a few months, on hire to LUT. An option by the PTE to purchase LUT was eventually exercised in 1976.

Local government reorganisation from 1st April 1974 enlarged the Passenger Transport areas and brought them under the control of the newly-created metropolitan counties of Greater Manchester and Merseyside, the clumsy SELNEC name giving place to Greater Manchester Transport (GMT). The Wigan transport undertaking was swallowed by GMT and those of St. Helens and Southport by Merseyside.

Further Cuts

There were more severe cuts in the Northern area in 1970-71. The Manchester-Glasgow and Liverpool-Edinburgh services, which had always operated as stage carriages between Kendal and Penrith and north of the border, now carried local passengers everywhere north of Kendal. Frequencies everywhere were reduced and many services completely withdrawn. Some of these curtailments followed the introduction of new regulations governing drivers' hours of work which exacerbated the already serious staff shortages at many depots. Pressure from the industry brought some relaxation towards the end of 1971. An agreement with the Unions granting a 5-day 40-hour working week on Mondays to Fridays, with weekend working covered by volunteers and part-time employees, was disastrous for a company with so many weekend holiday service commitments. While it was not too difficult

to get volunteers for coaching duties, covering late Saturday duties on stage carriage services proved well nigh impossible at some depots. The ruinous situation arose of hired vehicles running services while Ribble buses stood in their garages for want of men to drive them.

The Carlisle city services were converted to one-man operation with double-deck buses equipped with fare boxes on 3rd June 1972. Services in the Clitheroe area were drastically cut in April 1974. Yet there were still pockets of expansion such as Skelmersdale New Town where a local network was built up together with new through services to Liverpool. A new 50-bus depot in the town replaced Ormskirk garage from 20th October 1974.

County Council Agency Agreements

Over the years, Ribble fares had risen faster than those of the municipalities and local government reorganisation in 1974 had extended the boundaries of many authorities so that services within them were shared by municipal and Ribble buses on different fare scales. Thus Accrington had gobbled up its neighbours to become Hyndburn, and the Burnley, Colne and Nelson Joint Transport Committee was now Burnley and Pendle, covering an even larger area. At this stage, municipal operators within Lancashire owned 62% of the county's buses, operated 54% of the mileage and carried 77% of the passengers. Ribble's 42% of the mileage carried only 22% of the passengers, reflecting the rural and interurban nature of many of its operations.

The County Council promoted schemes of rationalisation of fares and services so as to get the best value from subsidies and the first of these, covering the Burnley and Pendle area, came into force on 22nd August 1976. Ribble was to receive £60,000 to reduce its fares to the level of the municipal operator who was to have control of all operations. This scheme was to run for two

The Leyland National became a common sight in the Ribble fleet, as in most NBC subsidiaries, from 1972 onwards. By this date, one-man working of full-sized single-deckers had been agreed and almost all of Ribble's examples were of the 11.3-metre length, though some with single-door and 52 seat capacity as in the case of 429 seen here.

The transfer of the Carlisle area services of United Automobile Services Ltd. to Ribble in January 1969 brought with it 21 Bristol vehicles, then seeming quite alien to the fleet apart from the single VRL double-deck coach prototype. Five were 45-seat Bristol LS5Gs with Eastern Coach Works bodies, new in 1956-57, of which No. 263 was typical. This was a model familiar in Tilling fleets but not hitherto seen in a former BET company. Note that the lower-case fleet name had not then been adopted.

(lLeft) R. Prescott and Sons' Bamber Bridge Motor Services was the last regular independent stage-carriage operator into Preston except for Fishwicks, and this former Leyland demonstrator, a lowbridge MCW-bodied Atlantean, had been acquired in November 1960. It was one of three buses transferred to Ribble on 1st April 1967, becoming No. 1966.

(Below right) The destination equipment was repositioned on 1960 Atlantean 1647 when it was converted to one-man operation in October 1969 to make it more accessible to the driver but the arrangement was not generally adopted. It is pictured in Morecambe with the recently-introduced lower-case fleet title.

One of the first Albion Lowlanders, 747 EUS, with Alexander body, was exhibited in Glasgow colours at the 1961 Scottish Show. Acquired by BBMS in November 1963, it was then the only Lowlander to operate in England badged as an Albion – the model was sold as a Leyland, south of the border. Becoming Ribble 1968, it is seen in Lord Street, Southport on a short-working of the X27 Liverpool-Skipton limited stop service.

years and was to set the pattern for similar agency schemes which usually provided for the removal of protective conditions restricting the carriage of local passengers; Ribble buses took over, or participated in, some municipal services.

The Burnley and Pendle scheme was implemented in three stages, the second of which linked three routes to form a direct service between Accrington and Nelson worked jointly by Ribble, Hyndburn and Burnley and Pendle buses. In December 1976, Skipton depot closed and some operations were taken over by West Yorkshire Road Car Co. and Pennine Motor Services.

The most radical scheme affected Lancaster and Morecambe where two municipal bus systems had been amalgamated in the 1974 reorganisation. A new network

came into operation on 2nd April 1979 with Ribble and Lancaster City buses sharing urban and rural routes. The joint operations of Pennine Motor Services were also integrated. Each operator saved four buses and combined operating costs of £130,000. Schemes for Accrington, Blackburn and Darwen followed.

The County Councils wanted to reinstate public transport to areas from which it had been withdrawn and sponsored the opening of school buses to ordinary passengers. Services such as Knott End-Preesall were licensed to Ribble but sub-contracted to locally-based Birch Motor Services. A scheme to link Clitheroe, Nelson and Burnley with neighbouring Pendle villages was at first operated by hired Great Manchester PTE midibuses but two Bristol LH buses were acquired to operate a

Two Seddon Pennine IV 19-seat buses were hired from Greater Manchester PTE in 1978 for an experiment with local subsidised services in the Ribble Valley. The Pendleton destination was an outlying district of Clitheroe, not the Salford suburb. No. 1730 was known as M730 during its stay. They remained until October 1980 when two 35-seat Bristol LHS6Ls were placed in service under the 'Betty's Bus' name. A diagram of the route was shown on the sides of the bus.

modified network after a three-month trial period at the end of 1978. This became known as 'Betty's Bus' after the regular driver, Mrs Betty Gray. A similar service, the Kirkham Roamer, supported by Fylde Borough Council, connected outlying villages with Kirkham and the regular driver, Walter Johnson, became equally well-known to his passengers. The first 'Community Bus', a 16-seat Ford Transit/Dormobile No. 1001, was named the Fell Runner and connected Langwathby and neighbouring villages with Penrith. Supported by Cumbria County Council, it was manned by volunteer drivers but maintained by Ribble.

The Last NBC Years

All services were placed under the microscope during the NBC-sponsored Market Analysis Project (MAP) in 1979-82 whereby passengers' travelling habits and needs were examined in detail, on a district basis. The last conductor-operated journey on the Ribble system ran from Chorley to Blackburn on 30th January 1982, the culmination of a process which commenced in 1958.

In 1985, Cumbria County Council reduced revenue support, resulting in further severe cuts in services in the north and the following year there were more withdrawals, particularly in the Furness area, in preparation for deregulation.

Successful minibus networks had been launched by other NBC companies and it was decided to adopt these vehicles on suitable parts of the Ribble system with increased frequencies on urban routes. 'Minilink' networks were introduced as follows, using 20-seat Mercedes Benz vehicles in a red and yellow livery:-

24. 8.86	Kendal Town Services and South Lakeland
27. 9.86	Clitheroe
4.10.86	Chorley
11.10.86	Fleetwood, Cleveleys
19.10.86	Preston-Penwortham
25.10.86	Preston-Bamber Bridge/Gregson Lane
26.10.86	Barrow, Grange, Windermere and Darwen
26. 1.87	Lancaster, Morecambe.

From the beginning of the school term in September 1986, Ribble won several County Council tenders for school services which were available to ordinary passengers. This resulted in the reopening of Appleby out-station (closed in May 1985) and Sedbergh (closed only two weeks earlier).

The Changing Express Scene

Following the sale of the stage carriage services of the old North Western company in 1972, that company was put

The Langwathby community 'Fell Runner' (1001) was a 16-seat Dormobile-bodied Ford Transit, manned by local residents and maintained at Penrith depot. It operated from 1979 to 1982 when it became a service vehicle.

The diversion of the X43 service on to the M66 motorway led to a big increase in loadings and this Leopard PSU3E (1123) with 45-seat Duple Dominant body provides its own advertisement. It is one of 25 vehicles delivered in 1979-80.

Leopard PSU3B with 45-seat Plaxton dual-purpose body is seen on the National Express Blackpool-Sheffield service in August 1983. Originally No. 67 in the fleet of West Riding Automobile Services, it was on loan to Ribble for several months from the non-operating NBC subsidiary, Associated Passenger Transport of Lincoln.

BUS STATIONS

Preston's new municipal bus station was opened in 1969 and this picture of the parking area shows a cross-section of the Ribble bus fleet in the early 'eighties. From left to right can be seen a Leyland Olympian, a Park Royal-bodied Leyland AN68 Atlantean, a Leyland National, a Marshall-bodied Bristol RE, more Nationals and more double-deckers including some Bristol VRTs.

The massive Victorian ironwork of Southport bus station, formerly the terminus of the Southport and Cheshire Lines Extension Railway, opened in 1884. It was opened as a bus station in the summer of 1954 and doubled as a depot from September of that year. It was closed for redevelopment by North Western on 3rd October 1987, the facade being retained. Two Nationals, a Bristol VRT and a Park Royal-bodied Atlantean can be seen towards the end of Ribble operation in this area.

Waterloo Interchange, Crosby, was designed to feed passengers into the Merseyrail network, the Crosby-Liverpool bus services being substantially reduced by order of Merseyside PTE in 1977. It is seen just before deregulation in 1986, the three Atlanteans having already been given North Western decals over their Ribble livery. The practice of deviating from the main road to serve the Interchange was abandoned at deregulation.

Although still carrying National Travel West fleet name, this 1980 Leopard PSU5C with Plaxton 46-seat body and toilet, was already No. 70 in the Ribble fleet when photographed at London Victoria in July 1984.

Leyland Tiger 112 with 48-seat Plaxton body was one of three transferred from United Automobile Services in April 1985 when six months old for Rapide services. All three were sold to Amberline in March 1988. Number 112 was caught by the camera at Golders Green bus station in November 1985.

under Ribble management. Lower Mosley Street bus station, Manchester was officially closed at midnight on 13th May 1972 though it saw some limited use for a time, services being transferred to Chorlton Street, a more central location.

The express services between the North West and London came under one control with the merger of North Western and Standerwick interests and in July 1973 it was agreed that Ribble would take over the 'local' express services between Manchester and Bradford (X12), Barnsley (X19), Sheffield (X48), and Mansfield (X67). From 6th February 1974, North Western's name was changed to National Travel (North West) Ltd., one of five companies formed to administer the national express network of the National Bus Company. This new organisation gradually took over the longer Ribble express services, the company supplying coaches on a contract basis, painted in the new corporate white livery.

Apart from the main line routes, the multi-purpose services of old were giving place to weekend services with a specific goal such as a seaside resort or holiday camp. The spread of the motorway network assisted this trend as people wanted fast transport to the destination of their choice.

In 1973, the Yorkshire-Blackpool pool split into two sections, Doncaster-Barnsley-Blackpool, (joint with Yorkshire Traction) and Leeds-Blackpool, (joint with West Yorkshire), the Leeds services J1-6 becoming X81-

86. The frontier town of Keswick was breached, several services running through to Workington and Whitehaven, jointly with Cumberland Motor Services.

By 1977 X14, Burnley-Morecambe, X55, Colne-Blackpool, X66, Blackburn-Manchester and X71, Liverpool-Blackpool had been withdrawn, some parts being replaced by National Travel services. An hourly X61 Liverpool-Blackpool was given local status between Burscough and Tarleton connecting with a reduced X60/70 at Preston. Many more services were converted to one-man operation, the changeover on X27 resulting in the use of five coaches instead of four because of the extra running time needed. From 31st July 1979, X61 was extended to Fleetwood every two hours and the famous X60/70 was withdrawn though a National Travel service covered the motorway route. A replacement X6 service between Manchester and Preston was unsuccessful and was withdrawn in November 1980 together with the X12 Manchester-Bradford route.

In a route exchange, the Oldham-Blackpool pool was handed over to Yelloway in 1976, the latter giving up their Blackpool-London service which was integrated with the National network. The excursion business from Bury (formerly Auty's Tours) was also sold to Yelloway in 1978.

Deregulation Begins

The Transport Act, 1980 began the process of deregulation.

Number 126, a Leyland Tiger with 48-seat Plaxton body to Rapide standard, combining National and Sandpiper liveries, visits Bury Interchange in September 1985. This was one of ten such coaches leased from Arlington Motors in 1984 and returned to them in 1987.

The ultimate in double-deck coaches, in which field Ribble were the undoubted pioneers, were these Plaxton Paramount 4000s of which ten (171-80)took to the road in June 1986. Unfortunately No. 173 was destroyed by fire on the M6 during its first week in service. Number 179 is seen in Accrington when new. The nine survivors were sold to Amberline in March 1988.

Ten coach-seated Leyland Olympians with 72-seat Eastern Coach Works bodies, were placed in service early in 1986 and No. 2173 is seen in Bury in red, grey and white Timesaver livery en route from Manchester to Nelson in October 1987.

Services covering a minimum distance of 30 miles no longer needed to be licensed and for shorter services, an applicant would automatically be granted a licence unless the existing operator could prove that the grant was not in the public interest. This reversed the onus of proof which had applied since 1931, whereby the applicant had been required to prove that the existing services were inadequate.

Long distance services freed from licensing became more flexible as there were no longer railway objections to changes. The National Travel network was challenged by British Coachways, a consortium of well-established independent operators, leading to reduced fares and improved services, but the opposition disintegrated as some of the participants dropped out. National's strength was its universal network of travel offices, agencies and repair facilities which the newcomers lacked. Some municipalities tried their luck at long distance work, perhaps the most remarkable being the service between Blackpool and Dover worked jointly by Burnley and Pendle, Leicester and Maidstone. Lancaster and Merseyside PTE collaborated in a Liverpool-Heysham service connecting with the Isle of Man steamers. None of these ventures was of lasting importance.

The National Express network used its fleet very intensively and economically, scheduled coaches being allocated to routes regardless of ownership. Two- and

Ribble's first 15 Leyland Nationals (371-85) were delivered in traditional cherry red livery and with 44 seats. They were repainted and reseated to 48 before entering service in November 1972. Several of the class were converted to 52-seaters later by removing the centre exit door.

Bristol VRT 1984 was re-registered NCK 984K before entering service in September 1971. With a Gardner 6LX engine and Eastern Coach Works 70-seat body it was hardly typical of Ribble as it stood at that date. It is seen equipped for one-man operation on the Carlisle city services.

three-day cycles of operation ensured the return of vehicles to their home depots for maintenance. Conversely, Ribble had saved vehicles by using coaches on odd stage carriage journeys and this was no longer possible.

Many Ribble medium distance expresses carried passengers for less than 30 miles and therefore were still licensed. Some of these were marketed under the 'Timesaver' label and given route numbers in a 7xx series. Thus X43, Skipton-Colne-Manchester became 743 (but X43 was retained as a motorway service) and X61 became 761 and was withdrawn between Blackpool and Fleetwood in February 1981. Services 738, Barrow-Blackpool (Mondays, Fridays and Saturdays) and 760, Clitheroe-Blackburn-Blackpool ran during the 1982 season and, over the Christmas and New Year period 1982-83, there were new routes specifically aimed at shoppers. These included 708, Ingol-Fulwood-Ribbleton-Manchester, 710, Lammack-Manchester and 763, Fleetwood-Blackpool-Manchester. Summer 1983 saw services originating in the former LUT area such as 736 and 737 to Blackpool and

Southport. The Blackpool coach started from Little Hulton and Walkden on Mondays, Wednesdays and Fridays and from Wingates and Westhoughton on Sundays, Tuesdays and Thursdays and the Southport coach vice versa. Operation on selected days was indicative of the greatly reduced demand on services of this kind.

Some 'Timesaver' services were for peak hour commuters such as 705, Parbold-Skelmersdale-Liverpool, 715, Scaws Estate-Penrith-M6-Carlisle and 780, Fleetwood-Preston.

During 1983, the clock was turned back and several express services were returned by National Express to Ribble which took over administrative control of National Travel at Liverpool, Manchester and Blackpool from 1st June 1984. The returned services were either very local , for example X8 Blackburn Area-Blackpool or weekend routes on which all or most of the passengers travelled to one destination such as the summer routes to Skegness, Middleton Towers, Pwllheli, Scarborough and Filey. In 1985, the National Travel name began to be phased out in

This stylish Park Royal bodywork was adopted by several NBC companies for use with the Leyland Atlantean AN68 chassis. Number 1363 was one of 104 such vehicles placed in service in 1974-76. Many operated on Merseyside and subsequently passed to North Western where they had long lives.

Bristol VRT 1446 with curved windscreen was one of 20 placed in service in 1979, originally powered by the Leyland 501 engine, and having full-height bodywork, as indicated by the depth of the between-decks white band, instead of the low-height version more usual on this chassis. Most of the batch, including this vehicle, were later fitted with Gardner 6LXB engines. It was working on Carlisle city services where experiments were made with various automated ticket systems.

favour of 'Kingfisher Ribble'. The network was now confined to primary routes and included several of the upgraded Rapide services for which 23 vehicles were needed. Other coach operations were marketed under the 'Sandpiper' name.

Prelude to Privatisation

Under the Transport Act 1985, the government was committed to selling off the NBC companies, converting municipal and PTE bus operations into commercial ventures and abolishing route licensing altogether outside London. Late in 1985, NBC held a general managers' meeting, addressed by Secretary for Transport Nicholas Ridley, who encouraged them to go away and prepare to make management and/or employee bids for their companies. At the end of the meeting, the general managers of the four largest companies, including Ribble, were told that they were forbidden from taking any interest in buying their companies.

The reason for this became apparent on 13th February 1986 when the Secretary for Transport announced (against the advice of NBC) that the four companies had to be split so that they might not be seen as so large as to be a deterrent to competition. Thus, whilst the company's staff was engaged in the mammoth task of preparing for deregulation, its management was further diverted by splitting the company into three competing parts. The first part of the split was accomplished by transferring the Carlisle and Penrith area operations to Cumberland Motor Services Ltd. on 23rd February 1986.

The south-western part of the system comprising the Merseyside depots, Skelmersdale and Wigan was transferred to a new North Western Road Car Co. Ltd. on 7th September 1986. To avoid the necessity of applying for licences for such a short period, North Western buses ran on hire to Ribble until 25th October 1986, after which deregulation was a reality and Ribble stood on the threshold of a new era.

CHAPTER 8
THE AGE OF DEREGULATION

The run-up to deregulation of the bus industry started about a year before the actual day – 26th October 1986. Operators had to advise the Traffic Commissioners of the services they intended to run commercially by 28th February 1986 so that county and other authorities would know what would need to be put out to tender. As all the artificial boundaries between transport operators were to be set aside and the municipal undertakings converted into companies, all the protective agreements of the past would be null and void.

A very high proportion of Ribble services was unremunerative and therefore would have to go out to tender and there was no guarantee that the company would retain them. On the other hand, there would be opportunities to gain tenders at the expense of other operators and the removal of restrictions would enable local passengers to be carried over hitherto prohibited sections of route. The forthcoming partition of the company would excise the profitable routes worked on behalf of the Merseyside PTE. However, the centralised nature of the organisation, particularly the Engineering Department, would leave a disproportionately high share of overheads with the new, lean Ribble company.

It was against this background that the company's management proposed to move into densely populated Greater Manchester and to broaden the base of operations in parts of its traditional area by launching networks competing with municipal companies. It was a time of great uncertainty as the results of tendering were often not known until close to D-day, making fleet requirements difficult to estimate.

It was decided to reopen Bolton depot, which had been used as a store since 1981, and to base local service buses at the coach depot at Hulme Hall Road, Manchester. New minibus sub-depots were opened at Barrow-in-Furness, Chorley and Darwen. Many additional double-deck buses were needed and 81 were bought second-hand as recorded in chapter 10. There was an adequate supply as many operators whose networks shrunk were disposing of surplus vehicles at low prices.

D-day

On 26-27th October 1986, Ribble buses appeared on a number of services in the Manchester area including the subsidised all-night routes. New Minilink networks commenced in Darwen, Lancaster and Morecambe. On the other side of the coin, Blackpool Transport and Fylde Transport won substantial tenders in the Fylde, running into Preston from Fleetwood and Lytham St. Annes; Carriages Ltd. competed on the Fleetwood town services; a local coach operator, Mercer's was competing in the Longridge corridor and in Leyland; Blackburn Transport

was running between Clitheroe and Manchester and GM Buses ran between Blackburn and Preston on Sundays. Several rural services were lost to local coach operators.

The first three months were a standstill period to enable operators to assess the situation and decide their future strategy. From 26th January 1987, GM Buses withdrew from Central Lancashire and, soon after, Ribble started running on some Bolton local routes and in Urmston. Blackpool Transport expanded in Fleetwood and Cleveleys following Ribble's withdrawal on Sundays and weekday evenings. Burnley and Pendle won several contracts in Accrington, Blackburn and Great Harwood and penetrated to Preston. On 6th April, United Transport opened a big network of Zippy minibus services in Preston and, although this initially competed with Preston Transport, strong resistance drove it to seek routes to Kirkham, Bamber Bridge and Penwortham which competed with Ribble. Tendered services were won by Ribble in Stockport and the Hyndburn circulars were converted to minibus operation.

In an ICC report, Ribble was adjudged the ex-NBC company with the least enviable record, being placed last in the performance league with a net loss of £4.18 million on a turnover of £17.67 million in the period ended September 1987. There was worse to come. In November 1987, Ribble lost the contract services to the BNFL factory at Salwick, undermining the whole Fylde operations. New operators were finding their way on to the National Express network on a contract basis and revenue from long-distance operations was being gradually eroded. Devonshire Road garage, Blackpool was closed and demolished and the site sold; the coaches were moved to the now under-used Coliseum coach station. The night service contracts in Manchester ceased in January 1988 following a change in PTE policy. Barrow and Lancaster municipal companies were being particularly troublesome; both extended as far as Kendal and Lancaster's buses were running to Blackpool, Preston and even Southport for a short time.

The Management Buy-out

After the company had been split up, the embargo on a management buy-out was lifted and the general manager, I.A.E. Chapman, together with the traffic manager, chief engineer and a new finance director, began their preparations. Uncertainty reigned for a time as a group of less senior officers, (known colloquially as the B Team as against Chapman's A Team) also prepared a bid for the company. Early sales of NBC subsidiaries to their managements had mostly been concluded at prices lower than the net book value of their assets and, in a few cases, there were 'claw back' clauses in the sale agreements

Many Nationals soldiered on well into the days of deregulation. A single door 11.3 m model of 1976, No. 727, waits for its departure time on the turning circle at Green Haworth, Oswaldtwistle on the Hyndburn Circular in June 1985, when the legislation which laid the foundation of the new policy was on its way through Parliament.

Leyland Olympian No. 2132 was one of seven which entered service in 1983. Its Eastern Coachworks body seated 45/32. It is working the Hyndburn Circular in April 1985 against a background of Blackburn Cathedral. The use of buses in all-over advertising livery brought more revenue but local commercial radio stations were themselves competing for advertising.

Deregulation day saw Ribble buses operating in the heart of Greater Manchester. Park Royal-bodied AN68 Atlantean No. 1621 was one of 27 acquired from Southdown Motor Services and was similar to Ribble's own Atlanteans of 1973-74. It is turning out of Parker Street into Mosley Street, Manchester on a route from Chorlton to Shaw, an extended version of what had once been a Manchester Corporation tram route, in July 1989.

Leyland Atlanteans No. 1622 and 1433 are seen in Preston depot in May 1987. Number 1622, with East Lancashire body, was one of six 1971/5 buses acquired from Blackburn Corporation in 1986 while 1433 was new to Ribble in 1976. Just over a year later, 1622 was caught by the camera on Morecambe promenade, after conversion to an open-top bus, as shown below left.

(Above) Conversion of the Hyndburn Circulars to Minilink operation brought these 25-seat Renault S56 vehicles with Dormobile bodies on to the road in 1987. Number 643 was one of 14 and is seen in Blackburn in May 1989.

Three dual-purpose Bristol VRs with coach-seated ECW bodies were acquired from South Midland Motor Services in 1986 and No. 2040 was painted in this double-deck coach livery. The paper label in the windscreen reads 'Kids Still Half Fare', reflecting a dispute between the company and Lancashire County Council when it was argued that children should be subsidised like other concessionary passengers. The scene is Lancaster bus station in April 1987.

Two virtually identical ECW-bodied Bristol VRs stand side by side in Blackburn depot yard in 1988. That on the left is No. 2036, ex-North Devon (and originally Western National) while the other is 1987, new to Ribble in 1972. Both carry notices showing that they have been operating Lancashire County Council subsidised services and 1987 is proclaiming the 'New Ribble'.

The destination display on Reeve Burgess-bodied Mercedes Benz L608D No. 549 is most uninformative as it is running a Fleetwood town service, straddling the tram track in Lord Street, then Britain's only thoroughfare with a street tramway along its full length. There were 64 of these vehicles of which 501-21 had 19 coach seats while 522-64 had 20 bus seats.

The whole 1985 single-deck order comprised Leyland Tigers but only one, No. 900, had a service bus body, a Duple Dominant type with 49 seats. No. 900 takes a break at Preston in March 1987.

It was many years since there had been a Daimler in the Ribble fleet and these three Fleetlines were part of a group of 18 dual-door buses bought from South Yorkshire PTE. Caught by the camera eight days before deregulation in October 1986, they had been painted in Ribble colours but still had their Sheffield destination blinds. They were CRG6LX models and had bodywork built by Eastern Coach Works – unusually for that bodybuilder in recent times, to the operator's preferred style, based on East Lancashire practice. Respectively, they were 1709, 1714 and 1713.

Yet another livery variation was carried by Leyland Leopard PSU3E No. 1101, seen at Manchester's Hulme Hall Road depot against a background of the electrified Manchester-Altrincham railway line, now the Metrolink. This 47-seat Duple-bodied coach, new in 1979, was used on a Manchester-Nottingham service which was not continued under deregulation, the photograph dating from August 1986

Number 1405, the first of the ECW-bodied AN68 Atlanteans of 1976, reverses off Preston bus-station in September 1987, attended by United Transport Zippy Fiat and Freight Rover Sherpa minibuses.

whereby the government would take a proportion of the profits from any subsequent sales of particular valuable properties.

However, by the time Ribble came to be sold the situation had changed. Because of the delay caused by the split, the company was inevitably near the end of the queue; deregulation had come and gone, a number of outside bodies such as Stagecoach and Drawlane had shown an interest in buying companies and the government endeavoured to circumvent the imposition of 'claw-back' clauses by asking for higher prices which allowed for the full potential value of the properties. In the final bid, Mr Chapman, by then managing director, and two fellow directors formed a property company, Dimple Estates, in conjunction with two property developers. If their bid were successful, the major properties were to be transferred to Dimple.

Initially, 26 parties had shown an interest in buying Ribble but, ultimately there were four sealed bids of which the management's offer was successful. It was for some £8 million against a net book value of assets at the sale date of £5.6 million. On 2nd March 1988, the three directors became the owners of the company, with contributions from eight other officers.

The New Broom

The first actions of the new regime were to sell the company's central stores and parts organisation to the Galbraith Group – the local Leyland truck dealers – and to withdraw from National Express, the contract and 25 vehicles being taken over by Amberline of Speke which

was shortly to be come a subsidiary of Crosville Wales and, subsequently the privatised National Express company. This was followed by Ribble's take-over of the Preston-based Zippy minibus fleet and the sharing of Manchester depot by United Transport's Stockport-based Bee Line Buzz Company. A new through service between Blackpool and Accrington via Lytham St. Annes, Preston and Blackburn echoed the great days of the trunk services. Apart from the East Lancashire-Manchester limited stop services, on which the demand was sometimes too good for the available accommodation, summer coach services to the coastal resorts were mainly confined to a few weekends.

Blackpool and Darwen depots were closed in August 1988, operations being shared between Fleetwood, Preston and Blackburn depots. The following month, Ribble took over the Bee Line minibuses of United Transport with 192 of the 225 minibuses, bringing Ribble's minibus fleet up to over 350 vehicles, second only to GM Buses.

In December 1988, North Western started competing with Ribble in Blackburn and Darwen. Intense competition persisted in Lancaster and Barrow though, in March 1989, a limited accord was made with the Lancaster company covering Sundays and Bank Holidays. The reduction of coaching work made Burnley depot uneconomic and it was closed on 3rd April 1989, buses being out-stationed at the Burnley and Pendle depot at Queensgate.

Competition was often met by offers of special day return fares or multiple-journey tickets, though restrictions and limitations on the use of the latter often confused passengers.

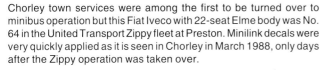

Chorley town services were among the first to be turned over to minibus operation but this Fiat Iveco with 22-seat Elme body was No. 64 in the United Transport Zippy fleet at Preston. Minilink decals were very quickly applied as it is seen in Chorley in March 1988, only days after the Zippy operation was taken over.

The three-axle Talbot Pullmans of United Transport probably gave the best ride of any of the minibuses. After acquisition by Ribble in March 1988 their Zippy decals were soon replaced by Minilink as shown in this scene two months later and, under Stagecoach ownership, they have travelled far and wide.

Several ex-Greater Manchester PTE buses came into the Ribble fleet after deregulation. Number 1645 (upper) was one of 12 purchased direct in 1987 and is seen in Bolton in March 1988 on a route which was once the exclusive preserve of the PTE, the 582 to Leigh. It was a 1972 Atlantean with Park Royal bodywork. The Northern Counties-bodied Atlantean AN68A (below) came to Ribble in July 1989, as an inter-company transfer within the Stagecoach Group. It was still in the mainly green livery of East Midland's Frontrunner-South East fleet when photographed in Blackburn two months later.

This Bristol VR with standard ECW body, No. 2045, came to Ribble in 1990 from Magicbus where it was No.102, but was new to Western National. Only the statutory lettering revealed the owning company's identity.

Number 583 is a Mercedes Benz 709D 23-seat vehicle with body by Alexander. It was completely anonymous when working a Bury local service at the Interchange in May 1990. It was one of 26 new vehicles of this type.

The Sale to Stagecoach

One of the parties which had shown an early interest in buying Ribble was the Stagecoach Group whose chairman, Brian Souter, had made a tour of inspection in 1987. However NBC, in accordance with Government policy, had imposed a condition that no one purchaser could buy more than three non-contiguous companies, thus ensuring that there would be no stifling of competition. By March 1988 when Ribble was sold to its management, Stagecoach had already bought Hampshire Bus, Cumberland and United Counties and were, therefore, not in a position to buy Ribble from NBC. However, Mr Souter had obviously been impressed by what he had seen and, with his acquisition of Cumberland Motor Services Ltd. from 23rd July 1987, had become Ribble's northern neighbour. The Group had a good record of success and had already bought a number of ex-NBC companies throughout the country. Its policy was to stabilise the position as far as possible and reach such limited agreements as the law allowed with other companies with whom competition had been intense and wasteful in the past.

Early in April 1989, Stagecoach bought the East Midland company which had extended its operations into Manchester since deregulation and, on 21st April 1989, he completed the purchase of the vehicles and goodwill of Ribble from its management. The properties remained with Dimple and those necessary for continued operation were leased to Ribble. Ian Chapman became part-time chairman until his retirement and Brian Souter temporarily took on the role of managing director before handing over to Cumberland's managing director, W.B. Hinkley.

As a result of Ribble's successful predatory attack, Barrow Transport went into liquidation on 26th May 1989, improving the company's position in the Furness region. The new owners decided that it made sense to have only one company serving the whole of Cumbria so the services worked from Barrow, Ulverston and Kendal depots were transferred to Cumberland from 18th June 1989; Ambleside depot had closed in May.`

An out-station was set up at Fylde Transport's Squires Gate depot in July 1989, thus eliminating dead mileage from Preston and Fleetwood and in September, the predatory North Western services in Blackburn and Darwen were bought out. An arrangement with Preston Borough Transport resulted in the withdrawal of much of the Zippy network in Preston while Preston withdrew from South Ribble. In November, a similar accord with Blackburn took the latter's buses off several out-of-town routes while Ribble abandoned the former North Western services.

The standard Stagecoach livery has been condemned not so much for its own lack of appeal but because it has replaced many well-loved liveries. Its use on all the Group's fleets is pragmatic as it reduces the cost of transferring vehicles between companies. Northern Counties Atlantean 1673, ex Greater Manchester PTE via East Midland/Frontrunner South East, is seen in Bolton depot yard in November 1989. Number 1452 (below) is a very similar vehicle but nine years younger, having been taken over with the bankrupt business of Barrow Borough Transport in May 1989. It is standing in Blackburn being overtaken by Reeve Burgess Mercedes Benz L608D No.553 in all-over advertising livery.

The first new vehicles to be delivered to Ribble under Stagecoach ownership were ten Leyland Olympians with Alexander bodies with 82 coach seats, Numerically the last of the batch, 2189 threads its way through a group of Merseybus vehicles at Hood Street Gyratory, at the start of a Liverpool to Blackpool journey.

The Drawlane Agreement

From 1st October 1989, the Stagecoach Group made an agreement with its nearest rival, Drawlane, which controlled the North Western and Crosville companies. Ribble's routes wholly within Manchester, together with those of the East Midland company's Frontrunner North West operation, were sold to Drawlane who passed them to North Western as caretaker pending the formation of a new Bee Line Buzz Co. Ltd. Ribble continued to run into Manchester from Bolton and East Lancashire but Hulme Hall Road depot passed to Bee Line. The acquisition of Mercer's in November restored order to the Preston scene.

Stagecoach philosophy left no place for Central Workshops which the Group's managing director, Mrs Ann Gloag, reputedly described publicly as a 'drain on resources' and 'a bastion of trade union militancy'. Decentralised management made the large Head Office building surplus to requirements and the office block and Frenchwood Workshops, which had been doing outside

work as Ribble Engineering Ltd., were closed, with many redundancies. All routine maintenance was done at depots or by Cumberland at Kendal.

The year 1990 was marked by a general review of services to achieve economies without loss of facilities. There was extended collaboration with Lancaster City, ending the bitter struggle in the Lancaster and Morecambe district. Blackburn and Fleetwood depots became minibus only, the latter being closed in favour of a parking area near the docks; the Zippy name was extended to services in the North Fylde and Over-Wyre areas.

By May 1992, the once 1,200-strong Ribble fleet was reduced to 354 vehicles based at eight depots as follows:-

Preston	90
Fleetwood	16 (minibuses only)
Lancaster/Morecambe	55
Blackburn	24 (minibuses only)
Clitheroe	47 (including Burnley out-station)
Chorley	47
Bolton	75
	354

Much research has been done into the early vehicles of Ribble by the PSV Circle, Ribble Enthusiasts Club and others but there are still mysteries which have not been cleared up. In the immediate post-1914-18 War years, it was still the practice for bodies switched from one chassis to another to take the registration number with them, creating great confusion for the historian. The five vehicles taken over from Hodson in June 1919 (four Karriers and a Leyland X type) had all been open-top double-deckers. Two dated from 1913, one from 1915 and two of the Karriers, built on ex-army chassis, were recent acquisitions. It has been speculated that at least one of the Karriers had

been converted to a single-deck bus before sale of the business to Ribble. One of the 1913 buses was withdrawn almost immediately while at least two others are known to have survived until 1924.

There were plenty of second-hand military vehicles for sale cheaply and the fleet was augmented by the purchase of eight AEC YC chassis, three in 1919 and five in 1920. At least three are known to have had open-top double-deck bodies fitted initially but by 1923 they were all running as 32-seat saloons. Some bodies were supplied locally by the Preston Motor Body Building Co.; others came from Birch Brothers, the London operator and

This covered Leyland charabanc, CK 477, was never a Ribble vehicle but was probably similar to CK 447 which was a 1913 vehicle in J. Hodson's fleet. The registration number was almost certainly transferred from an earlier vehicle. It was named 'Prestonian' and conveyed Dick Kerr's Ladies football team to and from their matches for several years. The reason for the upside-down number on the dash panel is unknown. The engine followed conventional practice of the period in most aspects, with four-cylinder side-valve layout, but the provision of two sparking plugs per cylinder was noteworthy, probably implying dual ignition for reliability.

bodybuilder. Two further chassis of the same type, with 32-seat bus bodies, probably by Birch, came in April 1920 when the Preston branch of the BAT was merged with Ribble. They had originally come from the Macclesfield branch and others of the same batch went into the North Western fleet when that company was formed in 1923.

Four examples of the very similar Daimler Y chassis, also ex-army, joined the fleet in 1920 followed by nine in 1921, five in 1922 and nine in 1923 by which time the supply of ex-army chassis was drying up. At least two of the 1920 deliveries had charabanc bodies as did two more transferred from the BAT's Barrow branch in 1922.

The intake for 1922 included five of the lightweight Vulcan VSD chassis, built at Southport with 20-seat bodies by Northern Counties of Wigan, a sixth following in 1923. Many operators favoured small vehicles of this type to pioneer new routes but, apart from acquisitions, no more small buses were to grace the Ribble fleet for over a decade nor were further orders placed with Northern Counties for many years despite its proximity.

The Leyland Connection

In June 1923, a Leyland G7 demonstrator with 32-seat Leyland body painted blue and white, was tried on various routes in the Preston area for about a month after which it was sold by Leyland to Cumberland Motor Services. Ribble was sufficiently impressed to place an order for the larger SG7 type of which 11 were taken into stock in 1923 and two in 1924. These were large vehicles in their day, measuring just under 27ft 6in long, with a full width cab, two doors and seats for 38 or 39 passengers. The engine

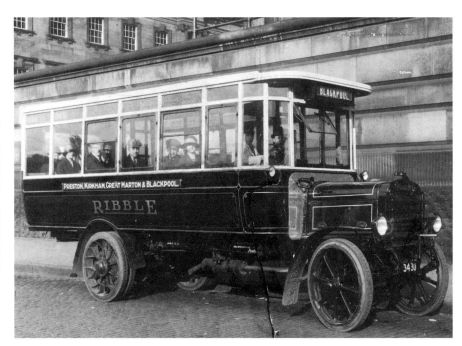

(Right) Fourteen of these Daimler Y saloons were placed in Ribble service in 1921, most being withdrawn in 1927, after pneumatics had been fitted. The overhauled ex-army chassis were bodied by Birch Bros., the well-known London bus operators, who built many such 28-seat bodies for several BET and BAT companies. Note the route board, a refinement which disappeared quite early, in furtherance of Ribble's policy of switching buses from one route to another and making six buses do the work of seven!

(Below) Despite its network of rural routes, Ribble did not buy many small buses, preferring to use larger buses which the fleet greater flexibility. Exceptions were these six Vulcan 20-seaters which arrived in 1922. The chassis were manufactured at Southport and the bodies by Northern Counties Motor and Engineering Co. Ltd. at Wigan. The Vulcans were numbered C47-51, the leader being No. C50.

Full-fronted Leyland SG7 (C67) was new in late 1923 and remained in service until 1930. It seated 38 in its dual entrance body though the rear entrance was mainly used. It is seen outside the Harris Library, Preston en route to Leyland, a highly competitive route until 1935. Note the smaller front wheels as an aid to steering these heavy vehicles. All the SGs were fitted with pneumatic tyres by about 1927. Note the early form of the fleet title, slightly more spread out than the later seriffed style.

The Leyland SG9 had a more powerful engine being rated by the RAC as 40 hp compared with the SG7's 36 hp. Number C84 was the first of 17 of these buses entering service in 1924, having 38 seats, though the last 12 seated only 36, an early example of Ribble's policy of giving greater passenger comfort. These were the first half-cab buses which improved access to the engines.

was partly alongside the driver. This was the beginning of a relationship between Ribble and Leyland Motors which was destined to last for six decades. The proximity of the Leyland works to Preston and clear signs that Ribble was likely to emerge as the dominant operator in the area made the company an obvious target for the Leyland sales force. Leyland Motors had gone through a lean period and it was the custom of such companies as Ribble and Crosville, both of which bought Leyland chassis and bodies in quantity after ex-army chassis were no longer available, that restored their fortunes.

In the case of Ribble, the relationship was closer, as the company was able to give the manufacturer feedback on performance on the road and influence vehicle design. In 1924, nine of the SGH7 type (the H denoted a higher radiator) were delivered followed by 17 of the more powerful SG9 type with an engine rated by the RAC at 40 hp compared with the 36 hp of the SG7. The SG9s introduced the half cab layout, a development suggested by Ribble to improve engine accessibility, though the first of the type went not to Ribble but to Rawtenstall Corporation. Thirty-nine more SGs were purchased in 1925 though all but four were on the 26ft SG11 chassis with rear-entrance bodies seating 35 or 36 passengers.

The G and SG models had straight chassis as used for

lorries, as then usual and, indeed, most ended their days with hauliers after sale by Ribble. They were rugged and reliable but the four steps were difficult for elderly people to negotiate. From 1926, tyre technology has reached the stage where pneumatic tyres were available for heavier vehicles and the earlier models were converted.

The Leyland Lion

Leyland revolutionised its range for 1926 by producing a new range of vehicles with lower chassis specifically designed for passenger work. The L range included a double-decker (the Leviathan) and four types of single-decker, the forward-control Lion and Leopard, normal-control Lioness and the small Leveret. The Lion emerged as the most important model; it was fitted with a 5.1 litre 4-cylinder engine and equipped with pneumatic tyres and four-wheel brakes. The first models, designated LSC1 or PLSC1, were 25ft long with a 14ft 6in wheelbase but a longer variant (PLSC3) appeared in 1927 with a length of up to 27ft 6in and a 16ft 5in wheelbase. This replaced the Leopard of which only two were built. Leyland produced a square but attractive body for the Lion with options of forward, rear or dual entrances.

Ribble bought new only Lions but took over Lionesses

The Lion PLSC offered more comfort and a better road performance than its square-cut lines might suggest. It played a big part in Ribble's expansion. Seen here are (above), four of the 1928 deliveries of PLSC3 models; (right) C159, the second of the initial batch of PLSC1 models and (below), in service in Preston is C460, one of a batch of ten PLSC3 models with 32-seat Leyland bodywork dating from 1928. It was one of the last of the type to remain in service, being withdrawn in 1939.

The Titan TD1 opened up new possibilities for double-deck operation of inter-urban routes, leading to scenes like this, showing C752 on the Blackburn-Wigan service in May 1930, soon after entering service – some 50 Titans were placed in service that year. The 6.8-litre petrol engine gave such vehicles the ability to keep up with the typical pace of contemporary traffic.

and Leverets with subsequent acquisitions. The 1926 order consisted solely of 47 PLSC1 Lions with front-entrance Leyland bodies and the Lion was adopted as the standard service bus for the next three years. Thirty-seven PLSC1s and 36 PLSC3s came in 1927 and 72 PLSC3s in 1928, the last two having Massey bodies, probably ordered by Lancashire and Westmorland Motor Services. Contemporary press reports state that the normal 31- and 35-seat capacity of these buses was reduced to 28 and 32 respectively to give greater passenger comfort. To the 192 Lions bought new were added a further 60 PLSC1s and 21 PLSC3s taken over from other operators up to 1931, giving a grand total of 273. Some of these had rear-entrance bodies. Two bonneted Lionesses and seven 20-seat Leverets were also taken over.

The Lions were just as rugged and reliable as their predecessors but offered greater speed and passenger comfort at a crucial time in the company's expansion. Most of them were withdrawn from service without modification between 1937 and 1939 but many saw further service with other operators. Crosville took 12 in 1939, fitting utility bodywork to six of them in 1943 and after sale in 1950, nine ran for the Forestry Commission until about 1960, giving them a working life of over 30 years. One, CK3825 (295), was restored privately and taken over by Ribble in July 1981. It was hired out to special parties, participated in special events and rallies but is now in store.

More New Leylands

Leyland consolidated its lead over other manufacturers at the 1927 Commercial Motor Show by unveiling the new T series, comprising the Titan double-deck and the Tiger single-deck which reduced the floor level even further to about 2ft 4in. Both were equipped with a 6.8 litre six-cylinder overhead-camshaft engine. At the time, Ribble had no use for double-deck buses and its 1928 order included 40 Tiger TS2 models with bus bodies fitted with coach seats and interior luggage racks. These were required for the network of express services introduced that year and whilst the exterior appearance was somewhat utilitarian, the appointments compared favourably with the many canvas-roofed vehicles then in service with other operators. The Tiger was a speedy vehicle and the 29 seats were reasonably comfortable for a long journey. With further expansion of express services, a further 30 were added to the fleet in 1929, this time with well-spaced bus seats for 26 and a roof-mounted luggage rack. There were thus 70 vehicles available for long distance services, an enormous fleet at the time. They were reseated to 30 in 1934 when delivery of new coaches enabled them to be cascaded to bus duties.

In 1929, the PLSC Lion was replaced by a new LT1 Lion which, broadly speaking, was a 4-cylinder version of the Tiger and rather resembled it in appearance. Ribble placed an initial order for 25 with 30-seat front-entrance

The Leyland Tiger brought six-cylinder smoothness and new standards of speed capability, though legal requirements only allowed these to be used sparingly. The vehicle shown, C604, about to leave Leyland's works in May 1929, was the first of a batch of 31 of the TS2 type with 26-seat bodywork for use on the rapidly expanding express services. They were re-seated to accommodate 30 in 1934 for bus duties, this one being sold in 1938 though it had a long life with independent operators, often the case with such vehicles, being rebodied and not withdrawn until 1959.

The Lion had graduated to the LT series and the Leyland body designers to a new curvaceous style by the time the LT2 appeared in 1930. Two examples are seen manoeuvring at Tithebarn Street bus station, Preston in the mid 'thirties amid other types. The LT2 was to remain a familiar sight in most parts of the company's territory through the 'thirties.

The 1931 delivery of 52 Tiger TS3 models were intended for long-distance services and so the Leyland bodies had well-spaced seating for 26 passengers and luggage carriers on the roof, but the era of bus-style vehicles on such duties was drawing to a close, so they soon began to look dated despite their well-proportioned lines.

bus bodies to which were added four ordered by Armstrong and Siddle and three by County Motors. The company now had a need for double-deck buses for use on the intensive urban routes in the Liverpool area and the Titan was ideal for the company's needs. Its unique design, with a sunken offside gangway on the upper deck where the seats were arranged in rows of four, resulted in an overall height of just about 13ft, nearly two feet less than the Leviathan. It was thus suitable for rural use on routes where there were low railway bridges and overhanging trees. Seventeen Titan 51-seaters came in 1929, all with open platforms and staircases, three being allocated to County Motors, then being operated as a subsidiary. Fifty more Titans with fully-enclosed rear ends were delivered in 1930. Double-deck operation was now extended to frequent interurban services such as Preston-Chorley-Bolton and the company standardised on the lowbridge design as there were dangerous railway bridges at several strategic points, such as Fylde Road, Preston and at Garstang where the Knott End railway line crossed the road.

There was a further intake of 25 Lions of an improved version (LT2), 22 of which had 30-seat bus bodies the odd three having been ordered by the Furness Omnibus Co. with a 35-seat specification. This highlights Ribble's policy of providing extra passenger comfort at the expense of five seats. There were more Tiger TS2s, 43 with 30-seat bus bodies, 22 with 26-seat coach bodies and nine buses on the shorter TS3 chassis. These, too, had been ordered by Furness and six of them were operated under the Claremont fleet name until October 1930. The 1930 Leyland bus body was much more curvaceous, particularly at the rear end and the windows were slightly arched at the top.

The 1930 deliveries totalled 144 new vehicles but even this massive figure was surpassed in 1931 when the intake was 153 comprising 37 Titan TD1s, 52 Tiger TS3 26-seat coaches and 64 Lion LT2 30-seat buses. The company was able to clear out the remaining high-framed SG buses and had a fleet in which every unit was mounted on a purpose-built passenger chassis.

However, the numerous takeovers had brought a vast influx of acquired vehicles, the total between 1925 and 1931 being 590 as far as can be accurately ascertained. Of these, 238 were Leylands, a reflection of the predominance of the marque in northern England for full-size buses. These were normally integrated with the fleet and disposed of when they reached the normal age. The remainder comprised some 30 different makes, many of them relatively obscure and for which parts were hard to find. These were usually disposed of quickly, some being re-acquired with future purchases, though appreciable numbers of the more reliable models remained in the fleet for some years. These included the large Tilling Stevens and Bristol fleet of the Merseyside Touring Co. Ltd. and several Maudslays.

The years 1929-31 saw 394 second-hand vehicles entering the Ribble fleet and the strain on the resources of the Engineering Department must have been enormous. Presumably all were examined by competent people before purchase in order to determine a sale price and there was then the task of bringing many buses up to the company's standards. After 1931, it was rare for second-hand vehicles to be taken into the fleet and if the terms of the acquisition included the vehicles, they were usually sold for what they would fetch as soon as possible even if they were broadly compatible with the Ribble fleet.

Ribble's batch of 36 coaches of 1933 were a landmark both within the fleet and among Leyland passenger models, being the first production examples of the new generation of Tiger and Titan (TS6 and TD3 respectively), which had a much neater as well as more compact front-end design than their predecessors. Here, an AA man on point duty at the Three Nooks Corner on the Preston-Blackpool road stands back as Ribble C1377 and C1383, with Leyland and English Electric body respectively, show off their performance in the August Bank Holiday dash to the sea in 1934. One of the 1931 batch of LT2 buses, 1157, is third in line, with more coaches prominent among the other traffic.

Ribble Individualism

The enormous intake of 383 new vehicles in 1929-31 was the result of a combination of factors – expansion of the business, the cost benefits of replacing large numbers of obsolescent high-framed vehicles and the availability of money to do it. It was naturally followed by some years when purchases were low, only 88 new vehicles being purchased in the four years 1932-35. During the 'twenties, the company had been content to accept standard Leyland bodies but by now it felt that it was in a position to influence body design and demand features to suit its own requirements. The policy was underlined by some problems with Leyland's first metal-framed bodies. Capt. Betteridge put together a design team which evolved a number of distinctively Ribble features which were incorporated into additions to the fleet in the later 'thirties.

Deliveries in 1932 were limited to six all-Leyland Titan TD2 double-deck buses which were outwardly similar to the TD1s though a relaxation in Construction and Use regulations enabled them to be one foot longer, and there were some mechanical changes. Attention was then given to introducing true luxury coaches to the fleet as the earlier coaches, with good passenger facilities hidden away in box-like bus bodies, compared unfavourably with some competitors' vehicles. The whole vehicle intake for 1933 comprised 36 luxury coaches, the bodywork order being equally divided between Leyland with 31 seats and English Electric with 26; all were initially used on extended tours developed from the former Merseyside company's business. These were the

first products of Betteridge's design team and, although there were detail differences, the overall effect was of identical vehicles, with a sun roof and curtained windows.

The Merseyside company's Leyland, Bristol and Tilling Stevens coaches were used on Ribble express services pending the appearance of a new design and in 1934 they were augmented by two AEC Regals taken over with the Blackburn excursion business of Kenyon, Coleman and Robinson. There seems to have been a continuing shortage of coaches resulting in the coaches of acquired businesses being taken into the fleet whilst service buses were rejected. Thus eight Leyland Tigers came with the company's share of the Liverpool firm of James Pearson and Sons, taken over jointly with Crosville in May 1935; 11 Tigers from Arthur Christy (Bolton) Ltd and a Tiger, two AEC Regals and two Albions from F. Snaylam, Bolton, both in 1938.

The locally based English Electric Co. was given a further order in 1934, this time for 12 lowbridge bodies on Leyland TD3 chassis, a redesigned model with a longer radiator which improved the appearance enormously. They were the first diesel-engined vehicles in the fleet and all subsequent double-deck buses were so fitted. A diesel engine was fitted to a 1933 Leyland-bodied coach (1372) in September 1934 but removed after three months, all the company's coaches retaining petrol engines during the 'thirties. In the same year, the company took delivery of six Dennis Ace 20-seat buses, also with English Electric bodies, to replace older acquired stock on the Bowness-on-Solway routes in Carlisle. One might have expected the Leyland Cub to have been chosen and the probable

The first manifestation of what became a clear company style came with the Tiger TS7 coaches, firstly by English Electric and then to virtually identical design by Duple, as represented here by C1539 in a photograph taken in October 1936, after three months' service. These vehicles were capable of an unflustered 60mph, and their petrol engines were almost inaudible when idling.

explanation of the purchase of these 'Flying Pigs' was to let Leyland know that they must not assume Ribble to be a captive market.

The Betteridge Look

New buses for 1935 comprised five Lion LT7s with Leyland metal-framed 36-seat bus bodies, one of which had been ordered by Brookhouse Motors, and five TD4s, four with English Electric bodies and one (1490) with a Leyland metal-framed body. The principal event was the appearance of the first 18 of a fleet of Tiger TS7 coaches with 31-seat English Electric bodies. The Betteridge design specified a half canopy with a distinctive triangular bulkhead pillar echoing the rake of the windscreen. Downswept moulding lines produced the streamlined effect beloved by 'thirties designers. Deliveries continued into 1936 when no fewer than 70 coaches were received, 20 by English Electric and 50 by Duple to the same general design. They were followed by a further 46 similar coaches mounted on the lightweight Leyland LZ2 Cheetah chassis, bodied to the same specification by Brush, traditionally a supplier to BET companies but never before to Ribble.

The record total of 190 vehicles delivered in 1936 also included 34 Leyland TD4 double-deck buses, the body order for which was divided between Burlingham (8), Roe (8), Eastern Counties (8) and Leyland (10), the latter being some of the last V-front metal-framed bodies produced. All bodies except the Leyland were of similar general appearance with raked front and, unusually in those days, heaters on both decks. There were also 35 Cheetah service buses with 30-seat bodies of which 25 bore the Eastern Counties name while 10 were by Eastern Coach Works following the separation of the bodybuilding activity from the bus company of that name. The buses had a family resemblance to the coaches, with half canopy and sliding door; all Betteridge vehicles, irrespective of type, shared a rather shallow, square cut windscreen. A seventh

Dennis Ace, this time with a 20-seat Dennis body, was also purchased.

Experience with the 1936 diverse body programme led to a policy of dividing bus body orders mainly between Brush and Burlingham, with some single-decks coming from Eastern Coach Works. Duple who were coach body specialists, clearly emerged as the preferred builder in this field. The remaining years until the war dried up supplies early in 1941 saw 663 new vehicles added to the fleet as shown below. The 1940 double-deckers were of the newly-introduced TD7 model and 40 had Leyland metal-framed bodies. Hundreds of older vehicles were sold and many saw further service elsewhere.

LEYLAND CHASSIS 1936-41

Year	SD buses	DD buses	Coaches	Total
1936	39	34	116	189
1937	41	35	43	119
1938	139	54	25	218
1939	169	48	18	235
1940-41	31	59	1	91
Total	419	230	203	852

BODIES 1936-41

Maker	SD Buses	DD buses	Coaches	Total
Brush	100	88	72	260
Burlingham	159	76	9	244
Duple	—	—	102	102
EEC	4	—	20	24
ECOC/ECW	156	8	—	164
Leyland	—	50	—	50
Roe	—	8	—	8
Total	419	230	203	852

Single-deck chassis comprised 309 Cheetahs (237 buses and 72 coaches); 309 Tigers (178 buses and 131 coaches) and four Lion buses, the last of the type to be bought. All the Tiger buses had diesel engines, 79 of them of the 6.2 litre L type. The one Cheetah coach which went into service in 1941 was Ribble's last new petrol-engined vehicle. Vehicles for the Standerwick fleet are not included in these tables.

There were some variations in body style, later coaches having a curved waistrail while the 1939 saloons had 32 seats and reintroduced the slightly curved upper edge of the windows reminiscent of the restyled Leyland bodies of 1930-32.

Ribble was the largest user of the lightweight Cheetah

Bus passengers also benefitted from six-cylinder petrol-engine refinement. The Leyland Cheetah thus powered was Ribble's choice for most of its single-deck bus needs in 1936-38, and deliveries continued until 1939, though the oil-engined Tiger had taken over as the more numerous choice by then. In 1938 Eastern Coach Works supplied the bodywork on that year's entire intake of Cheetah buses, amounting to some 121 examples, all with 30-seat bodywork – C1814, seen here, was one of the first to arrive, in February of that year.

The oil engine, standard on Ribble double-deckers since 1934, appeared on the company's single-deckers from the first time in 1938, though a much bigger delivery came in 1939 when C2172 was one of 89 Tiger TS8 models with Burlingham 32-seat bodywork. Similar bodywork was built for 40 more by Brush. This one is thought to have had a standard 8.6-litre engine, but others of this batch had semi-experimental engines of 6.2-litre capacity.

The standard Ribble double-decker outline of the late 'thirties is conveyed by this view of C1721, the first of a batch of twelve Titan TD4 models with bodywork by Burlingham, dating from 1937. Brush also built bodywork to almost identical design. The double-deck version of the livery differed from that on single-deckers in the use of crimson rather than white for window surrounds and rear dome. It was one of the minority of such buses not rebodied, running much as shown until being scrapped in 1952.

chassis, powered by a 4.7-litre petrol engine and based on components from the Cub range. The model did not enjoy great popularity and Ribble's success was to a great extent due to meticulous observance of the manufacturer's recommended vehicle weight. The bodywork was not skimped on this account but the seating capacity was 30 for buses, with generous legroom and 31 for coaches. Several of the buses had sliding roofs for use in the Lake District.

Another noteworthy acquisition was an AEC Regal built with 7.7-litre oil engine and a Burlingham coach body to Ribble specification when new in 1939, to the order of AEC, to act as a demonstrator for Ribble. AEC had several times demonstrated in the past without response except for some Regals for Standerwick in 1938, but the onset of war may have influenced purchase.

Whilst future difficulties could not have been foreseen, Ribble entered the war with a fleet of which the average age was 33 months, an enviable position which eased wartime maintenance problems considerably.

Wartime Buses

In 1942 the government 'unfroze' a number of chassis and bodies which had been partly completed when factories had been turned over to wartime activities and a further 10 Leyland TD7s were received, three bodied by East Lancashire and seven by Leyland. The latter had been ordered by the Scottish operator, W. Alexander and Sons, and arrived with their distinctive route indicator layout though this was modified after the war.

During the next three years, the company received a total of 58 buses built to the Ministry of Supply's austerity specification with only two opening windows on each deck, wooden seats and squared off 'domes'. Twelve were Daimlers (five CWG5 with 5-cylinder Gardner engines and 8 CWA6 with AEC engines) and the others were Guy Arab Mk II (all but six with 5-cylinder Gardners, the others with 6-cylinder engines). Like most utility buses they were painted in grey livery. The bodywork was divided between Brush (10), Northern Counties (23),

Ribble reverted to Leyland bodywork for 40 of the 59 Titan TD7 models placed in service in 1940. Number 2338 is seen before delivery in May. At that stage, vehicles were still receiving the full pre-war livery, complete with elaborate lining out.

Duple (4), Roe (13) and Park Royal (8). The latter, mounted on Guy chassis, introduced highbridge bodies into the Ribble fleet for the first time since the ex-Waterloo and Crosby NS buses were scrapped. They were used on the Carlisle city services and the experience influenced post-war fleet policy.

Five 1930-31 TD1s were also given utility bodies by Northern Counties in 1943-44 and a sixth received a second-hand Leyland body of unknown origin. Three were also given diesel engines. Most of the unrebodied 1931 TD1s survived until 1946-48 but several were then sold to Crosville where they were rebodied and remained in service until 1956. The rebodied TD1s were withdrawn in 1950.

Several coaches were commandeered for military use and not all were returned. Others were converted for use as ambulances though, apart from isolated incidents, in the company's area only Merseyside was subjected to severe aerial attack. Some vehicles were converted to operate on producer gas generated in a trailer but the government's directive on these conversions was cancelled before the programme was completed, to the profound relief of all concerned.

Wartime utility buses entered service in grey livery though most of the fleet retained standard colours during the war years unlike others where grey became usual. Standard fleetnames and numbers were applied, but clearly someone could not believe that the number of C2423, a 1944 Daimler CWA6 with Brush lowbridge body, should have been applied lower on the bonnet side so as **not** to be readily visible.

Guy Arab II 2439 (ACK 829), new in 1944, had Roe bodywork, originally seating 55. It is shown after the end of the war, having been fitted with 53 upholstered seats and with an extra opening window on the nearside. However, the tiny wartime headlamps remain and a need for some remedial work to corroded waist rails on both decks is evident.

The White Ladies were somewhat deceptive creatures – basically lowbridge buses on the Titan PD1/3 chassis, though dressed up to appear more glamorous for use on shorter-distance express services by their external design. Burlingham built the bodywork incorporating full-fronted cabs, rounded window outlines and other details to give them a 'coach' look, and perhaps a touch of reaction to years of wartime gloom. The first one, 2518, is seen before entering service in June 1948.

In common with all other operators, Ribble came out of the war with a fleet which, because of shortages of skilled labour and materials, had been under-maintained. The intake of new vehicles just before the war minimised mechanical problems and the greatest neglect was in the bodywork. Bodies made in 1940-44 were often of poor quality and pre-war bodies had been subjected to much greater wear and tear during the war years. Leyland Motors had been employed on building tanks and armoured vehicles and was slow to get back into full peacetime production. Bureaucratic control of materials created shortages and bottlenecks and the demand for new vehicles was insatiable. Massive orders were placed with Leyland and the company resisted the temptation to ease its problems by placing orders with different manufacturers resorting instead to an ambitious programme of rebuilding and rehabilitation which went on until 1951.

There was a change in double-deck policy, perhaps as a result of the experience with the highbridge Guy Arabs, and it was decided to use this type of vehicle wherever possible especially on urban services where the lowbridge type's side gangway restricted passenger movement and slowed down fare collection. The Traffic Department then produced what was known internally as the 'Bridges Traffic Circular' which listed every potentially dangerous bridge anywhere near a bus route in the Ribble area; it was reissued periodically for many years but the occasional low bridge accident still occurred.

Destination indicator apertures were enlarged in depth from 3in. to 5in and, on double-deck buses, incorporated into a sexagonal layout below the three-track route number; existing buses were modified on overhaul. New service buses had rear route number blinds fitted at cantrail level.

The first post-war buses, delivered between November 1946 and January 1947, were 21 Leyland PD1s with 56-seat highbridge bodies by Burlingham (2449-69) followed in 1947 by 48 PD1As 10 bodied as highbridge by Leyland and 38 as lowbridge by Brush (2470-2517). In 1948-9 the original highbridge buses were all fitted with O.600 9.8-litre engines, as used in the PD2, their 7.4 litre engines being transferred to pre-war petrol-engined vehicles. The Brush bodies did not wear well and, in 1955, 22 of them received new 8ft wide lowbridge Burlingham all metal bodies with platform doors; most of these received O.600 engines in 1959.

For the 1948-49 orders, Ribble specified 8ft wide chassis, newly-authorised for restricted use, each individual section of road having to be approved by the road authority and the Traffic Commissioners until 1950. While some quite narrow roads were authorised, Burscough Street, Ormskirk was refused on the grounds that, as it was exactly 16ft wide, two 8ft buses might attempt to pass with disastrous results. This led to the diversion of services via County Road. The company was offered 42 highbridge all-Leyland PD2/3 buses in 1948 due to the cancellation of an order from Cape Town and these entered service on Merseyside at the end of 1948. They were recognisable by a non-standard indicator layout with single track route number box and an unusually large number of half-drop windows. They were rebuilt to standard layout on overhaul. There were also 28 lowbridge buses with Brush bodies; they had rubber glazing and hinged front upper-deck vents and somehow emphasised the extra width. Three with Leyland bodies which had been ordered by Scout were exchanged for three new Leyland PS1/Burlingham coaches.

A further 100 all-Leyland lowbridge PD2/3s were added to the fleet in 1950 of which 50 had hand-operated two-leaf platform doors and 30 more or less identical buses but on PD2/12 chassis and with power-operated four-leaf doors, purchased in 1952, carried the last new Leyland double-deck bodies purchased by Ribble.

An order for 65 Leyland PS1/1 single-deck 7ft 6in wide chassis with 31-seat Burlingham coach bodies was intended mainly for the Standerwick fleet but, to ease the shortage of coaches for Ribble services, 14 instead of the intended seven were taken into stock in 1948-49 and three more were exchanged with Scout as mentioned above.

Double-deck Coaches

A dramatic move was the order for 30 49-seat double-deck coaches on PD1/3 chassis for use mainly on limited stop services between Liverpool/Manchester and Blackpool/Morecambe and between East Lancashire and Manchester where exceptionally heavy duplication was needed. They were christened 'White Ladies'. All seats were forward facing and there were luggage racks over the rear wheel arches and a small boot beneath the rear platform which, being level with the saloon floor, was reached by two steps. The upper deck layout incorporated the side-gangway and there were opening roof-lights protected by bars. The five-bay Burlingham bodies were full-fronted, the original grilles being modified to improve engine cooling in 1951-52. They were unusual for Ribble in having full number and destination displays at the rear as well as at the front.

Despite the cramped upper deck layout, they were successful for their intended purpose, the longest regular scheduled journey being Manchester-Kendal. A further 20 on PD2/3 chassis were delivered in 1950-51 but with four-bay bodies by East Lancashire Coachbuilders of Blackburn; they had the modified front grille from new. They were the first new vehicles to carry fleet numbers in the new series.

All the original 'White Ladies' ended their days on stage carriage work, the PD1s being reseated to 53 and

The adoption of highbridge Burlingham bodies for the first post-war double-deck bus deliveries marked a change in policy, possibly influenced by the experience of the eight wartime Guys in Carlisle, but more likely a manifestation of the new general manager's ideas. Leyland Titan PD1 No. 2466 is seen much later in its life at Skelhorne Street, Liverpool against a background of Lime Street station's roof. By this time its lower and upper cream bands had been eliminated.

Ten all-Leyland PD1As entered service in 1947, again with 56-seat highbridge bodies. They outlasted the Burlingham version by about three years, being withdrawn in 1961. The upper cream band has been painted over in this latter-day view, again in Skelhorne Street, Liverpool.

The Burlingham-bodied Leyland Tiger PS1s were the only new single-deck coaches taken into the Ribble fleet in the immediate post-war years. They seated 31 instead of the usual 33 and there were 62 of them - 14 for Ribble and 48 for Standerwick. They were significantly heavier than pre-war coaches, turning the scales at 7 tons compared with 6 tons 6 cwt for a 1936 Tiger of similar capacity. This coach was originally numbered 2552 but became 705 in the renumbering scheme. After withdrawal in 1959, it was exported to Yugoslavia with five others.

Lowbridge buses were still needed on many Ribble routes and 38 of the 1947 PD1As had 53-seat Brush bodies which echoed some features of Ribble pre-war designs and Brush wartime utility bodies. The inward-tapering destination display, all under one glass, with the new 5 in. screens had been adopted as a new standard and pre-war double deck buses were so fitted on overhaul. Like many early post-war bodies built from the poor-quality timber common at the time, these deteriorated rapidly and over half the batch were rebuilt in 1955 with 8ft-wide metal-framed Burlingham bodies with platform doors. Their 7.4 litre engines were replaced by O.600 engines at the same time. The upper picture shows No. 2505 in original condition when new while below is No. 2485 with a new Burlingham body, working the long Liverpool-Chorley service. No. 2505 was one of those that survived unrebuilt, lasting until 1958.

painted red between 1955 and 1958. However the PD2s, which remained on express duties until 1960, retained their coach seats and livery until withdrawn in 1961. Mention must be made of the solitary 'Red Lady' (2648) which had a service bus version of the Burlingham body with exposed radiator, half cab and open platform. It was exhibited at the Commercial Motor Show in 1948 and remained in service until 1960 but no more were purchased.

The Rebodying Programme

The double-deck rebodying programme carried out in 1947-50 involved 148 pre-war buses on Leyland TD4 and TD5 chassis. Burlingham 56-seat highbridge bodies, similar to those on new PD1s, were fitted to 68 vehicles which were used mainly on urban services. Five bodies were transferred to 1939 TD5s in 1951-52 but retained their 1936-37 fleet numbers. In 1948, 25 TD5 buses were fitted with Eastern Coach Works lowbridge bodies similar to those used as standard by Tilling group companies.

Following the sale of that group to the British Transport Commission, these bodies could not be sold to outside companies otherwise it seems likely that more would have been ordered. Orders for 1949-50 were placed with W. Alexander and Sons of Falkirk and when unrestricted use of 8ft wide buses was permitted, the order for 55 bodies was changed and 25 were delivered to the new width, the chassis being modified accordingly. The Alexander bodies had a neat appearance with some resemblance to Leyland designs but with quite different flush glazing.

The double-deck programme continued into 1951-52 when the wartime Daimlers and Guys, which were reseated to Ribble's standard 27/26 layout in 1948-49, were refurbished in one of two ways. Sixteen 1937-40 Metropolitan-Cammell highbridge-bodied Titans were purchased from Wallasey Corporation and their bodies mounted on six Daimlers and ten Guys, the Wallasey chassis then being sold for scrap with the utility bodies. The other 42 were sent to Bond of Wythenshawe for a thorough body overhaul, rounded domes and sliding

Large-scale rebodying of the TD4 and TD5 types of Titan made a considerable impact on the Ribble scene in the post-war years. For many years the bulk of the Carlisle town services were operated by such vehicles after fitting with new Burlingham highbridge bodywork in 1947. Seen here passing the Rotunda in the early 'fifties is No. 1619, a 1936 TD4 originally fitted with Eastern Counties lowbridge body – it remained in service in this form until 1958, like most of the type, lasting as long as buses with similar Burlingham bodies on new PD1 chassis.

Leyland No. 1772, new in 1938, was one of 25 TD5 models which received new Eastern Coach Works bodies in 1948, giving them a 21-year life. The general design was similar to that used by the Tilling Group companies on Bristol K chassis, though Ribble maintained its 53-seat capacity compared with the usual 55 on this type of body.

When Eastern Coach Works bodies became unobtainable when the Tilling Group sold out to the British Transport Commission, Ribble turned to Alexander of Falkirk for further bodies to complete its refurbishment of pre-war double-deckers. The Ribble order to rebody 55 TD4s and TD5s in 1949-50 marked the beginning of Alexanders' business as a supplier to English operators. The 1950 order for 30 was to the new 8ft width, the chassis and rear axles being modified. Number 2047 remained in service until 1961, passing then to Blair and Palmer of Carlisle where it ran for another two years.

Although looking only slightly different from its original form in the early post-war livery with mudguards in the same colour as the body, no lining out and sans serif fleetname, Cheetah No. 2103, one of the Burlingham-bodied batch dating from 1939, had lost its quiet-mannered ways, having received one of the 6.2-litre diesel engines from a Tiger of the same age. It is seen at Whalley. The C prefix to the fleet numbers was dropped when they began to be displayed openly on the front and rear panels.

A comparison of the 7ft 6in and 8ft wide versions of the 35-seat Burlingham bus bodies. Number 219 (formerly 2710), a Tiger TS7 new in 1936, was purchased as a chassis from Devon General and carries its final livery while below is new Tiger PS2/5 No. 238 (formerly 2788) in original livery. With the advent of underfloor-engined chassis, they soon became obsolescent, though the PS2s continued in service until 1962-65.

windows being fitted. At one time the Guys were concentrated at Ulverston but eventually the drivers complained and they were distributed in ones and twos throughout the system. Being non-standard they were unpopular and all the wartime buses were withdrawn in 1954-56.

During 1946-48, 40 1939 Cheetah buses received the experimental 6.2 litre diesel engines from TS8 buses of the same age which were then fitted with 7.4 litre units. The quiet running Cheetahs then became noisier than the contemporary PS1s as gear ratios designed for high-revving petrol engines were retained. There was a small single-deck bus bodying programme using 35-seat front-entrance Burlingham bodies. Twenty 8 ft wide bodies went on to new PS2/5 chassis in 1950, and 27 of the old width were fitted to old TS7 chassis. Of these 16 had been 1935-36 coaches but the others were bought second-hand, four from Yorkshire Woollen District Transport and seven from Devon General; all were fitted with 7.4 litre diesel engines.

The coach rebodying programme was much more complex and space is not available to give full details. There was some exchange of chassis between Ribble and Standerwick. The objective was to combine the best

chassis with the best bodies, everything being overhauled individually. Chassis and bodies for disposal were put together before sale.

To use the available resources to the best advantage, the programme was carried out in stages, mainly during the winter months. During 1948-49, 25 of the older petrol-engined coaches and four Lion LT7 buses dating from 1933, 1935-36 had their mainly English Electric bodies removed and were fitted with reconditioned Burlingham (7) or Duple (22) 31-seat coach bodies from TS8s. This was a stop-gap measure involving four TS6s, four LT7s and 21 TS7s and only enough work was done for them to run for two seasons. Most were withdrawn in 1950, three surviving a year longer.

An order was placed for new Duple 31-seat bodies which were fitted during 1949-50 to one 1934 TS6 and 34 1938-39 TS8s, all of which had been previously fitted with 7.4 litre diesel engines. These, together with six Standerwick vehicles which received similar treatment, were regarded as first line coaches and most remained in service until 1958. They were numbered 715-48 in the new scheme. The 1950 order for new Duple bodies was modified to the 8ft width and 20 TS7 chassis dating from 1935-37 were overhauled, fitted with 7.4-litre diesel

The 54 Leyland Tiger TS6, TS7 and TS8 coaches, rebodied by Duple and re-engined with 7.4-litre diesel engines in 1949-50 were, with the 14 PS1s, Ribble's front-line coach fleet until the arrival of the Royal Tigers in 1951. The entire TS8 batch, plus one TS6 from the Christy fleet, were rebodied to 7ft 6in width whilst the 20 done in 1950 on TS7 chassis were 8ft wide. Right: No. 1955 (later 739) of the TS8 batch rebodied in 1949 is seen in Grasmere, while, below, 1497 (later 758), a 1936 TS7 is seen just after rebodying to 8ft.

Originally a 32-seat Burlingham-bodied service bus (2201), new in 1939, Leyland TS8 coach 774 was one of 12 with old Duple bodies which were virtually completely rebuilt in the Frenchwood works in 1950-51, the external trim becoming similar to that of the White Ladies. Number 774 is seen on a Leeds-Blackpool service in Keighley. The whole batch was withdrawn in 1956.

Standards of comfort on Ribble's standard double-deckers rose appreciably in the late 'forties. The PD2 chassis offered quiet interior noise levels, especially with Leyland-built bodywork, and platform doors were introduced for suitable services from 1950. Seen here is 1307, a PD2/3 of the batch which introduced this feature, and also marked a breach with the old fleet number sequence, beginning a new series for double-deck buses at 1301. Units of this batch spent their entire service lives working on the long Lancaster-Keswick service until withdrawal in 1964-66.

engines and entered service in 1950-51, being renumbered 749-68. Four Standerwick vehicles (35-38) were also done. The first eight footer (1504, later 761) went into service between Liverpool and Edinburgh on 17th May 1950. One of the batch (768) was a 1935 TS6 ex-Christy, made conspicuous by its WH registration number. After withdrawal in 1961 it was sold to Progress Motors of Chorley who ran it until 1972 when its chassis was 37 years old! It has since been preserved.

The 1950-51 programme was designed to augment the coach fleet by lengthening the life of 50 vehicles to be used only at peak holiday times. The 25 1939-40 TS8s chosen for this exercise had been 32-seat service buses; they were fitted with second-hand 31-seat Burlingham (4) or Duple (21) coach bodies and, together with 24 TS8s with their original Brush coach bodies, were painted in reversed coach livery. The 1941 Cheetah coach made up the 50 'weekend coaches' as they were termed; it retained its petrol engine until 1952 and was fitted with a Duple body older than its original one. It was withdrawn at the end of the 1952 season but most of the others ran until 1953. The weekend coaches were numbered 1151-1200, on the end of the single-deck coach series.

The final stage of the programme was devoted to the rehabilitation of 12 of the 1939 TS8 saloons which were fitted with Duple coach bodies which were so extensively rebuilt that they scarcely resembled the original vehicles. Gone were the downswept flashes and mouldings, the result being rather squat, unattractive vehicles. The exercise was spread over three years, 1950 (3), 1951 (7) and 1952 (2) and all 12, numbered 769-780 were withdrawn in 1956.

New vehicles were now arriving in substantial numbers and the rebodying programme came to an end. It had enabled Ribble to make do with pre-war chassis until new underfloor-engined vehicles came into service thus avoiding the obsolescence factor experienced by many operators who invested heavily in traditional front-engined chassis in the five immediate post-war years.

The choice of the Sentinel-Beadle underfloor-engined single-decker was a none-too-gentle nudge to Leyland to hasten its own efforts in the same direction. This is the first one, placed in service in May 1949 and described in early records as of type SB but seemingly identical to the rest of the batch designated STC4 when they were delivered the following year. The body structure had affinities to Beadle designs for Tilling group companies but, together with Sentinel's four-cylinder engine, with its Ricardo indirect injection, was quite unlike anything else in the fleet.

The Underfloor Era

Although Leyland had long since announced the development of an underfloor-engined chassis, Ribble believed, rightly or wrongly, that they were being unacceptably slow. There were many restricted routes where duplication could be eliminated if larger single-deck vehicles could be built. Sentinel had been famous for its steam lorries which had the engine mounted under the frame, so it was a natural step to use a similar layout for diesel vehicles, both goods and passenger. The latter were at first a joint effort with coach-builder Beadle which had developed a lightweight form of integral construction. A complete vehicle, for the Western National Omnibus Co, had been exhibited at the 1948 Commercial Motor Show, upstaging other makers, including Leyland, which had nothing more than a horizontal version of the O.600 engine on display.

Ribble ordered six of the initial design, built to the then maximum dimensions of 27ft 6in by 7ft 6in. This was the SB model, later designated STC4, powered by a four-cylinder engine with five-speed overdrive gearbox. When the first was delivered in May 1949, it was put on service 109, Preston-Leyland-Chorley which passed the Leyland works and was restricted by the low and narrow Pack Saddle bridge on the A49 near Euxton. It was an unlikely choice for Ribble, Sentinel being a firm with very little experience of bus manufacture. Some faults had to be rectified by Ribble and Sentinel before the rest of the batch arrived in February 1950. With the relaxation of dimensions to 30ft by 8ft, Sentinel produced the STC6 with 6-cylinder 9.1- litre indirect-injection Sentinel-Ricardo engine; this was of monocoque construction with a 44-seat Sentinel body with Beadle overtones. Fourteen of these were ordered and, on their arrival in 1951, all 20 Sentinels went to Carlisle where, despite being non-standard, they continued to run until 1962-63.

By this time the integral Leyland Olympic HR44 was in production, Leyland having co-operated with the MCW body-building organisation, in those days composed of the quite distinct Metropolitan-Cammell and Weymann factories. The first of a Ribble order for 30 was shown at Earls Court in October 1950. The Olympic seated 44 passengers, a big advance on the 30-34 single-deck norm and was powered by the 9.8 litre O.600 engine. However, the model most favoured by Ribble was the Royal Tiger, a chassis with similar mechanical features to the Olympic and able to accept bodywork of the operator's choice. Ribble's initial orders, made from the drawing-board, were for 246, made up of 136 41-seat coaches (including 16 for Standerwick) and 110 44-seat buses. All but six of the coaches had heavy all-metal bodies with centre entrances; these were the first Leyland coach bodies to be produced since the 'thirties. The odd six, for Standerwick, had front-entrance bodies by Duple and these were transferred to Ribble in 1963.

The all-Leyland Royal Tiger coach had an integrated ventilation and heating system and individual air vents above the seats fed by fans on either side of the front destination display. The lower front panels of the Leyland body were swept under but Ribble had them modified to make a deeper vertical skirt. The 44-seat service buses had a new design of Leyland body with power-operated front doors. The first coach (781) entered service in March 1951 and the first bus (298) in December 1951.

There was a further intake of Royal Tiger coaches in 1953, 45 for Ribble and 20 for Standerwick. The Ribble order included 20 with air brakes and centre-entrance Burlingham bodies fitted with 32 individually adjustable seats for extended tours. They initially gave the company an advantage in the competitive tour market but their eight year life on these duties was too long. They were reseated to 41 in 1961 and transferred to express work.

High taxation on fuel turned the thoughts of engineers

towards more fuel-efficient lightweight vehicles and the prototype Tiger Cub, (408) with Saunders-Roe 44-seat alloy bus body entered Ribble service in January 1953. It was powered by the 5.76 litre O.350 engine and had apparently been exhibited at the 1952 Commercial show but the chassis had been changed before delivery. A further 49 buses of this type went into service, mostly in 1954, followed by 15 coaches with centre-entrance Burlingham bodies. The Tiger Cub coaches were fitted with Eaton two-speed axles and were very economical, an average of 20 mpg being experienced even on a hilly route such as Blackpool-Newcastle-upon-Tyne. Fifty-eight more Burlingham bodied coaches went on the road in 1956-58 but all had front entrances. Ten bore Auty's Tours fleet name from 1956-59 though five of them (982-6) were legally owned by Ribble.

For the 1958 summer season, the coach fleet (excluding Standerwick) comprised exactly 300 vehicles, 165 Royal Tigers, 73 Tiger Cubs, 14 PS1s and 48 rebodied TS8s with a total seating capacity of 11,500.

A New Double-Deck Era

The company's double-deck policy was now to use highbridge double-deck buses wherever possible and to retain lowbridge types only for routes with physical limitations. Leyland had given up bodybuilding in 1954 and the 1955-56 orders were for 120 PD2 chassis with Metro-Cammell (75) and Burlingham (45) 61-seat bodies. Of the Burlinghams, 40 had power-operated sliding doors; 25 of the Metro-Cammells had four-leaf folding doors.

These were the last new traditional double-deck buses to enter Ribble service as the relaxation of box dimensions in 1956 to permit 30ft by 8ft double- as well as single-deck buses on two axles caused a radical rethink on bus design. Although other operators used rear platform buses to the new dimensions, Ribble saw that fare collection would be improved if loading and unloading could be placed under the supervision of the

The final batches of rear-platform double deck buses were purchased in 1955-56. Earlier deliveries had Metro-Cammell bodies on PD2/13 chassis with air pressure brakes. The body styling resembled the somewhat austere Orion design but, in practice, was rather heavier. There was a reversion to the vacuum-braked PD2/12 in 1956 when the body order was divided between Metro-Cammell and Burlingham, both the vehicles shown dating from the latter year. No. 1495 was one of the Metro-Cammell buses while below No. 1438 of the Burlingham batch, with just a hint of the pre-war 'Betteridge' outline evident in its lines. Both vehicles are seen in Liverpool.

driver and were sufficiently confident that an order was placed for 105 of the new PD3/4 chassis with 72-seat forward entrance Burlingham bodies; this batch had manual gearboxes. The full-fronted cab had the nearside bulkhead unglazed to give the driver a clear view of the forward entrance. The first bus entered service on Preston local service P2 in September 1957 and deliveries continued for over a year.

Meanwhile, Leyland had been developing a rear-engined double-deck model and various prototypes were tested on Ribble routes from 1954 onwards. The original concept had been a low-height vehicle with orthodox seating but when the first production PDR1 Atlanteans appeared at the end of 1958, they were of normal height. Ribble placed initial orders for 100 service buses and 15 coaches. Of the service buses, 70 were highbridge 78-seat models and 30 were lowbridge 72-seaters, the latter, disappointingly, having a side gangway and rows of bench seats at the rear of the upper deck. This was because the spiral-bevel rear axle necessitated the floor height directly over it to be of about the same level of that of a conventional double-decker of the period. Bodywork was by Metro-Cammell and deliveries commenced in November 1959 and continued until April 1961. They were generally allocated to the long-distance stage carriage services.

The first coach (1251) had a Metro-Cammell body shell finished by Weymann and was delivered with 51 seats of which only 16 were on the lower deck; one upper deck seat was quickly removed. To the rear of the lower saloon there was a spacious luggage compartment, a servery and a toilet; seats and footrests were individually adjustable and there were reading lights for each seat. The coaches had air suspension on the front axle and the type was christened 'Gay Hostess', the adjective having not acquired its present dual meaning. The testing of the prototype is described in chapter 6.

There were many mechanical problems with the early Atlanteans and the company reverted to PD3s with full-fronted, forward-entrance Metro-Cammell bodies 8ft 2.5in wide for the 1961-62 orders; these were PD3/5s with semi-automatic gearboxes. There were 95 of these elegant vehicles which replaced many of the ageing double-deck buses of the immediate post-war era. A further 36 identical vehicles were purchased in 1963 but, in the meantime, there was a return to the PDR1 Atlantean with a further 14 lowbridge service buses and 20 59-seat Weymann-bodied coaches. These were the second generation White Ladies; they had plainer lines, double seats and lacked the servery and toilet of the Gay Hostess class. They were used on the medium distance express services from Liverpool and Manchester and achieved very high mileages, No. 1283 exceeding the million mark. The last one (1267) was withdrawn on 31st December 1977.

Surprisingly, the next double-deck buses came from Scotland being low-height Albion Lowlander LR1s with full-fronted Alexander 72-seat bodies. There were 16 in all, delivered over several months in 1964-65. The Lowlander had a flat floor and normal seating on both decks but the lower deck had a low ceiling and tended to be somewhat claustrophobic. A further vehicle of this

Following the legalisation of 30ft long double-deck buses on two axles in 1956, Ribble placed an order for 69 vehicles to the new dimensions, on PD3/4 chassis, followed by a second order for 36. Delivery started in September 1957, the Burlingham bodies seating 72 – 41 upstairs and 31 below. The entrance, with a sliding door, was placed in a forward position where the driver could supervise loading and unloading, thus easing the job of the conductor who at busy times had more fares to collect. This broadside view of No. 1501 shows the well-proportioned lines of the model. Several were fitted with illuminated offside advertisement panels when this was in vogue in the 'sixties. Withdrawals were spread over six years – 1971 to 1976.

The rear-engined double-deck bus was expected to be a low-height vehicle but the original Atlanteans were highbridge vehicles. Ribble's first Atlantean service buses arrived in November 1959 and had 77 or 78-seat (44/34 or 44/33) Metro-Cammell bodies. A year later 95 were in service of which 25 had special lowbridge bodywork with a side gangway and bench seats to the rear of the upper deck. These seated only 72 (39/33). Number 1692, seen at Lower Mosley Street, Manchester, was a 1958 highbridge 77-seater while 1808 (of a later similar batch of 1962), standing in Blackburn bus station, was a lowbridge vehicle, fitted with an as yet unused illuminated advertisement panel.

Mechanical problems with the PDR1/1 Atlanteans influenced Ribble's decision to revert to PD3s for most of their 1961-62 double-deck requirements. The 72-seat Metro-Cammell bodies on these 95 PD3/5s were 8ft 2.5in wide. These buses were used extensively on Merseyside area services and the last six were not withdrawn until 1981 when operations with conductors ceased.

The Leyland Atlantean began to make its appearance in the fleet in 1959 but, in addition to bus versions, Ribble took the opportunity to develop a coach which took the concept much further than the White Lady idea, being intended for the London service and offering more comfort and facilities than had been attempted previously. The Gay Hostess title may seem strange nowadays, but at the time simply conveyed the intention of providing something akin to airline glamour and cheerful service. Two Standerwick examples head for London on the then far from complete M6.

The Lowlander was a rather strange hybrid, designed by Albion using largely Leyland components, including most of the PD3 front-end, but with a new drop-centre rear axle, allowing low-floor proportions. Alexander modified its body design for the model to provide for Ribble's preferences for a full-fronted cab.

Fitting the Albion Lowlander drop-centre rear-axle to the Atlantean produced a low-height bus with continuous centre gangways on both decks. The style of the 72-seat Alexander bodywork on 10 PDR1/2 Atlanteans followed a BET Group specification as economics dictated a move away from individualism. The move away from the earlier angular bodies was very welcome. Number 1876 (above) of 1966 poses in the yard behind Frenchwood offices when new. Fifteen bodies to the same specification but with a quite different interpretation of a rounded outline were built by Northern Counties of Wigan the following year as exemplified by No. 1957 (below) working a Blackpool express service duty. These were the first Northern Counties bodies since the 1939-45 war. Although Leyland and Daimler were not associated at the time, the PDR1/2 was fitted with a Daimler gearbox, this being as used on the Fleetline and specifically designed to provide a direct transmission line to a drop-centre axle.

type, but not full-fronted, came with the Bamber Bridge Motor Service takeover in 1968. By this time, Albion was owned by Leyland and the Lowlanders were powered by Leyland O.600 engines.

Alexander 75-seat bodywork was again specified for 10 Atlanteans placed in service in 1966; these were on the PDR1/2 chassis with Daimler gearbox and a further 15 followed in 1967 but with Northern Counties 72-seat bodies. The latter received fleet numbers 1951-65, leaving a gap in the series from 1877 to 1950. The explanation was the non-availability of matching registration numbers as ECK 877E upwards had been allocated to coaches in that year. This gap was never filled as two Weymann lowbridge-bodied Atlanteans and the Albion of BBMS were numbered 1966-68 followed by the five Atlanteans and five PD3s from the Scout fleet.

At this time, there was a school of thought within the company that the double-deck bus may be on the way out so no further orders were placed for the time being.

The Leopards

The Leyland Leopard, which came on the market in 1959, was a medium-weight chassis powered by the O.600 engine and about one ton lighter than the Royal Tiger. Air brakes were standard and the coach version, designated L2, had the option of an Eaton two-speed axle (L2T). Ribble's first order was placed in 1961 for 35 coaches and, surprisingly, the attractive Harrington Cavalier body was chosen. Twenty 32-seat L2Ts replaced the now ageing Royal Tigers on extended tours and the other 15 originally had 41 seats though 10 were reseated for 32 in 1962 for use on Kingfisher tours. Six of these were changed back to 39 or 41 seats in 1968. The 20 tours coaches were reseated to 41 in 1966, their seats being transferred, after retrimming, to new Bedford VAM coaches with Plaxton bodywork which took over the tours programme. The relatively noisy performance of the latter led to their premature sale in 1969.

Six more Leopards which had been ordered by Scout before takeover entered the fleet in November 1962 but these were built to the new 36ft length (designated PSU3) with 40-seat bodies by Duple Northern and a toilet compartment. They had been intended for the London service but did not see such use until the winter of 1969-70 when they went on loan to Standerwicks. They were numbered 701-6, a reversion to the beginning of the coach series, and 702 was specially seated for use by Preston North End FC from 1963 to 1967.

The Leopard was an economical model and became Ribble's standard single-deck vehicle for the next few years. In 1963-64, 141 chassis were purchased of which 90 carried 53-seat bus bodies by Marshall of Cambridge, a relative newcomer. Of forty-one 49-seat coaches, 20 had Harrington Cavalier bodies while 21 were supplied by Plaxton. All were numbered in the Ribble series but, following a change in accounting policy, 10 went to Standerwicks with S-suffixed numbers and four to Scout with S-prefixed numbers. Henceforth, the subsidiaries' new coaches were owned by Ribble but leased to them. The balance of 10 were dual-purpose vehicles with 49 coach seats in an upgraded version of the Marshall bus body. An eleventh vehicle of similar general appearance was mounted on the first production Leyland Panther rear-engined chassis, entering service at Preston depot in July 1964. The mechanical units were similar to those of the Leopard but there were many teething troubles and Ribble ordered no more Panthers.

In the years 1965-68, a further 273 Leopard chassis were added to the Ribble fleet and 53 to those of the subsidiaries. Bodywork of the 155 buses was of similar appearance but orders were divided between Weymann (41), Metro-Cammell (19) and Marshall (95). However, because of the 45-seat limit for one-man operation, deliveries for 1966-67 were largely on the 30ft 10in long PSU4 chassis with 44 seats. The 21 PSU3s which came in those years were of 45-seat capacity and most of the earlier 53-seat buses had eight seats removed and luggage pens installed. Dual-purpose vehicles had proved popular on the medium distance express services and 68 were added during these years, 10 with bodies by Weymann, 28 by Marshall and 30 by Willowbrook.

The company stayed with Plaxton for luxury coach bodywork and 40 more 49-seat coaches were added to the main fleet. For the London services there were 44-seat coaches with toilets of which 17 joined the Standerwick fleet with two more carrying the Scout name until 1968. Many vehicles were exchanged between the three fleets during this period and, as the motorways were extended, older coaches tended to be transferred to Ribble for less arduous duties.

Bristols and Nationals

The sale of the BET bus companies to the Transport Holding Company and the subsequent establishment of the National Bus Company was not the reason for Ribble changing its allegiance from Leyland to Bristol chassis. The share exchange between Leyland and Bristol enabled the latter marque to be sold outside the nationalised group and it had become widely recognised that the Bristol RE with horizontal rear-mounted engine was perhaps the most successful of the early generation of rear-engined single-deckers. The first order for 10 RELL6L models, with dual-entrance NBC-pattern 41-seat Eastern Coach Works bus bodies, was placed before the sale; they had Leyland engines and went into service on one-man operated urban services in Crosby and Chorley in 1968.

Further Bristols came to Ribble in January 1969 with the Carlisle operations of United. These comprised five LS5Gs and 16 MW5Gs, all except one with 45-seat Eastern Coach Works bodies. Three Bristol KSW6B double-deck buses were allocated fleet numbers 1979-81 but the transfer of these was cancelled and three delicensed PD2s put back on the road instead. All the ex-United vehicles had 5-cylinder Gardner engines and were equipped for one-man operation. Some were already 12 or 13 years old and all were withdrawn between 1970 and 1974.

Between November 1970 and July 1972, 89 short-length Bristol RESL6L 47-seat saloons entered the fleet, 49 bodied by Marshall and the remainder by Eastern Coach Works. All had Leyland engines, but the first 23 rear-engined VR double-deck buses which arrived in 1971-72, had the Gardner 6LX.

The link with Bristol took on a new and distinctively Ribble character with the appearance, at the 1968 Commercial Vehicle Show, of the first Bristol VRL double-deck coaches. The VR model had been first seen at the 1966 Show when two prototypes had been exhibited with the vertical engine mounted longitudinally behind the offside rear wheel. This was abandoned for production versions in favour of the VRT with transverse rear engine but its potential as the basis of a double-deck coach was not lost on Harry Tennant, Ribble's chief engineer. The result was a most striking vehicle with special 60-seat ECW body with centre entrance and stairs. Powered by a Leyland O.680 engine, its 36ft length, newly authorised for double-deckers, was visually emphasised by its low build. Apart from a one-off Daimler for Walsall Corporation exhibited at the same show, this was the first British home-market 36ft long double-deck vehicle.

The vehicle was allocated to Standerwick for the Lancashire-London services and a further 29 entered service in 1971-73. Unfortunately, the type suffered from

The long and the short of it. Further relaxation of the Construction and Use Regulations permitted 36 ft long vehicles and the 53-seat capacity of the PSU3 Leopard saloons, the first of which entered service in 1964, equalled that of the lowbridge PD2 double-deckers still in use. A side effect was the need for more space in some garages. The Marshall bodywork was to BET specification with some features in common with the Alexander and Northern Counties Atlanteans. Union resistance to one-man operation and manoeuvrability problems in some rural areas led to the adoption of the 30ft 10in long PSU4 44-seat bus in some cases from 1966. Wigan bus station is the scene in the upper view of No. 502, one of the original PSU3s of 1964. Note the Lowlander in the background. Short-length 640, seen at Penrith, was the original Formby town service bus for which it was painted in reversed livery and reduced to 36 seats in 1967, but it reverted to its original layout before migrating north. Many of the PSU4s were transferred to Cumberland Motor Services in 1978.

The Bristol RE single-decker was only available to state-owned operators when introduced in 1962, but when offered more widely later, Ribble was among those attracted. As it turned out, the initial order began to arrive in March 1968 just as Ribble, along with other BET operating companies, was acquired by the Transport Holding Company which held the shares in the nationalised companies.

Number 221 was numerically the first of ten of the RELL6L type with ECW bodywork with 41-seat capacity, dual doors and a standing capacity of 31, the latter later reduced to 25. They were used on Liverpool-Crosby and Chorley town services, but the vehicle is seen at a later date.

inadequate design development and proved unreliable in service, the model's reputation not being helped by an overturning accident, even though the cause lay with another vehicle. The vehicles were sold off by National Travel in the mid-'seventies.

However, Ribble continued as primarily a Leyland user and welcomed the arrival on the scene of the Leyland National, a joint enterprise between Leyland and the NBC. The concept of an integral-construction single-deck bus using some of the techniques of volume car production had begun as a purely Leyland project, aimed at what was seen as an extended market for single-deckers as city services were converted to one-man operation. The

large scale use of one-man operated double-deckers was not foreseen at that stage. The NBC came into the project in 1969 and production started in 1972 at a new factory at Workington. The specification included the Leyland 510 engine, a turbocharged 8.2-litre unit mounted horizontally at the rear and air suspension, the latter one of the most successful features which influenced its general adoption.

Ribble was one of the earliest users, 50 examples of the 11.3-metre length with two-door 48-seat bodywork entering service in 1972-73; subsequently the single-door version, seating 49, was favoured of which there were 40 in 1973-74 and 112 between 1976 and 1978. Interesting individual vehicles included a 10.3-metre example delivered in October 1973 which was almost immediately converted to electric traction with a four-wheeled trailer carrying the batteries. It found a home on Crosville's Runcorn busway services and was sold to that company in 1978 after three years on hire. Prototypes of the simplified series B in both short and long form as well as the National 2 with O.680 engine were taken into the fleet, a clear indication of the continued close liaison with Leyland on technical matters.

Ribble's production National 2 deliveries began in 1980 were of the shorter version which by then was 10.6-metres due to the more rounded windscreen of the National 2; 65 of these single-door 44-seat buses entered service up to 1982. The final 21 Nationals, delivered in 1982-83, reverted to the 11.6m length with 52-seat bodies and many of the dual-door buses were rebuilt to the same layout from 1979 onwards. By the end of 1985, only eight dual-door buses remained. Several were equipped to load

Facing page: Stylish was a justifiable description of the Bristol VRL double-deck coaches, which anticipated later trends in the design of such vehicles in both layout and to some degree in appearance. The first one, 50S in the Standerwick fleet, is seen here when new. The ECW bodywork seated 50 and the centre entrance and staircase position meant that forward vision for all passengers was good.

Foot of opposite page: There was no doubt about Ribble's change of ownership when, in 1971-72, 23 Bristol VRT double-deck buses with 70-seat ECW bodies reversed the trend towards standee single-deck buses which had prevailed for some years. Ribble engineers soon appreciated the rugged quality of the Gardner 6LX power-units. These vehicles were equipped for one-man operation from new but No. 1992 was crew-operated when seen leaving Carlisle bus station, a flap to the right of the front fleet title having been dropped to cover the 'Pay as you Board' sign.

Ribble was an early user of the Leyland National and 50 of the 11.3 metre type were delivered in 1972-73, all with a centre exit-door. The first Nationals were delivered in cherry red with 44 seats but they were repainted into NBC poppy red and reseated to 48 before entering service. Later Nationals had 49 seats with no exit door and many dual-door buses were rebuilt as front-entrance 52-seaters later in life.

The first 10.3 metre National to come into the Ribble fleet was No. 461, a 41-seat bus. delivered in October 1973. It seems possible that it never ran in service for Ribble as, in 1974, it was converted to battery-electric operation, its batteries being carried in a four-wheel trailer, authorised by special ministerial dispensation. In this role it went on hire to Crosville for, use on the Runcorn busway services, in November 1975 and was sold to them in 1978, becoming XEB 461 in their fleet.

wheelchairs. Following dissatisfaction with the Leyland 510 engine, the 11 1983 Nationals were powered by Gardner 6HLXB (10) and one 6HLXC turbocharged units.

Between 1977 and 1980, a further 60 Bristol VR double-deck buses were purchased, all with Eastern Coach Works bodies with the, by then, standard seating layout of 43 upper deck and 31 lower deck. The Leyland 501 engine was specified until the 1980 order for 11 vehicles which arrived fitted with Gardner 6LXB engines; all the others were converted to Gardners in 1982-83. The only other Bristol service buses acquired during this period were two small LH 35-seat models for the community services in the Ribble Valley.

More Double-deck Buses

Despite the NBC policy of using Bristol-ECW products, certain companies with long associations with Leyland products were able to make a case for continuing them. In 1973 NBC placed an order for AN68 Atlanteans with Park Royal bodies, dual-door examples of which had been put into service by London Country Bus Services. Seventy single-door vehicles were allocated to Ribble who specified various improvements to the design. Side seats were eliminated thus improving the entrance area. The driver's compartment, forward ascending staircase and side panel were integrated in one unit, the driver's position being 10in higher than normal. Good all-round vision was ensured by fitting a deep, electrically-heated, double-curvature windscreen and the extensive use of plastics produced an attractive interior finish.

Black masked front destination indicators with lower-case lettering and very small route numbers were a retrograde step; some buses were fitted with the standard route numbers.

Seats were provided for 43 upstairs and 30 downstairs, with 10 standing. Delivery of the first order was spread from December 1973 to January 1975; further orders totalling 66, including 20 diverted from Midland Red, were fulfilled by July 1976. These had one more lower-deck seat. The new Atlanteans, which were used to replace PD3s on Merseyside, had fleet numbers from 1301 up, thus returning to the beginning of the double-deck series. A delivery of 20 standard low-height Bristol VRT with ECW bodywork was made in 1977, though this time with vertical Leyland 501 engines equivalent to those in the Nationals. A further batch of 29, supplied in 1978-79, were of normal overall height. Delivery of a further 50 ECW-bodied Atlanteans continued until February 1981 and, as Merseyside's requirements were fully met, allocations were made to Blackpool and other depots. The last two had Transign electronic destination displays. Number 1470 was converted experimentally in 1980 to run on LPG; there was a cleaner emission and less vibration but it used 58% more fuel so the project was abandoned. The final 11 VRTs, delivered in 1980, were Gardner 6LXB-powered, many of the 501-engined vehicles being converted to 6LXB from 1982.

Leyland's B45 semi-integral double-decker was intended to replace the Atlantean, Fleetline and VRT models, NBC being particularly interested in its capability, with suitable bodywork, to supplant the VRT with standard low-height ECW body. The first bodied prototype, with Gardner 6LXB engine, was accordingly completed by ECW and finished in Ribble colours, entering service for evaluation in 1980. This followed the new concept of the body giving rigidity to the chassis and was preferred to fully integral construction which limited body choice. The model was christened 'Olympian' and, between 1981 and 1985, a further 79 of the type were ordered, 14 of the later deliveries having coach seating for Timesaver and

The Leyland Atlantean resumed its position as the favoured choice for additions to the fleet in the 1973-76 period, when batches of the AN68 version of the chassis by then current were delivered, complete with Park Royal bodywork of a style being supplied to several NBC companies. Number 1317 is seen here when new in January 1974. From mid-1972 Ribble's vehicles received Lancashire rather than Preston registration marks and hence this vehicle was RTF 628M, though the position was further confused with the setting up of the new local vehicle licensing offices which became operational in 1974, with a redistribution of marks which caused hitherto unfamiliar letters to appear on Ribble vehicles.

The full-height ECW body lacked the elegance of the Park Royal product when mounted on the Leyland Atlantean AN68 chassis. New in 1976, No. 1429, bearing both NBC and Merseyside PTE logos, leaves Crosby bus station for the city centre on a one-man operated journey in 1977.

The first Leyland Olympian entered service with Ribble in August 1981 and several further orders were placed, all with Gardner 6LXB engines and ECW low-height bodywork seating 77 as a service bus or 70 as a coach. Passengers board No. 2110 at Bolton bus station in March 1982 and in a contrasting scene in the Pendle village of Downham, No.2114's electronic destination shows 'Bus Full', a display rarely, if ever, needed in the 'eighties.

similar limited stop duties. Production buses had the lower deck capacity increased to 32 while the coaches seated 42/28.

The designers of the AN68 Atlanteans had eliminated most of the PDR's problems and the Olympian was a worthy successor. In 1984, Ribble acquired its last, and most unusual, PDR1 Atlantean, a Metro-Cammell-bodied open-top bus which had originated with Devon General in 1962; it was used briefly in the Lake District and at Fleetwood. In 1985, it operated the special service 401 in Liverpool to the Garden Festival grounds. At the end of that year the double-deck fleet consisted of 321 buses, little more than half the total in the post-war boom years.

The Modern Coach Fleet

Ribble disliked Bristols for coach work and had only one batch of 10 Leyland-engined RELHs with 49-seat Eastern Coach Works bodies in 1972. They were delivered in NBC white livery and lost two seats in 1977 when luggage pens were fitted. Ribble continued to buy Leyland chassis for coach duties and, between 1969 and 1980, acquired 180 more Leopards and many more transferred from the Standerwick fleets. Orders for 1969-71 specified Plaxton bodywork – 30 on 36ft long PSU3As and 36 on the 30ft 10in PSU4 chassis. Of these, 25 were for the tours fleet with 36 seats and 11 for general coach duties with 43. From 1973 the preferred coachbuilder on Leopard chassis was Duple, 113 of the new Dominant bodies of 47 or 49-seat capacity being purchased.

The establishment of the National Travel fleets with their corporate white livery divided the coach fleet into two parts. Many existing coaches were repainted and there were transfers between companies. Deregulation of express services in 1980 led to an expansion of the National Express network and the extensive inter-working of different companies' fleets. Frequent reorganisations added to the movements and changes of ownership of vehicles. Often only the legal ownership changed, the coach continuing to do the same work. Motorway services needed fast, powerful vehicles and the advent of the premium Rapide services brought new standards of comfort.

In 1972, Ribble tested a 12m PSU5 (701) which had been exhibited at the Commercial Motor Show. It represented NBC's concept of a specialised motorway coach and its 46-seat fully-carpeted Alexander M body, finished in the new white livery, incorporated small double-glazed side windows, sound insulation and a toilet. It had a chequered career, being successively lent to National Travel (South East), renumbered 1200, sold to National Travel (North West) and withdrawn in 1983 after two further renumberings.

The Leopard was replaced in the Leyland range by the TRCTL11 Tiger, 43 being taken into the fleet new in 1983-85. The Tiger was powered by the Leyland TL11 engine developing 218 bhp at 2,100 rpm; it came in two lengths, 11.3 or 12.0m and examples of both were acquired.

The transfer of the 147-strong Manchester-based National Travel fleet to Ribble from 20th May 1984 brought more Leopards and Tigers into the fleet. Bodywork was by Duple except for eight Plaxton Paramounts and seven Willowbrooks, and 15 were built to the Rapide specification with 48-seats and toilet. Some were leased from Arlington Motors and went back at the end of the lease in 1987.

Four Metroliner three-axle double-deck coaches were included in the transfer but they were on loan to United and never, in fact, operated for Ribble. Five similar vehicles, used on the Liverpool-Newcastle service, came from Crosville following labour troubles there in 1986. A Mercedes-Benz-powered Neoplan double-deck coach was finished in the livery of Anglo-Continental Travels and worked a shuttle to Spain. A further 10 Plaxton Paramount 4000 double-deck coaches, two with Gardner 6LYT engines, were acquired for National Express services in 1986.

The 12-metre Leyland Leopard exhibited at the 1972 Commercial Motor Show in NBC corporate white livery and numbered 701 in Ribble's fleet had Alexander M-type bodywork of similar design to that being supplied to the Scottish Bus Group. The possibility of it being the precursor of an NBC motorway coach standard was in mind, such a line of thought having been proposed by the recently-appointed NBC Chairman, F. J. (later Sir Freddie) Wood, but this was not pursued.

The Bristol chassis was not favoured by Ribble for express duties and only 10 RELH coaches with 49-seat ECW bodies came into the fleet. In white National livery with tiny Ribble name over the front wheel-arch, No. 1018 (top) leaves Lower Mosley Street bus station, Manchester (soon to be closed) when new in 1972 while, six years later, No. 1016 of the same batch, (centre) in Ribble dual-purpose livery is seen en route to Liverpool on the limited stop X27 service. An almost contemporary Duple-bodied Leyland Leopard PSU3B/4, No. 1022 of 1973, (bottom) typifies Ribble's choice for coach work for almost two decades.

Number 1150, a 1983 Leyland Tiger with Duple Dominant 51-seat body, was a one-off to replace No. 1098, a 1978 Leopard burnt out in September 1982. In the upper picture, taken at Blackpool in July 1986, it wears the Kingfisher livery used for a short time to replace the tarnished National image. Below, it is seen in Whitechapel, Liverpool on the 761 Liverpool-Blackpool service in February 1990 in the new coach livery of red, grey and white.

Partition and deregulation

At the end of 1985, Ribble still owned 923 vehicles of which 67 were delicensed and 42 were awaiting disposal. In the 1986 partition, 73 were transferred to Cumberland and 252 to North Western leaving a total of just over 500 full-size vehicles operating under the Ribble name.

After the decision was made to operate minibuses, 90 Mercedes Benz L608D vans were converted by Reeve Burgess. Twenty-one had 19 dual-purpose seats and 43 had 20 bus seats; the other 26 were diverted to North Western. A further 40 Fiat (Iveco) 49-10s with 19-seat Robin Hood bodies and a Freight-Rover Sherpa with 16-seat Dormobile body made up the initial minibus fleet which entered service just before deregulation. Mention should be made of the solitary factory-registered Leyland Lynx 51-seat service bus (901) acquired in 1986. In happier times this might have been the forerunner of a new single-deck fleet.

Second-hand Buses

For the expansion into Manchester and other pre-deregulation projects in 1986, no fewer than 81 second-hand double-deck buses were purchased, mostly from other NBC companies. Ribble would have preferred all Leyland Atlanteans but these were not available and the final tally was as follows:-

From Southdown Motor Services Ltd.
27 AN68 Atlanteans/Park Royal (new 1974-75)
 3 Bristol VRs/ECW (new 1972-74)

From Midland Red Coaches
 5 Daimler Fleetlines/Alexander (new 1971)

From Midland Red (North)
10 Daimler Fleetlines/Alexander (new 1969-71)

From North Devon Motor Services
 5 Bristol VRs/ECW (new 1970-73)

From South Midland Motor Services Ltd.
 3 Bristol VRs/ECW (2 with coach seating -new 1970-3)

Strangers in the camp. Four Alexander-bodied Daimler Fleetlines stand in Burnley depot yard in July 1988. Left to right are 1732 ex-Midland Red (North) 6193; 1719, 1723 and 1721, all ex-Midland Red Coaches but originally Fife Scottish.

From Northumbria Motor Services Ltd.
4 Bristol VRs/ECW (new 1974)

From Blackburn Transport
6 AN68 Atlanteans/East Lancs (new 1972-75)

From South Yorkshire PTE
18 Daimler Fleetlines/ECW (new 1974-75)

All the Bristols and Daimlers were Gardner-engined. The Midland Red (North) buses were in very poor condition and only two were recertified after the first year's Ribble service. One of the Northumbria VRs had been used regularly on the route across the tidal causeway to Holy Island and two dustbins were filled with seaweed when its chassis was cleaned prior to entering Ribble service. These vehicles were numbered in three series – 1601 up for the Atlanteans, 1701 up for the Daimlers while the Bristols continued the existing 2000 series from 2035 up.

A further 12 AN68 Atlanteans with Park Royal bodies, dating from 1972-73, were bought from Greater Manchester PTE in 1987 and seven similar vehicles from Plymouth Transport in 1988. The latter included five with dual doors; the centre exit was crudely panelled over on the exterior by Ribble and a bench seat for three fitted inside.

Privatisation

The takeover of the United Transport Zippy services in March 1988 almost coincided with the sale of Ribble to its management and brought 75 minibuses, all less than one year old. There were 40 Fiat 49-10s, 35 with 19-seat Robin Hood bodies and the other five 22-seat Elmes. Freight Rover Sherpas converted to 18-seats by Carlyle numbered 25 and there were 10 three-axle Talbot Pullmans. Six months later the Bee Line services in Manchester and Stockport yielded 188 minibuses all but 50 being Carlyle bodied Sherpas. The others were Dodge S56s with Northern Counties 22-seat bodies.

The collapse of Barrow Borough Transport in May 1989 came just after Stagecoach bought Ribble from its owner-managers. This brought further minibuses, five Dodge/East Lancs 22-seaters and one Renault/Reeve Burgess 25-seater. There were also 11 Nationals and seven Atlanteans. However, within a month, all these were transferred to Cumberland Motor Services along with the 10 Talbot Pullmans and 79 other Ribble vehicles based at Kendal and Ulverston. Other units of the Barrow fleet were leased and were returned to the lessor.

The 230 buses transferred to the Bee Line Buzz Company on its formation in September 1989 comprised 179 minibuses formerly owned by the United Transport subsidiary, Manchester Minibuses Ltd., eight 1973 Nationals, three Leopard coaches dating from 1974-76, three of the 1973-74 Park Royal Atlanteans and the 37 surviving Atlanteans from the 1986-87 second-hand purchases.

Inter-group Transfers

The Stagecoach Group regarded the buses of the constituent companies as one fleet, hence the bland corporate white livery with red, blue and orange stripes and vehicles have been transferred in and out of the Ribble fleet regularly to meet short- and long-term commitments in the various companies. In 1989 30 Atlanteans and five VRs were received from East Midland companies while in 1990, three Mercedes-benz L608Ds, seven Atlanteans and one VR, all originally new to Ribble, were received back from Cumberland. Other VRs have come from Magicbus (4) and United Counties (2). Two Mercedes-Benz 709Ds came from Magicbus and two L608Ds and three Tiger coaches from Cumberland. Hampshire Bus supplied three 1989 Dennis Javelins with Duple 63-seat bodies, for use on service 142, Blackpool-Morecambe, in exchange for three 1980 Leopard coaches, originally with National Travel (West). Seven Leopard buses with Alexander bodies came from Highland Scottish in 1991, the same company supplying 14 Leyland Olympians, new in 1983-85. Transfers in and out of the fleet are bewilderingly frequent; some are only temporary, to meet changes in the requirements of contract services.

Formerly in the Manchester Minibuses' Bee Line Buzz Company fleet, Freight Rover Sherpa 3237 with 18-seat Carlyle body (top) turns out of Oldham Street into Piccadilly, Manchester in March 1989 after acquiring Minilink decals. The livery was red and yellow. From the same source came 3448, a Dodge S46 with 22-seat Northern Counties body, still in the City Sprint blue and grey colours when parked in Stockport bus station in December 1988.

Seen at Bolton in May 1989, AN68 Atlantean 1651 with Park Royal bodywork was one of seven acquired from Plymouth in 1988. Its original centre-exit was rather crudely panelled over before it entered Ribble service, a bench seat for three being fitted.

Atlanteans with Northern Counties bodywork from the fleet of the Greater Manchester PTE were sold in large numbers after deregulation and this one eventually came home again. A product of the Stagecoach-Drawlane rationalisation it became Ribble 1681 in July 1989 having latterly been in the East Midland Frontrunner South East fleet in Essex. It stands in Bolton depot alongside a 1981 10.6 metre Leyland National 2, No. 843.

A hopeful sign was the allocation to Ribble by Stagecoach of 10 new coach-seated Leyland Olympians with 82-seat Alexander bodies in late 1989. It is passing through Blackburn on a through service to Blackpool in March 1990.

Group policy provides for a small injection of new vehicles annually. In 1990, Ribble received nine Olympians with Alexander 51/31 coach bodies, followed by seven with bus bodies in the following year. The 1991 programme was for 12 Olympian double-deck coaches with Alexander RL bodies. Twenty-six Mercedes-Benz 709Ds with Alexander 23 or 25-seat bodywork were also added to the fleet in 1990 and December 1992 saw the first of a further 19 similar 25-seat vehicles enter service. 1993 has seen the return from the associated Cumberland company of many ex-Ribble vehicles which were displaced by a new fleet at Carlisle. These new orders seem paltry compared to the enormous orders of past years but they are better than some fleets which are receiving no new vehicles whatsoever.

Under its new ownership, Ribble has adapted to the completely changed circumstances of post-deregulation bus operation. The transition has not been easy but the fleet is smart and well turned out and the future seems assured.

CHAPTER 11
RIBBLE PEOPLE

Major Harold Edward Hickmott, ('Hicky' to his friends), who was the driving force of Ribble during its first 25 years, was born in 1882. A Yorkshireman, he had trained as an engineer at Vickers at Barrow-in-Furness and had had experience running buses in Sussex in 1914. He had served in the fledgling Royal Air Force. He was joined in 1920 by another ex-officer, Captain Harold Leonard Betteridge, who became the company's engineer. His pre-war experience had been with motor manufacturers. Both men were autocrats and were always known by their military ranks. Years after they had passed on, the dining rooms at Frenchwood were known as A Mess and B Mess and the senior staff corridor was termed the quarter-deck! Betteridge was a competent engineer but very unpopular with the staff. He introduced the league table based on fuel consumption. Two drivers were allocated to each bus, one early and one late, and they were disciplined if fuel used was above average. If consumption was excessive, the depot foreman was disciplined as well. Suspension without pay was used ruthlessly as a disciplinary measure.

In 1929, Horace Bottomley joined the company as assistant to the managing director. He had started his career as a parcel boy with Huddersfield Corporation Tramways in 1914 and from 1924 held various positions with United Automobile Services. He had a strong personality and commanded respect at all levels. He played a big part in the multitude of take-overs of the next few years and stamped his individual style on Ribble.

After Hickmott retired on 31st December 1944, the office of managing director was held by a member of the BET executive staff, the first incumbent being J.W. Womar. Bottomley was appointed general manager, thus ensuring continuity of management as ill-health had resulted in the Major relinquishing some of his duties before retirement. He guided the company through its post-war expansion and was personally responsible for many innovations. Wit' in the company, he was always referred to as 'H.B.' and one wag said that Ribble was the only company to put the general manager's initials on the pencils. He, too, had health problems, and died suddenly, aged 61, in 1962. His achievements were aptly summed up at his memorial service at Lytham in the words of the Rural Dean – "Ribble is everywhere and Horace Bottomley put it there".

Capt. Betteridge retired prematurely in 1946 being replaced as chief engineer by A.S. Woodgate from the neighbouring North Western company; he became assistant general manager in 1949 and was succeeded as engineer by Harry Tennant who held the position for many years. The first traffic manager was Thomas Robinson, who had been the 'R' in KCR Services. He was assisted by the traffic superintendent, Jack Tipping, a former Wigan

Corporation inspector, who travelled between depots on a motor-cycle and sidecar. Robinson was succeeded in 1931 by F. A. Dickinson from the Llandudno Coaching and Carriage Co., which had been swallowed up by Crosville. He presided over operating matters until his retirement in 1959.

Tribute should be paid to the great men who chaired the Board of Directors. W.S. Wreathall held this office during the 'thirties and was succeeded by John Spencer Wills who went on to take charge of the whole BET empire. His place was taken in 1947 by R.P. Beddow, a lifelong BET employee, who held office until 1968. Although he had a home in Dover, Mr Beddow liked to get his Dover sole from Fleetwood. He would personally telephone the local superintendent, Jimmy Wilson, who would buy a box of fish and see it on to Standerwick's 'Fleetwood feeder' at 7.20am. After transfer to the service coach at Blackpool, a telephone call would be made to Victoria Coach Station, resulting in the Standerwick and East Kent representatives supervising its placing on a coach to Dover.

In the 1960s, he became frustrated by the endless bureaucracy. At the 1967 Annual Staff Dinner at the Savoy Hotel, Blackpool he deplored the proliferation of committees which deliberated *ad nauseam* whilst achieving next to nothing at a time when there were serious problems to be solved.

The last chairman in the BET era was A.F.R. Carling, CBE, who had been managing director from 1956

The senior officers of northern bus companies gave Major Hickmott a farewell dinner just prior to his retirement on 31st December 1944 and signed their names on the menu. The signatures are those of J.W. Womar (North Western), E.H. Edwardes (Lancashire United), A.T. Evans (United Automobile Services), W.J. Crosland Taylor (Crosville), D.E. Bell (Yorkshire Woollen District),, C.R.H. Wreathall (East Yorkshire), N.H. Dean (Yorkshire Traction), R.T. Ebrey (a former secretary of Ribble; Western Welsh), H. Bottomley (acting general manager of Ribble) and J.C.Dean (West Yorkshire).

to 1968. A former traffic manager and general manager of Southdown, he was a dedicated bus man who took an energetic interest in all the company's activities and inspired his colleagues by his infectious enthusiasm.

In 1962, Bottomley was succeeded as general manager by George Brook who came from North Western. He was an accomplished accountant and markedly improved the company's financial position, selling surplus properties and adopting new procedures to avoid unnecessary taxation. He had such a different approach to the job compared to Bottomley's that one official was heard to say "he doesn't care whether a bus runs or not so long as it pays". He declined to speak to senior officials together, insisting in having them in his office singly. He became the first chairman in the NBC era and took responsibility for the whole North West group. He, in turn, was followed as general manager by W.S. Leese, also from North Western.

Leonard Waller was appointed traffic manager following Dickinson's retirement. Starting as a junior clerk at Skipton, he had worked his way up to a position known as 'Liaison Officer' which was really the general manager's special investigator. When he went on to become general manager of Trent, his place was taken by E.W.A. (Ted) Butcher who, on completion of his training, had come to Ribble as district traffic superintendent, Skipton, with responsibility for just nine buses. He quickly advanced to eastern area superintendent, assistant to the traffic manager, assistant traffic manager (when W.J. Hart retired) and ultimately traffic manager. He is remembered for his friendly approach and his successful modernisation of the old-fashioned bureaucratic procedures which had grown up over the years. In 1968 he was the first BET man to be appointed as general manager of an ex-Tilling company when he went to Bristol, being followed as traffic manager by his deputy, D.D.N. Graham.

Under the NBC management changed much more frequently, perhaps too frequently for the company's good. One humorist suggested that a permanent notice should be erected in the Frenchwood offices foyer inscribed 'Your general manager this week is.......'. Space precludes mention of them all.

The Takeovers

Many staff taken over with other businesses remained with the company for many years. W.J. (Joe) Hart, who became assistant traffic manager, came with Parsons' Motors in 1925 and his lengthy diatribes about the old days heralded by 'I remember the time...' were well known to his colleagues. The Bristows from Carlisle migrated south, one to Clitheroe and the other to Bolton. Fraser Lawson, manager of Merseyside Touring Co., was a head office accountant for many years, making his way from his home in Crosby by bus to Southport, train to New Longton and bus to Preston! Bob Spensley, a Merseyside conductor, became an inspector and a Preston town councillor. He made a name for himself gathering in evidence for complex traffic court cases and persuading members of the public to come along to testify to their difficulties. One of the last such takeovers was Jack Williams, traffic manager of Scout, who brought a breath of fresh air to everything he touched. He went to Carlisle as northern area superintendent, but sadly died of cancer within quite a short time.

Management and Discipline

Stories of draconian discipline in the early years probably magnified in successive telling. Certainly suspension without pay seems to have been meted out very freely, not just to platform staff but to others as senior as depot foremen. However, labour relations must be viewed against the conditions and practices of the time and Ribble was probably little different in this respect from contemporary companies elsewhere. In times of severe unemployment only the most senior drivers and conductors had a

The late 'fifties and early 'sixties saw the retirement of many long-serving employees. W.J. Hart who had joined Ribble with the take-over of Parsons' Motor Services of Chorley in 1925 retired as Assistant Traffic Manager in 1962 and this picture was taken at one of many presentations - this one from the Central Area management staff. Left to right T. B. Pound, Depot Engineer, Blackpool (Devonshire Road), T. Rawstrone, Inspector (Kirkham), J. H. Kershaw, Central Area Supt., C. D. Parr, District Traffic Supt., Preston, T. B. Maund, District Traffic Supt., Blackpool, W. J. Hart, H. Bottomley, General Manager, J. Wilson, District Traffic Supt., Fleetwood, K. Keegan, Senior Depot Clerk, Blackpool and C. Kenvig, Inspector-in-charge, Garstang.

A high proportion of Ribble's staff stayed with the company for long periods and, to some observers at least, the mental picture of the typical crew of the post-war period is very like that seen here, with both driver and conductor grey-haired. Checking watches was part of the ritual at the beginning of a duty and this scene was a familiar sight. The type of uniform was rather conservative, still retaining a distinctly military look in a period when other operators were beginning to adopt rather 'softer' styles. The photograph was taken by the Lancashire Evening Post, evidently soon after Royal Tiger coach 877 had entered service in 1951, and shows Conductor Shannon at the completion of 30 years' service. Thus his career went back to the very early days of the company.

guaranteed 48-hour week, there being 36-hour men, 24-hour men and others with no guarantee at all who had trained in their own time and stood outside the garages waiting for someone to fail duty in order to get a day's work. Nevertheless, most employees stayed in the company's service for very many years and these included people taken over with other businesses. Many of them were shareholders and were very conscious of their duty to the travelling public.

Old habits died hard and vestiges of the autocracy of the formative years could still be encountered as late as the 'sixties. One district traffic superintendent whose office adjoined the bus station, always went home to lunch on a particular bus. If it was raining, the duty inspector had to wait at the office door with an umbrella so that his boss did not get wet crossing the road and vice versa when he returned.

The Central Organisation

Ribble was a very centralised company with most real decision making vested in Head Office officials. Vehicle overhauls were done at the Central Workshops, Frenchwood into which vehicles would disappear to be virtually dismantled and reassembled, emerging sometimes as long as three months later. Nowadays, many of the tasks are considered unnecessary, an opinion long held by many operating people especially when faced with newly-overhauled buses which required immediate mechanical attention on return to their depots!

One of the most labour-intensive sections of Head Office was Ticket Audit where every waybill was analysed and revenue apportioned to the appropriate route. In the days of the Willebrew ticket system, 39 girls were needed to compute revenue from the pieces sliced out of the Willebrew ticket. It took an average of three months to train them because they did not have to record the fare

value remaining on the clipping but the value below it. Once they had mastered the art, they punched the values in to old fashioned adding machines at an incredible speed. When the Setright system replaced the Willebrew, much of the revenue apportionment was done by the conductors and depot clerks and the 39 girls were reduced to seven. Ticket Audit also had the job of making all the necessary calculations in connection with the myriad joint working agreements in which Ribble was involved and advising the Traffic Department when the company was seriously over-run or under-run. Some of these agreements, particularly with municipal operators, were very complex, mileage being calculated in the case of Accrington Corporation to four places of decimals, equivalent to just over six inches.

For many years, the day-to-day affairs of the Traffic Department were supervised by the chief traffic clerk, John Swarbrick, (known to all and sundry as 'Jaz') who was one of the company's first clerks and scrutinised every Traffic Circular, Notice and important letter in draft. His pedantic style was detectable in all kinds of documents as everyone drafting something for his scrutiny would carefully copy phrases from other writings that he had approved. His dry wit is well remembered. "We have a booking agent at Stacksteads", he would say, "he's a tobacconist, a retired policeman with only one eye. Do you think he'd be able to understand what you've written?"

In the days before national standard timetable references such as NSu for Not Sundays, Jaz had devised a complex system of 102 code letter combinations for every occasion such as N for Not Sundays and CP for Mondays, Wednesdays and Thursdays only. In the Traffic Department, clerks used these in conversation saying, for example, that a Thursday journey ran on 'Q days'.

The Traffic Department prepared drivers' and conductors' rosters for the whole company. There were sections which corresponded to the operating areas which

Also posed with a Royal Tiger coach, in this case the prototype, No. 781 at its 'christening' shortly before entering service in March 1951, are most of the company's senior personalities of the time. From left to right are seen Harry Tennant, Chief Engineer; A. S. Woodgate., Assistant General Manager; R. P. Beddow, Chairman; J. W. Womar, Managing Director; Horace Bottomley, General Manager.

at one time numbered seven; they were gradually reduced to four, corresponding to the engineering areas. There were other specialist sections dealing with Fares, Vehicle Allocation, Season Tickets – known locally as Contracts – (all of which were prepared at Head Office), Staff Matters, Private Hire and Tours and Publicity. They were headed by senior clerks, most of whom had joined the company around 1930 and carried an enormous amount of knowledge in their heads. Several of them retired or died within a short time and much of this knowledge was lost.

The weakness of this centralised organisation was that it produced too many specialists who were out of touch with the realities of life outside. One senior roster clerk, a brilliant man in his field, insisted that, as the official running time for a particular section of route was seven minutes, no alteration could be made, even though at peak hours it took half an hour because of traffic congestion. He was eventually persuaded to try it for himself and after that more notice was taken of similar complaints.

On the Road

New depots or outstations were originally run by drivers or conductors-in-charge who made sure that the buses ran out on time and dealt with basic administrative matters as well as working duties themselves. They worked very long spreadovers and were often rewarded, as the depot expanded, by promotion to inspector thus entitling them to work even longer hours without any overtime pay. The next grade was resident inspector and then district traffic superintendent, a non-uniformed rank. On the engineering side, a mechanic-in-charge might rise to depot foreman, a grade which was re-designated depot engineer in post-war years. Many of these were very dedicated men,

working all night to ensure that every vehicle was on the road on busy summer Saturdays.

Driving standards on the road were monitored by engineering road inspectors who wore inspectors' uniforms with a distinctive cap-badge though when visiting bus stations they often wore cloth caps to avoid attracting questions from the public that they could not answer. They also carried out driving tests for new employees or conductors who had passed through the Driving School. The latter was established after the war, being available for conductors with at least two years' service who successfully survived a grilling not just from their depot superintendent but from the Area superintendent. They also signed an undertaking not to leave the company's service for at least one year. The School was in an old AEC Regal coach, new to W. Salisbury and Sons in 1934, with desks and various mechanical components on tables. The chassis of this vehicle is preserved with the Leyland body from one of the 1933 TS6 coaches. It was supervised by Arthur Dunn, a genial character with legendary driving skills. The bus would visit the depots and the trainees would be expected to attend in their own time for two weeks, working two part shifts before and after the school session from 10.0am to 4.0pm. After that they practised at the depot with the local driving instructor, also in their own time, until sufficiently proficient to undertake the PSV test.

In retrospect, Ribble treated its people very tolerantly. A few of the old hands who had been promoted in pre-1939 days found it difficult or impossible to adjust to post-war conditions when men no longer jumped when told to and everything became more complicated. There were cases of people whose health suffered as a result of their efforts to keep the job going during the war; others could not

Major
H. E. Hickmott
Managing Director
1919-44

adapt to change and were quite unable to handle their jobs effectively but they were treated with consideration, moved sideways or otherwise allowed to see out the years until their retirement. There were none of the harsh redundancies which are a feature of today's business world.

After the formation of the National Council for the Omnibus Industry in 1942, with employer and employee representatives, every facility was given for trade union activity with some degree of consultation at every level. Platform staff were usually members of the Transport and General Workers' Union but some depots, such as Fleetwood and Lancaster, had the National Union of Railwaymen and Preston had both. Ribble enjoyed better labour relations than some companies in the 'sixties when many operators had serious labour problems, 1970 being Ribble's worst year.

Captain H. L. Betteridge
Chief Engineer
1920-46

(Below) The Directors' visits to garages often produced good group photographs. Here the Directors are seen in Burnley depot in July 1958. Left to right the group includes W. G. Hunniball, Assistant to the General Manager; N. P. Burrows, District Traffic Supt., Burnley; J. Holland, Depot Engineer, Burnley; H. Tennant, Chief Engineer; F. Keir, Area Engineer, Eastern Area; E. W. A. Butcher, Area Supt., Eastern Area; R. P. Beddow, CBE, Chairman of the Board of Directors; A. F. R. Carling, Managing Director; E. L. Taylor, Director; C. D. Quinn, Architect; A. E. C. Dent, Director; J. P. Senior, Assistant General Manager; H. Bottomley, General Manager; E. W. Arkle, Director; F. A. Dickinson, Traffic Manager; and H. W. Miller, Secretary.

The ceremonial handing-over of one of the first Marshall-bodied Leyland Leopards in June 1963. Left to right, George Brook, general manager, J. Davies, sales director Marshall, H. Tennant, chief engineer, J. Lees, home sales manager, Leyland.

Walter G. Hunnibal was General Manager in 1973-74

Irwin Dalton was appointed General Manager in 1974, serving in that capacity until 1977.

Fred Dark became General Manager in 1977

Ian Chapman, appointed General Manager in 1979, points to the long service certificate issued to the Ribble Enthusiasts Club in 1981, T. B. Collinge, founder of the club, looks on. The Ribble Enthusiasts Club has always enjoyed a particularly close relationship with the company. Ian Chapman, as the final Managing Director of the Company – in NBC days – found himself obliged to supervise the consequences of the Ridley directive to break up the Company. He subsequently led the successful Management Buy Out team, which later sold out to the Stagecoach concern.

SOME PERSONAL REMINISCENCES
by T.B. MAUND

I joined Ribble in October 1949 and during the next 18 years held positions at Head Office Traffic Department and Standerwick's and managed Blackpool and Preston depots.

In contrast to the concentration of power at Head Office, the supervisors in the field had much greater authority to deal with immediate problems than their opposite numbers in other companies. This included switching buses and crews between duties, arranging extra duplication and even hiring other operators if all else failed. Where bus stations were shared with a municipal operator, the contrast of authority was immediately apparent. In moments of crisis I have sent a Blackburn depot PD2 White Lady to Halifax where no Ribble double-decker had ever ventured before and on another occasion five Atlantean White Ladies went fully loaded from Blackpool to Glasgow! The latter was to somewhat premeditated as a substantial overload was anticipated. When bookings were stopped for the popular return Saturday from Blackpool, Western SMT offices would continue to book passengers from Glasgow with a Sunday return date, telling them that it could be changed to Saturday at Blackpool which, of course, was not true. People could not remain in their boarding houses until Sunday and turned up for the Saturday departure. On this occasion the overload compared with the chart was over 600 passengers, of which the five Atlanteans took about half! Although this happened every year, Head Office was reluctant to hire additional vehicles to cover it in case one

year it didn't happen, but it always did! Head Office would hire up to 200 vehicles on peak Saturdays and I usually had a few of my own up my sleeve.

Sleight of Hand

The 9.30am Blackpool-Glasgow service on summer Saturdays was a perennial problem and often had over 30 duplicates. Loading started at 8.0am and one conductor was allocated to three hired vehicles. There was a particularly cumbersome ticket system, dictated by the Scottish Group, which involved the writing out of a carbon-backed exchange ticket for every passenger. The conductor would deal with one coach before departure, travel with another and arrange to meet the third somewhere on the road. The local excursion operators were hired and, as the traffic was essentially one way, so were coaches from Penrith, Ingleton and the Lake District. Sometimes the local people would refuse two-day hires such as Glasgow because they needed coaches for Sunday morning excursions and, on desperate occasions, I persuaded them to relent by hiring them Ribble coaches for local excursions on Sunday morning.

There were manipulations with other depots' vehicles which could be used to good effect. Skipton had two coaches with layover in Blackpool; one worked the X16 from Skipton to Blackpool and the other the X7 from Southport. These were used with Blackpool crews for afternoon duties to Bradford and Huddersfield, the Skipton

Blackpool and its intensive summer services made huge demands on resources of vehicles and staff, giving rise to all kinds of subterfuge to get round the problems. Ribble, as the incumbent operating company, had to work with other companies' vehicles coming in on jointly operated services. This is a posed view, showing

the then new first White Lady double-deck coach on Leyland PD1/3 chassis, still with Burlingham poster in one of the windows in the bus station with Ribble, North Western and Lancashire United vehicles.

crews taking back Blackpool coaches which arrived back from Newcastle-upon-Tyne later in the afternoon. The coaches were exchanged on Sunday in Devonshire Road garage.

All depots had their little dodges that they used to get out of trouble. At Liverpool, the L3 Crosby service with a six-minute frequency was regarded as a legitimate source of buses for unforeseen duplication to Blackpool and it was a rare summer Saturday that saw a full service operating. Morecambe, with much less space than Blackpool, was a difficult station to work and their Lancaster service was sometimes raided in similar circumstances.

In the days before the Ashton-Lea by-pass and the motorways, Preston was a serious traffic bottleneck, particularly on summer Saturday mornings and Sunday evenings and the effects were felt over a wide area. Further north, Skerton Bridge, Lancaster, and Kendal town centre caused serious delays. Ribble inspectors devised various methods of minimising the effect of these problems. For example, at Blackpool Coliseum there were crew reliefs on five consecutive X60 departures between 1.0 and 2.0pm and, if these departed late, the evening departures between 6.30 and 7.30pm would be disrupted as most of the crews worked double trips with a break in between. Other depots' buses which had long layovers were often used to fill in and North Western coaches would be used to enable the through coaches to Derby and Nottingham to leave on time. The juggling inevitably led to North Western and Trent vehicles finishing up on the wrong runnings and this brought forth howls of protest from one or both companies almost every week despite the fact that it was done to give a good service to the paying public.

Day and night running on the Scottish services always led to coaches finishing at the wrong depots as the Scottish inspectors seemed to have no idea of English geography. Coaches would be lost to their rightful owners for days and sometimes longer. The Ribble superintendent at Manchester always regarded another depot's coach as a bonus and immediately allocated it to a duty which would take it anywhere except near its own depot. A favourite trick was to allocate a Blackpool coach to the Manchester depot working on Blackpool-Nottingham as this was a two-day cycle and the vehicle spent every other night in Blackpool garage. If the Blackpool staff were not alert, they would think that all was well whereas, in fact, there were two Blackpool coaches on Nottingham instead of one, resulting in a crisis the next time every coach was booked out. As Blackpool was such a good common denominator, other depots would appeal for help in tracing 'lost' coaches and they would often appear with a Manchester crew.

Carlisle depot had a control office run by a highly competent inspector who kept track of vehicle movements. In pre-motorway days it was difficult for vehicles to miss Carlisle and if I found that one of my missing coaches was coming south from Scotland with a 'foreign' crew, I would ask for it to be loaded so that it had to go into Preston coach station. A driver would then be sent there with instructions to board it, travel passenger to wherever it was going and then bring it back empty to Blackpool.

Overtime

Although most companies made righteous noises about observing legislation concerning drivers' hours, the services could not have been maintained during the staff shortages of the 'fifties and 'sixties without excessive overtime being worked. Breaches of the law were often unwitting as harassed inspectors, trying to cover a duty, often could not check to see what hours a driver had already worked. Every depot had one or more drivers who would almost literally work night and day. There was a driver at Blackpool who lived in an externally dingy but internally well-appointed terraced house, conveniently situated for both garages and Talbot Road bus station. He had what must have been the only telephone in the street and made sure that every inspector knew the number. One Saturday evening, he was working a 'special' at Blackpool Coliseum when the police rang to say that a Penrith depot driver had been knocked down by a tram on the promenade. He was not seriously injured but would have to stay in hospital overnight. He was due to take his coach on a tour

Leyland PLSC1 C295 originally entered the company's service in March 1927 and was sold in 1938, a creditably long life in those days. It became a showman's vehicle and was eventually purchased privately for preservation in December 1973. Ribble took it over in July 1981 and completed its restoration to full working order, using parts of similar vehicle HF 4535 (ex-Wallasey Corporation No. 8), another stalled preservation project. It has been used for promotional and publicity purposes.

of the illuminations at 10.0pm and then return to Penrith. Our 'night and day' driver immediately agreed to take this coach back to Penrith, caught the southbound night service back to Blackpool, and reported for his duty on the Sunday morning even though he had been told that other arrangements would be made to cover it.

On another occasion, the Union at Preston made a big fuss about a certain driver who had agreed, at short notice, to take a coach from Preston to Glasgow at 11.55pm. It was revealed that he had already worked a full split turn and the second part of a late duty but had misled the inspector. The man, a former lorry driver, said he couldn't understand what the fuss was about as he had often done that sort of thing and loaded and unloaded his wagon as well! A Preston depot conductress received 170 hours pay one week, two more than there are hours in the week.

The senior men at most Ribble depots, with service back to the 'twenties, were of a breed which was never replaced. Blackpool had a summer out-station at Middlesbrough, one crew (later a driver only) working the Middlesbrough-Hawes section of X32 every day from the end of June to the end of September. It was an easy duty lasting from about 9.30am to 4.15pm and the senior driver and conductor always elected to do it, allegedly to get away from their wives for three months, though that was never proved. They had good lodgings and both had part-time jobs working the tote at a Middlesbrough dog-track. One morning, the driver telephoned to say that he was ill and had to return home so would we send a second driver from Blackpool to work the Hawes-Middlesbrough trip. It was found that the driver had suffered a minor stroke and had driven the Royal Tiger coach from Middlesbrough to Hawes when he was very slightly paralysed. He never drove a bus again. These drivers were craftsmen, handling their relatively primitive vehicles with flair, changing gear on the crash box without using the clutch. In later years, wherever possible, would-be drivers were tested on a bus with a crash box and many applicants from municipal systems with all-synchromesh fleets failed.

A Head Office official who had started his Ribble career as a conductor at Church depot, told a story of an empty trip back from Manchester with a rear entrance PLSC Lion. On a long, straight and deserted stretch of road with a slightly rising gradient, he was quietly completing his waybill when his driver suddenly appeared beside him looking for a light for a cigarette. The Lion carried on driverless at about 15 mph with no deviation from the straight and narrow. The driver then climbed back through the front bulkhead window, puffing contentedly.

Inspectors

One of the most regrettable aspects of the present day is the almost total elimination of the people who played such an enormous part in making things run smoothly in the past – the inspectors – and one or two memories about them make an appropriate finale. At one time, a rather predictable inspector covered the Fylde coast area and I was travelling to Blackpool on a Preston depot coach when, at Freckleton, the conductor, a man of many years' service, stood up and said to the passengers 'Now then,

ladies and gentlemen, please have your tickets ready as me dad will be getting on soon and he'll want to see them'. After another mile and half, with no tip-offs from other drivers, we rounded a bend and, sure enough, there was the inspector! So much for surprise checking. Another day, a very steady inspector boarded a bus on which there was a rather garrulous conductor. 'Good morning' said the latter, 'Here, have an orange'. The inspector put the orange in his pocket and went to check the upper deck passengers' tickets. When he came down, he handed the orange back to the conductor saying 'You'd better have this back; there's an uncollected fare upstairs and I'm going to book you.

In the quiet days of winter, Blackpool inspectors would sometimes do ticket checking duty in the Preston area. One dark Friday morning, a particularly dry Blackpool inspector boarded a bus on the Leyland road. 'I haven't seen you before', said the driver, 'Which depot are you from? 'Penrith', said the po-faced Blackpool inspector. 'Good heavens, what time did you come on duty, then? 'Tuesday' said the inspector.

The first few Ribble buses were apparently painted grey but the familiar livery of cherry red and ivory soon took its place. In pre-war days the cherry red was lighter than in later years. Panels were lined out in gold, with black beading and the company's name appeared in gold shaded, serifed lettering on both sides. When coaches were introduced, the livery was adapted to the design of the bodywork, the fleet name giving way to a garter encircling a Gothic 'R'. From 1937, the coach livery was reversed, ivory becoming the dominant colour.

In post-1939-45 war days, the fleet name was modernised with block sans-serif letters and, in the 'fifties, the gold gave way to yellow, the change being so subtle that few observers noticed it; lining-out was scrapped and mudguards became red. In 1950 the cherry red on single-deck buses was extended to all but the waistband, and the three ivory bands on double-deck buses were reduced to two and then to one, at cantrail level. In the 'sixties, single-deck buses became very drab with no ivory relief at all. Coaches continued to carry reversed liveries adapted to their contours. In the late 'sixties, a new lower case fleet name style appeared.

In 1972, the National Bus Company adopted its corporate livery policy, companies being given the option of choosing 'poppy red' or 'leaf green'. Ribble chose poppy red which, compared with its traditional livery, gave the impression of an undercoat. By mid-1975 only two buses, both PD3s, remained in the old livery. Coaches were finished in an overall white livery with red and blue 'National' insignia, company fleet names becoming subsidiary to 'National'. 'National Holidays' was adopted for tours work.

From 1983 some coaches were appearing in 'Timesaver' livery of white with blue stripes and this was applied to coach-seated double-deckers in 1984. The following year, a system of different coloured stripes for different coaching 'products' was devised. Timesaver became red with grey stripes, Kingfisher vehicles had silver stripes and the Southport-based 'Sandpiper' coaches had a sand-coloured livery with gold stripes. Fleet titles in grey or red block letters were adopted. Variations on the latter included red and white with gold stripes and a black skirt. In 1986, the NBC relaxed its rules on standard livery and some Ribble vehicles appeared with a broad grey band, edged with white and fleet name in yellow block letters, the basic livery remaining poppy red. From mid-1986, 'local identity' slogans were added e.g. 'From Manchester serving the North West' or 'From Preston serving Central Lancashire'. Minibuses were originally finished in red and yellow with various stripes but there have been variations to adapt to the style of vehicles. A new express livery of cream and grey with red and yellow lines was overtaken by the Stagecoach group's controversial group livery of white with red, blue and orange stripes though, in 1993, many vehicles remain in earlier liveries.

FLEET NUMBERS

The company's fleet numbering policy seems to have originated about 1921, numbers being retrospectively allocated to earlier vehicles. Each chassis had a C number while the bodies were separately numbered with a B prefix. The C number was painted on the nearside of the chassis on the earlier types and low down on the bonnet side of later types. The B number appeared inside the lower saloon and for several years there seemed to be one different between the two on any particular vehicle. Numbers were allocated progressively irrespective of vehicle type and were given to all acquired vehicles even if they were not operated. If a bus was sold and then acquired again with a later purchase, it received a second number. Several ancillary vehicles were numbered in the same series as were pre-war Standerwick vehicles, though different fleet numbers appeared on the coaches.

By 1931, when C numbers had reached 1362, these were regarded as fleet numbers though they were not displayed on the front dash and rear panels until 1946. Fleet numbers had reached 2797 by 1950 when the system was changed as described below.

Staff had often complained that the progressive numbering of the fleet made it impossible to identify the type of vehicle just from the number. Fleet numbers were prominently displayed, front and rear, from 1946 and in 1950 a renumbering scheme was announced whereby blocks of numbers were allocated to types of vehicles as follows:-

1-200	Standerwick coaches
201-700	Single-deck service buses
701-1200	Single-deck coaches
1201-1300	Double-deck coaches
1301-up	Double-deck service buses

The blocks were estimated to contain twice as many numbers as would be needed at any one time, the double-deck block being left open-ended as it was not intended to renumber this type though new vehicles started at 1301. This system remained in use, more or less, for the next 35 years though in later years the 201- and 701- series were merged and overflowed into the 1200s and numbers above 2000 were used for low-height double-deckers. All the series were reused, some of them twice. Despite the apparent adequacy of the blocks, some renumbering was necessary as the numbers of new buses caught up.

The Standerwick series continued to be used for National Travel coaches and, with the return of coach operations to the companies, was continued as a series for top class coaches. Double-deck coaches have been numbered with the buses, the 1201- series having been abandoned. Ribble minibuses were numbered as single-deck buses but those acquired from United Transport carried numbers from 1 up (Zippy) and from 3060 up (Bee Line).

ROUTE NUMBERS AND DESTINATIONS

From the mid-'twenties, the company devised a route number system which was used only in time-tables and ultimately exceeded 200, with many suffix letters. Internally, the company had a system of 'Ribble references' used for crew instruction and revenue analysis; sometimes the Ribble reference was the same as the route number but more often it was not. A separate system for express services followed by 'ex' was started in 1928. In 1935-37, new service numbers were allocated progressively throughout the system and new vehicles were equipped with three-track number blinds to the front. Older buses displayed cards. The numbers were allocated territorially as follows:-

1-99	Preston, Lancaster and Fleetwood area
100-up	Other services from Preston, including the original 'trunks'
200-up	East Lancashire, including services from Bolton
300-up	Merseyside and South Lancashire
470-up	Kendal, Windermere, Sedbergh and Ingleton
500-up	Furness and Lake District
600-704	Northern Area - Carlisle, Penrith, Appleby, Keswick

Express services were in a separate series, generally prefixed by 'X', but the Yorkshire-Blackpool services were prefixed 'J'- for joint. Standerwick services were not numbered. Numbers were allocated to some extent with the units figure indicating a specific corridor. For example, all Manchester or Bolton-North services ended in '0', Liverpool services in '1' and Blackpool services in '2'. The Manchester-East Lancashire services all ended in '3'. The 'hundreds' blind carried letters as well as numbers and 'X1' was included, enabling numbers such as X100, X173 etc. to be displayed. The same rule was applied to some extent with ordinary services e.g. all services leaving Liverpool along the A59 had numbers ending in '1' (matching the expresses) and some of these, e.g. 101, 321, 341, remain today. In post-war years, some people in the company obviously did not understand the system, resulting

in such numbers as 201 and 411 being allocated to Liverpool services. Many separate numbers for short workings were abandoned during the war.

As it would have been difficult to accommodate all Ribble services between 1 and 999, separate local series were also used for town services, prefixed by the town's initial letter and 'S' and 'W' were used for special or school and workpeople's services. A little-known 'H' series was used for special Holiday Services for the Wakes Weeks. In the 'sixties, many services were renumbered to enable the service numbers and Ribble references to coincide and, in 1970, there was a campaign to eliminate prefix letters but it was never taken to its logical conclusion and one 'L' service remains in Liverpool to this day (but operated, of course, by North Western).

Early Ribble buses were equipped with destination blinds with quite informative displays, e.g. 'Bolton via Horwich', and some types had displays front and rear. By the late-'twenties, the depth of the blind was reduced to 3 in. and there were displays only to the front. A common blind was devised containing, in alphabetical order, all the principal towns in the company's area and such displays as 'Town Hall' and 'Railway Station'. For places not on this roll, a board was slotted over the aperture with an external light to illuminate it at night. Supplementary cards, listing intermediate places, were displayed in side or rear windows.

This system continued until 1945-46 when district blinds were installed, containing everything needed for a depot or group of neighbouring depots and the depth was increased to 5 in., older buses being modified on overhaul. Paper labels were often used for emergency displays. Rear service number equipment was fitted on post-war bus bodies but this fell into disuse in the mid-'sixties.

From 1973-74, the destination aperture was reduced again and lower-case lettering adopted. Many services have retained their numbers throughout the years but others have changed beyond recognition.

FLEET STRENGTH					
1919	5	1931	817	1960	1168
1921	18	1934	880	1965	1137
1924	61	1937	959	1969	1105
1925	94	1939	1055	1975	1150
1926	153	1940	1110	1980	910
1927	260	1942	1038	1983	800
1928	352	1945	1102	1986	923
1929	474	1950	1179	1987	532
1930	556	1955	1157	1992	354

The solitary Leyland Panther, 774, on an Omnibus Society trip in 1967. It was new in 1964, the Marshall body being almost identical to that on contemporary Leopard dual-purpose vehicles, but moving the engine to the rear brought a drop in reliability.

RIBBLE DEPOTS

Location	Code	Opened	Closed	Notes
AINTREE, Ormskirk Road	AY(AI)	1951	1989	To NWRCC 9.86
Reopened		1991		
AMBLESIDE, Compston Road	BJ	1931	1989	Replaced small out-station.
BARROW, Emlyn Street	(BA)	1986	1989	
Ironworks Road (rented yard)	(BA)	1988	1989	
Hindpool Road	(BA)	1989		Ex-Barrow Borough Tpt. to CMS 1989
BLACKBURN, George Street	AG(BB)	1928		Rebuilt 1985 Minibus only from 24.8.91
BLACKBURN, Foundry Hill	AH	1926	1980	Ex Pendle Motor Services Used as store until 1986
BLACKPOOL, Devonshire Road	AC(BL)	1937	1987	Coach depot
BLACKPOOL, Talbot Road	AC(BL)	1928	1988	
BLACKPOOL, Coliseum	(BL)	1987	1988	
BOLTON, Charles St.	AS	1925?	1929	
BOLTON, Goodwin Street	AS(BO)	1929	1981	Used as store
Reopened		1986		
BOOTLE, Hawthorne Road (I)	CL	1930	1979	Ex-Merseyside Touring Co. Rebuilt 1933-34
BOOTLE, Hawthorne Road (II)	CL(BT)	1979		To NWRCC 9.86
BURNLEY		1923	1926	
Trafalgar Street	AK	1926	1958	
Olympia Street	CA	??	1958	Coach depot
Turf Street		1934	1958	Workshop, ex-Wright Bros.
Centenary Way	AK/CA(BU)	1958	1989	
Queensgate	(BU)	1989		Burnley & Pendle depot
BURY, Millett St	BY	1956	1975	Ex Auty's Tours
CARLISLE, Corporation Road	BR	1931	1968	Ex Carlisle & District
Willowholme	BR(CA)	1968		To CMS 1986
CHORLEY, Eaves Lane	AR(CH)	1925		Ex-Parsons Motors
Brooke St.	(CH)	1986	1989	
CHURCH, Blackburn Road	BW	1930	1946	Ex-Rishton & Antley Motors
CLITHEROE, Pimlico Road	AL(CO)	1926		Ex-Pendle Motor Services Outstation of B'burn 1986
DALTON-ON-FURNESS, Station Road	BT	1930	?	Ex-Furness Omnibus Co. Outstation of Ulverston 1932
DARWEN, Gillibrand St.		1986	1989	Minibus out-station of B'burn
FLEETWOOD, Birch Street	BC(FL)	1931	1991	Ex-Lawrence Motor Services Rebuilt 1932, 1939
GARSTANG, Bridge Street	AF	1926	1989	Ex-Pilot Motors

Location	Code	Opened	Closed	Notes
GRANGE-OVER-SANDS, Kents Bank Rd.	BV	1958		Ex-Grange Motor & Cycle Co. To CMS 1989
KENDAL, Station Road	BG(KE)	1927		Ex-Lancs.& Westmorland Rebuilt on same site 1959 To CMS 1989
Shap Road	BG	1930	1959	Ex-Kendal Motor Co.
KESWICK	BH	1928	1971	Out-station of Ambleside
LANCASTER, Owen Road, Skerton	BA(LC)	1927		Ex-Lancs. & Westmorland Rebuilt on same site 1934
Dalton Square	BD	1929	1934	Ex-County Motors
LIVERPOOL, Collingwood Street	AW	1927	1960	Ex-Collingwood Motors
Hilbre Street	AW(LP)	1960	1980	To National Travel (West)
MANCHESTER, Trumpet Street	AV	1947?	1972?	
Hulme Hall Road	AV(MA)	1989		North Western depot until 1972. To Bee Line 1989
MORECAMBE, South Avenue	AZ	1927		Ex-Lancs.& Westmorland Sub-depot of Lancstr from 19??
ORMSKIRK, Knowsley Road	AX	1937	1974	Replaced by Skelmersdale
PENRITH, Brunswick Road	BK(PE)	1929		Ex-Armstrong & Siddle Sub-depot of Carlisle 1985 To CMS 1986
PRESTON, Park Road	AA	1921	1952	
Selborne Street	AB(PR)	1927		
SEAFORTH SANDS, Crosby Road South	AY	1930	1934	Ex-Waterloo & Crosby
SKELMERSDALE, Neverstitch Road	(SK)	1974		To NWRCC 1986
SKIPTON, Broughton Road	AP	1928	1976	Ex 'Old Bill' Motors Rebuilt on same site 1938
SOUTHPORT, Lord Street	CS	1954	1986	Ex-CLC Railway station To NWRCC 1986
ULVERSTON, The Ellers	CD(UL)	1932	1990	To CMS 1989. Closed 6.2.90
WIGAN, Wallgate	AT(WI)	1928		Rebuilt 1971, to NWRCC 1986
WINDERMERE		1986		Minibus sub-depot of Kendal To CMS 1989
FRENCHWOOD, Central Workshops		1926	1989	
Head Office		1937	1989	

In addition, there were many sub-depots or 'dormy-sheds' including Bowness-on-Solway (CC), Kirkoswald (BN), Appleby (BQ), Ingleton (BE), Sedbergh (BF), Kirkby Lonsdale (BB), Kirkby Stephen (BP), Shap (BL)and, in pre-war days, Rochdale (AJ). Express vehicles were out-stationed at different times at Middlesbrough (CF), Glasgow (BS) and Widnes (CE).Pennine Motor Services depots used Ribble documents and were coded as follows:- Skipton (AD), Ingleton (AE) and Settle (AQ). A new depot was planned for Accrington in 1939, to replace Church and the fuel tanks had already been installed when the outbreak of war led to the plan being scrapped.

New depot codes were allocated in 1982 and these are shown in parenthesis in the table above. Depots still open in 1982 for which no new code is shown were regarded as sub-depots of others.

NWRCC = North Western Road Car Co. Ltd. CMS = Cumberland Motor Services Ltd.

ACKNOWLEDGEMENTS

Special thanks are due to the Ribble Enthusiasts Club for exceptional help, in particular to Simon Watts, Records Officer and Ian Warwick, Editor of the Club's Bulletin, both of whom spared no effort to solve various queries. The Club's 1972 publication, *52 Years of Ribble* was a valuable source of reference as was Eric Ogden's Ribble book in the British Bus Systems series published by Transport Publishing Co. Ltd.

Arthur Caine, a retired Assistant Traffic Manager of Ribble, and a former colleague, brought his prodigous memory to bear on many events of the early years of his company service which started in 1930.

The Fleet Histories of the PSV Circle and Omnibus Society have been invaluable aids to describing the fleet and tracing the origins and disposals of many buses and coaches which wore the Ribble colours at different times. Individual members of the Omnibus Society have been generous in their assistance and particular mention should be made of J.S.M. Fowler of Doncaster for original research into the personal relationships of the founders; P. Deegan, W. Dodds, J.E. Dunabin, D. Grisenthwaite, C.W. Heaps and K.W. Swallow.

Roger Atkinson of the Ticket and Fare Collection Society generously made valuable items from his collection available for photography by R.L. Wilson who also offered a wide choice of pictures for use in the book. J.D. Howie, R. Marshall and D. Wayman provided an extensive range of pictures and it is regretted that considerations of space limited the numbers which could be used. Author and Publisher have agreed to produce a series of albums showing Ribble at work in different areas to extend the scope of the material available.

Queries on some of the early events in the Ribble story were solved in the library of the National Motor Museum, Beaulieu, the staff of which offered every assistance.

PHOTOGRAPHIC CREDITS

GHF Atkins	48(top), 49(bottom), 57(bottom), 116(bottom)
R Downham	123(top), 125(bottom), 129(bottom), 131(upper), 135(top)
E Gray	74(top right)
RN Hannay Collection	46(centre), 123(bottom)
WJ Haynes	33(top), 43(bottom left)
FJ Higham	28(bottom)
JD Howie 81	(centre right and foot), 83(foot), 84(lower right)
R Marshall	49(top), 51(bottom), 55(top right), 60, 85(lower left), 86(bottom), 88(top), 89(top and centre), 94(centre both and foot), 97(top both and foot), 98(both), 114(top), 118(top),122(bottom), 125(bottom),129(top two), 133(top),135(centre & bottom), 136(top), 138(bottom), 139(bottom),
TB Maund Collection	12(both), 15(top), 16(bottom), 21,23, 24(bottom), 34, 36(both), 37, 38(top), 40, 41(top), 46(top & bottom pair), 47(centre), 48(bottom), 54, 55(top left), 63(centre), 64(lower), 76, 79(all), 119(bottom), 140, 141, 147, 148, 151
Northern Counties	26(top), 101(lower)
E Ogden Collection	114(centre), 144(top two)
SL Poole	25(bottom), 32(both), 111(bottom),
FJ Reynolds	117(bottom)
Ribble Enthusiasts Club	
(Courtesy TB Collinge)	145 all 146 both
Senior Transport Archive	9, 10(top & bottom), 11(top), 13(lower), 14(top), 19, 20(both), 22, 24(upper), 25(top & second bottom), 26, 27(both), 28(top), 29, 31(both), 33(bottom), 35, 39(all), 45(bottom), 47(bottom), 51(all except bottom), 55(bottom), 56(both), 59(bottom), 61(all), 62(both), 64(top and centre), 66(all), 67(top and centre), 68(all), 70(both), 71, 72(all), 74(top left), 75(top), 77(top and bottom), 82(top right), 83(top), 86(top), 87(centre and foot), 90(both), 91(both), 101(upper), 102(upper), 109(lower), 110, 112(top), 114(bottom), 115(top), 118(lower), 119(top & centre), 121, 124, 126(both), 127, 130(both), 142, 143, 144(bottom), 145(bottom), 147
Senior Transport Archive courtesy BCVM	10(centre), 11(centre & bottom), 13(top), 14(lower), 15(centre & bottom), 16(top), 19, 20(both), 22, 24(upper), 25(top & second bottom), 26, 27(both), 28(top), 29, 31(both), 33(bottom), 35, 39(all), 41(centre & bottom), 43(top & centre), 44, 47(top), 50(both), 52(both), 100(both), 102(lower), 103(all), 104, 105(both), 106, 107, 108, 109(top), 111(top), 112(bottom), 120, 134, 146
EJ Smith	116(top)
KW Swallow	79(centre right both)
AA Townsin Collection	25(second top), 43(bottom right), 45(upper), 122(top)
D Waymann	85(lower right), 93(all), 95(all), 96(both), 99(centre), 133(bottom), 137, 139(top)
RL Wilson	57(top & centre), 67 (lower left and right), 74(lower), 75(centre and foot), 77(centre), 79(lower left), 82(top left), 84(lower left), 88(lower), 89(foot), 94(top), 97(centre right), 99(top and bottom), 115(lower), 125(top), 131(bottom), 133(centre), 136(bottom), 138(top & centre)
Unknown	49(centre), 55(centre), 59(top & centre)

INDEX

INDEX

Venture Publications and The Ribble Production Team

We hope you will enjoy reading this book, Venture's first. Venture has a wide range of material for publication covering the history of British bus companies and the bus and truck manufacturing industry. Railway histories will also be published from time to time. If you would like details of forthcoming titles please send a stamped addressed envelope to Venture Publications Ltd, PO Box 17, Glossop, Derbyshire SK13 9FA

The team involved in the production of this book and the second volume which is in the course of preparation is as follows -

TB Maund – the Author – is a native of Wallasey, on Merseyside and his interest in public transport was evident before he reached the age of three! His interests gradually expanded to include South Lancashire, North Wales and the West Midlands. Encouraged by the late Peter Hardy, he started to take an interest in historical research in 1941 and, recognising the enormous scope of the subject, decided to specialise on the Merseyside area.
He has contributed many articles to the technical press over many years and this is the sixteenth book of which he has been author or co-author. The *Liverpool Transport* series, published in five volumes between 1975 and 1991, is recognised as the most comprehensive history of road passenger transport services in the provinces.
Although originally a railwayman, he made the change to buses following war service in the army, joining Ribble Motor Services as a traffic clerk in 1949, after brief experience with a well-known independent operator in the South of England. During the following two decades he held various appointments, both with the parent company and the Standerwick subsidiary, successively managing Blackpool and Preston depots. His later years were spent with the United Transport group at first in Kenya and then in South Africa where he was general manager of three bus companies before transferring to the executive staff.
He took a great interest in training and further education, lecturing at colleges at Blackpool and Preston and at Rand Afrikaans University, Johannesburg.

Alan Townsin, Editor-in-Chief of Venture Publications Ltd, began direct involvement with buses when he became a draughtsman with AEC in 1951, spending four years at the Southall works. Two years with CAV, the fuel injection specialists, were followed by four as a chassis designer with Thornycroft at Basingstoke. In 1959, he took over the editorship of 'Buses Illustrated' for Ian Allan Ltd, at first on a part-time basis, and this continued when he joined the staff of 'The Commercial Motor' for two years in 1961. Then, in 1963, he joined Ian Allan on a full-time basis, editing both 'Buses Illustrated' and the trade monthly journal 'Passenger Transport'. In 1965 came a move to IPC Transport Press and the technical editorship of both 'Motor Transport' and the monthly 'Bus and Coach', becoming editor of the latter later that year.
The next move was to West Midlands PTE in Birmingham as press & publicity officer in 1972, then back to London in 1975 to join the Confederation of British Road Passenger Transport, soon better known as CPT, though nowadays called the Bus & Coach Council.
He reverted to being a writer in 1979, mainly for the Transport Publishing Company though also working on a part-time basis as technical editor of 'Coaching Journal' until 1988 and from time to time for other publishers. A native of Newcastle upon Tyne, he spent much of the war as a schoolboy evacuee in Penrith and says it was Ribble's coyness about its fleet numbers that really caused him to get hooked on buses as serious study.

John Senior brings to Venture a lifelong interest in road and rail transport. A keen photographer for nearly 50 years (he stresses he was an early starter with a Box Brownie taking Crosville Titans and Blackpool trams in 1945!) his interest rapidly developed - literally - when his father taught him to do his own processing as soon as photographic materials became available again after the war. He still has his first 'proper' camera, an Agfa Isolette which used a variety of 120 size films including Selochrome, FP3, HP3, FP4, HP4, Panatomic X, Ferraniacolour, Gevacolour, Ektachrome, and Agfa CT18. He began shooting colour 40 years ago when his career in the printing industry started, processing the films at work with his foreman's connivance. Processing took nearly 6 hours from start to finish. The 'day job' gave him a love of large format negatives, up to 40in x 30in on glass plates! After completing his apprenticeship he joined the staff of the Manchester College of Science and Technology as a part-time lecturer. Electronic scanning and computers came his way in 1960 whilst working for the Inveresk Group, and a move to Windsor as Process Manager combined that experience with magazine and newspaper production. Subsequently three years as a technical representative and trouble shooter for Fuji Film took him all over mainland Britain. A Fuji automatic 35mm camera joined the ranks and his transparency collection blossomed during his travels. Subsequently he purchased a Zeiss Super Ikonta which is now used for large format colour slides.
Contacts made during his years as a technical representative have stood him in good stead in his publishing career and he looks forward to continuing to use the march of technological progress in the production of Venture's books.

Venture Publications and The Ribble Production Team

Ken Swallow has had over 40 years professional experience in public transport. Retiring in 1989 as Director General of Merseyside PTE, he now maintains his connections with the industry as Northern Regional Officer of the Chartered Institute of Transport. His interest in transport outside his career was originally prompted at the age of 7 by the Llandudno & Colwyn Bay trams. From his first Box Brownie picture of an ex-Midland Johnson 0-6-0 he graduated to first one, then a second Kodak Sterling II, invariably using FP3 or HP3 film, and for good measure staining his parent's bathroom with Promicrol. His Sterling II era lasted until the '70s, spanning most of the period covered by those pictures reproduced in this volume and those earmarked for the later one. Even now, with a Canon autofocus SLR, he keeps his old Kodak to remind him of simpler pleasure.

Reg Wilson is a native of Stretford, Manchester and his interest in buses started with an admiration of the 'streamline' Manchester livery of the 'thirties. Holidays in Wales kindled an interest in Crosville and photography became a serious hobby when film once more became available after the war. He does his own monochrome developing and printing and has extended his interests to cine and video.
Reg is a noted expert on vehicle registrations, having helped with the compilation of several books on the subject. He has lived on the Wirral peninsula since 1955 and has recently retired from his career as an industrial chemist in the oil industry.

Roy Marshall was born in Nottingham in 1928 and took an early interest in buses. During the war he visited towns up to a hundred miles away, to extend his interest, including taking photographs for Bill Haynes using the family Box Brownie. He has spent 40 years in the bus industry starting with Skills and retiring from the managership of Burnley & Pendle in 1986. In his earlier days Roy received help and encouragement from Geoff Atkins. His cameras have comprised a 120 Zeiss, an Ensign Selfix and a selection of Rollies. A Kodak Retinette 1B and a variety of Pentaxes were used for colour.

David Waymann was fascinated from an early age by new unfrozen Leyland TD7s. Later his interest broadened to include the history and functions of the operating and manufacturing aspects of the whole mass transportation industry, road and rail. He photographs buses with an Olympus OM1 or a Canon AL1. Spare time involvements also include transport preservation and radical politics relating to transport.

John Howie can trace his interest in Ribble vehicles back to the mid-1950's when he moved to north Liverpool - this was re-inforced through school journeys to Ormskirk over a number of years.
During the 1960's he travelled the system extensively, building up a comprehensive photographic record in the process until he moved away from the area. He now lives in Surrey with his wife and daughter.

The **Senior Transport Archive** has grown from what were originally the private photographic collections of John Senior and his father, though the latter was not a transport photographer. With the production of histories of transport manufacturers and operators John Senior inherited vast quantities of official material, including photographs, sales literature and other records, house magazines and so on. Official collections of negatives were loaned and a darkroom facility created to print archive negatives up to 15 x 12in, or to enlarge from negatives up to whole plate in size. The quality of the official photographic content is second to none and has come to form the core of the present archive. Photographs loaned or donated by enthusiasts, together with those purchased for use in books, have swelled the numbers and there are now over 86,000 photographs alone. The collection contunues to increase and the books, magazines and official brochures are an invaluable source of reference. Venture Publications has access to this archive and its authors will be able to use it to further their research or to locate material to illustrate their works.
The archive is being computer catalogued and the next step will be the filing of photographs on CD disc for direct computer access. Offers of assistance will be welcomed, as will offers of additional transport related material for the archive.

Ribble History

A second volume, to be published in 1994, will cover the fleet in generously illustrated detail, describing the vehicles on a batch by batch basis and also their duties and their operating characteristics. In addition there will be more detailed descriptions of the depots, and bus stations, quoting their history and the areas served. The Standerwick fleet will also be described and illustrated in detail.

If you would like details of this second volume nearer to publication please send a stamped addressed envelope to:

Venture Publications Ltd, PO Box 17, Glossop, Derbyshire, SK13 9FA

marking your envelope Ribble 2 in the top left hand corner.

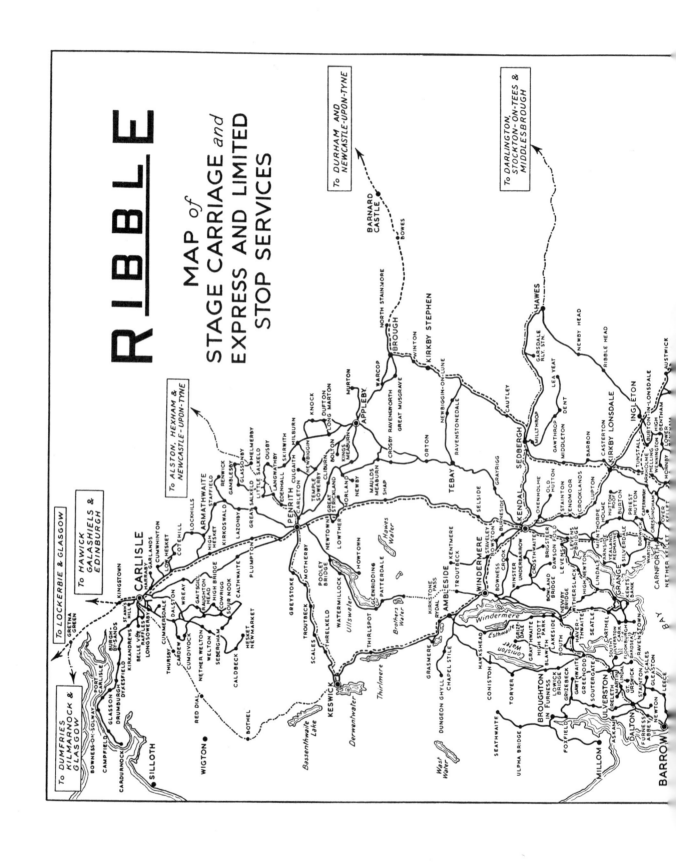